WITHDRAWN

RED FOR
DANGER

RED FOR
DANGER

by

L. T. C. ROLT

DAVID & CHARLES
NEWTON ABBOT
1971

ISBN 0 7153 4009 3

First published in 1955 by John Lane,
The Bodley Head Limited
New extended edition first published in 1966 by
David & Charles Limited
Second impression published 1971

Type set by Richard Clay (The Chaucer Press), Ltd.,
Bungay, Suffolk

Printed in Great Britain by
Latimer Trend & Co Ltd, Whitstable
for David & Charles (Publishers) Limited
Newton Abbot, Devon

CONTENTS

APPENDICES

ILLUSTRATIONS

ACKNOWLEDGEMENTS

Radio Times Hulton Picture Library; Stephenson Locomotive Society; *Picture Post* Library; Lieut-Colonel J. A. Burns of Cumbernauld by Glasgow; Messrs E. G. Graham and A. W. H. Pearsall of Morecambe; British Railways, Western Region; Messrs Turner and Drinkwater, Hull; Railways Inspection Dept, Ministry of Transport & Civil Aviation; *Daily Record*, Glasgow; *Daily Mail*.

PREFACE

IN THE preparation of this book I owe an immense debt of gratitude to the late Colonel G. R. S. Wilson, the Chief Inspecting Officer of Railways, and his colleagues of the Railways Inspection Department, Ministry of Transport. Press reports and other secondhand accounts of railway accidents are usually inaccurate and lacking in essential particulars. Moreover, they invariably omit precise reference to the most interesting feature of such accidents, the mistakes which caused them and the lessons learnt from those mistakes. Hence it would not have been possible for me to write this book at all, except in a very superficial and sensational form, had it not been for the most generous co-operation of the Railways Inspection Department in allowing me access to their records and full facilities for studying them.

The precise circumstances attending a major railway disaster are often the subject of controversy. Thus railwaymen and railway historians not infrequently disagree with the inspecting officers' findings. Yet in an accident inquiry no pains are spared to arrive at the truth so that, while the most conscientious investigator can be misled, to disregard the official account would be to abandon fact for hearsay. Each detailed account of a railway accident in this book is therefore based on the report of the inspecting officer concerned, with the addition, where it is recorded, of the actual evidence of witnesses.

In writing about dramatic events in the past an author is always tempted to embroider the facts with his own imagination at the expense of authenticity. But in this case any embroidery would be superfluous and unwarranted. For where every detail is recorded, even in some cases the sayings of the men involved, it is not necessary for the author to invent. He has only to give such material dramatic shape in order to bring the past to life more vividly than any fiction can ever do. I would like to emphasize, therefore, that the speech recorded in this book is authentic. It represents the conversation of the men concerned as recollected by them in evidence shortly afterwards and is not merely what I imagine such men might have said in given circumstances.

The records of the Railways Inspection Department go back to 1840 and consist of annual bound volumes of reports, statistics and returns, each of which is considerably larger and longer than this book. In dealing with such an overwhelming mass of material I have had to be guided by certain terms of reference. With but few exceptions I have confined my attention to major disasters although, from the point of view of the inspecting officer to whom the cause is more important than the consequence, a long casualty list has no technical significance except as regards the design of rolling stock and is often a result of unlucky chance. I have further confined my choice to accidents occurring on steam railways within a period of 100 years, from 1840 to 1940. I have thought it inappropriate to deal with accidents of more recent occurrence, for even in the case of the latest accidents which I have described I have considered it desirable to change or to withhold the names of the men chiefly concerned. Finally I must stress that my object has not been merely to relate a series of sensational stories of sudden death but to use these disasters to illustrate the way in which the present high standards of safety on our railways developed.

Certain other sources, additional to the Ministry of Transport records, to which I have referred in preparing this book are included in a short bibliography and I would here express my indebtedness to the authors concerned, as well as to those among my railway friends who have given me information and advice. I should make it clear that although I have enjoyed the co-operation of the Railways Inspection Department, this assistance has been confined to giving me access to material and has not extended to the use which I have made of it. In other words this book is in no sense of the word 'official' and carries no stamp of approval. Except where I have stated otherwise, any opinions given or conclusions drawn are entirely my own and I accept full responsibility for them.

L. T. C. R.

PREFACE TO THE SECOND EDITION

ELEVEN YEARS have elapsed since this book was first published, so in preparing this second edition I have added a chapter which brings the story forward to 1957. I have also taken the opportunity of correcting certain errors in the original text which have been pointed out to me by the Railways Inspectorate, Ministry of Transport. I would like to express my most sincere thanks to the Officers of that Department for their kindly advice and guidance in compiling the additional chapter.

1966   L. T. C. R.

Out of this nettle, Danger
We pluck this flower, Safety.

Henry IV (Part I)

1

INTRODUCTORY

A RAILWAY ACCIDENT is always news. Governments may fall or battles be fought and lost but no matter what the crisis of the hour may be, a derailment or a collision involving a relatively small loss of life will be sure to command a banner headline in the popular Press. All but the most lurid of road accidents pass without remark, but even the derailment of a few goods wagons involving no fatality or even injury will generally make a small paragraph in the news columns. Generations of railwaymen have complained with reason that such publicity is misleading; that it tends to obscure a safety factor so high that there are, in fact, few safer places on earth than a passenger compartment on an English train. But such publicity is, in part at least, the price the railwayman pays for efficiency. If railway accidents were as frequent as road accidents they would soon lose their news value. We should hear a great deal about 'the toll of the rail', no doubt, but individual disasters would cease to receive so much space.

There are, however, other factors which account for the news value of railway accidents. There is, of course, the morbid interest in details of sudden and violent death to which the popular Press has always pandered. Anyone who picks up this book expecting sensationalism of this kind is doomed to disappointment for he will find in it no gruesome descriptions of charred or mangled corpses. Violent death or mutilation may frequently accompany railway accidents but it is not peculiar to them. No, even if the macabre element be discounted altogether, the railway disaster is a tragedy with a dramatic quality which is practically unique. Other disasters, often claiming a far heavier toll of human life, frequently fill the pages of our newspapers. A volcano erupts; an earthquake rocks a town; fire destroys a great building; a ship is lost by storm at sea. Such calamities are almost invariably tragic in the sense that the Greeks understood the word. They reveal man as the victim of forces or circumstances against which he is powerless. Only very rarely in peacetime is he directly responsible for bringing comparable destruction upon himself or others. But in the case of disasters on the railway the reverse is true. As we shall see in the following chapters, the pure 'accident' – the accident caused by fate alone – is rare on the railway. Almost invariably human fallibility is responsible. The cause is found to be trivial – a single mistake on the part of engine driver, guard or signalman, fitter, shunter or permanent way man or some fatal lack of co-operation between them. It is in this contrast between trivial error and terrible consequence that the drama of the railway accident lies. Is it not the essential stuff of all great tragedy?

Over and above this, each railway accident represents but one brief incident in a much larger though less spectacular drama which has been going on ever since the first steam engine moved on rails; I refer to that struggle to eliminate the possibilities of human error which has engaged the ingenuity of generations of engineers. The railway disaster may represent the engineer's failure but never his defeat; always he has resolutely counter-attacked. From the terrible lessons learnt in the flaming wreck or the heap of shattered, telescoped coaches have come all those safety devices which combine to make the modern railway one of the most complex but at the same time most successful organizations which man has ever evolved. The automatic vacuum brake, the block system, the interlocking lever frame, facing point locks, catch points, track circuiting, automatic train control, all these and many other devices simple or complicated have been developed as a result of bitter experience. It may sound a paradox, but it is hardly an exaggeration to say that it is the accidents described in this book which have made our British railways the safest in the world.

To this long struggle for perfection there can be no end, for the goal is unattainable. No mechanical devices and no precautions however painstaking can ever be altogether proof

1(a). 'The Dickens Disaster': the wreckage of the Folkestone Boat Express on Beult Viaduct, Staplehurst, 9 June 1865

1(b). The scene at Abbots Ripton, 21 January 1876, after the disaster involving the Great Northern Scottish and Leeds expresses

2(a). Fall of the Tay Bridge, 28 December 1879: the scene on the day after the disaster

2(b). When the girders were salvaged they still contained the coaches of the doomed train

against mistakes. Man must ever remain a fallible mortal. Indeed, elaborate mechanical or electrical safety devices can sometimes defeat their own object by inducing too great a reliance in them at the expense of human vigilance. When we consider operational methods in the early days of railways the remarkable thing is that there were not more serious accidents. By contrast the railway disaster of modern times is the more poignant and tragic because some trivial fault or unlucky combination of circumstances can still defeat the best laid schemes, the finest organization.

That the misfortunes recorded in this book have been turned to profit we, the passengers, have to thank not only the signal engineers and the staffs of the railway companies but, to an equal degree, those most admirable guardians of the public safety Her Majesty's Inspecting Officers of Railways. The Railways Inspection Department has a remarkable record of continuous and exemplary public service over a period of 125 years, a span which covers practically the whole history of railways. Indeed, its present representatives may fairly make the proud claim that they received their original mandate from the father of railways – the great George Stephenson himself. For when the Government set up a Select Committee to inquire into the new railways and report upon the degree of supervision required in the public interest, George Stephenson wrote to Henry Labouchere, the President of the Board of Trade, setting forth his own views on the matter. This letter is reproduced as an Appendix to this book. The great engineer's advice undoubtedly guided the Board in setting up a department which, to the present day, has continued to act in accordance with the principle which Stephenson laid down. The golden rule throughout has been supervision without interference and it has often been assailed. Upon the one hand there were ranged those railway companies and railway engineers who would brook no Government supervision whatsoever. First and foremost of these was Stephenson's great contemporary, Isambard Kingdom Brunel, the engineer of the

Great Western Railway. Brunel told the Select Committee roundly that Government inspectors would receive no co-operation from railwaymen who could scarcely be expected to assist in shackling themselves although they would, *he hoped,* answer questions in a gentlemanly manner. Railway officials understood very well, he said, how to look after the public safety, and possessed more ability to find out what was necessary than any inspecting officer. On the other hand, serious railway disasters almost invariably provoked a clamour in both Press and Parliament for more active Government control by legislation.

Acts of Parliament passed in 1840 and 1842 empowered the Board of Trade to appoint railway inspecting officers who were recruited, then as now, from the Corps of Royal Engineers. They were to inspect and report upon newly constructed lines which could not be opened for public use without their approval. They were also to investigate the causes of accidents, and, although such proceedings did not receive legal sanction for another thirty years, they conducted their first inquiry into an accident at Howden on the Hull & Selby Railway in August 1840. From this date forward successive inspecting officers contrived with conspicuous success to steer a middle course between recalcitrant railway companies on the one hand and an indignant or alarmed public on the other.

The situation became most difficult in the late sixties and the seventies when the inspecting officers were urging the railways to adopt interlocking and absolute block working while an increasing number of serious accidents caused panic demands for Government intervention. But the department was fortunate to have at its head at this time Captain (afterwards Sir) H. W. Tyler who continued to defend the principle of non-interference when even one of his own colleagues, Colonel Yolland, expressed himself in favour of more direct Government control. Tyler would not yield to such persuasions. Responsibility for safety on the railways, he maintained, must remain with the individuals concerned. Any form of direct supervision or control by Government would be harmful because it would inevitably divide responsibility and by so doing weaken it. There was only one right but harder way to bring about reform and that was by persuasion and by pressure of public opinion. It was to the latter end that Tyler initiated the publication of accident reports which had hitherto appeared only in state papers, and also the annual issue of accident statistics. This principle of Tyler's which has implications which extend far beyond the sphere of railways, has prevailed to this day in the Railways Inspection Department. The history of railway legislation shows that safety measures have only been imposed by legal compulsion when persuasion had already caused the desired reforms to be almost universally adopted. The principle whereby the Government does not interfere with the day-to-day operation of our railways still holds good, and rightly so. But unfortunately the natural sanctions of individual initiative, public opinion and competition no longer operate with such salutary effect as they did in the days before railways became the monopoly of a state corporation.

Although the railway inspecting officers were not inventors of railway safety devices – that was the work of the great signal engineers – they displayed almost unerring judgement in singling out the best appliances and urging their adoption many years before they were brought into common use. What one generation has advocated the next has seen widely adopted. How difficult their job was may be gathered from some of their reports to which I refer in this book. The autocratic chairmen and chief engineers of Victorian railway companies frequently displayed a hostility which they made little or no attempt to conceal. Sir Daniel Gooch referred to 'minute and irresponsible interference', while a certain eminent chairman, when confronted by recommendations for interlocking and block telegraph installation, was heard to remark that it was high time they put such new-fangled gadgets into the fire and got back to the great days of Brunel and Stephenson. But the inspecting officers did not mince their words either, and ultimately the 'new-fangled gadgets' won the day. For it was another axiom of Captain Tyler's that a certain complexity of equipment was necessary to ensure greater simplicity and safety in operation.

The old hostility no longer exists today. Ever ready to advise and recommend but reluctant to order, the inspecting officer has become the railwayman's guide, philosopher and friend. One has only to read the Press reports of accident inquiries, or, better still, the reports made by the inspecting officers themselves to realize the contribution which these men have made to the efficiency and safety of our railway system. Each report is a model of scrupulous care and thoroughness in investigation, of a humane understanding of individual frailty combined with complete impartiality in the examination of witnesses who often, after a major disaster, labour under great stress of emotion. The inquiry which follows a serious accident inevitably and rightly attracts much publicity. Such occasions are now happily rare, but no railway mishap however trivial escapes the inspecting officer's attention so that the full extent of his work and its value is seldom appreciated outside railway circles. Authoritative but never dictatorial, the inspecting officers continue to uphold the best traditions of public service at a time when too many government officials have become our masters instead of our servants. The occasion of this book demands that due tribute should be paid to them.

In these days of supersonic flight when we can buy motor cars capable of exceeding 100 miles an hour by a handsome margin, we are no longer awed like our ancestors by the speed of the express train. But where potential danger and destructive power is concerned sheer speed is not the only factor to be considered; weight must also be taken into account and in this regard an express train, weighing, perhaps, as much as 600 tons, travelling at eighty miles an hour represents a destructive force which is still without parallel in transportation. With the finest of brakes, its stopping distance is considerable and it can take no avoiding action. Hence the need for every precaution that the wit of man can devise, precautions which sometimes seem, to the layman accustomed to the road or the air, needlessly elaborate. That this is far from the case the following chapters will show.

If the lethal power of the express train is still unequalled today, how much more was this true in the earliest days of railways. Our whole consciousness, even our unconscious reflexes, have become so adapted and attuned to high speeds, that for us to understand the impact of railways upon a world which had never known anything swifter than a galloping horse demands a considerable imaginative effort. On to the stage of a peaceful, bucolic England of coach, plodding wagon team or silently gliding canal boat the steam locomotive, breathing fire and smoke, made an entry as sudden and dramatic as that of the demon king in pantomime. Some saw in the new invention a source of wealth, others an instrument of universal brotherhood linking people to people, but to many it did appear to be an evil power. Its baleful breath would cause crops and stock to wither and die in any fields through which it passed. As for those who were foolhardy enough to travel behind the monster, even if they were not first asphyxiated by its headlong velocity they would certainly be whirled straight to death and damnation.

These first prejudices were all too soon overcome. The railways claimed their first victim at the opening of the Liverpool & Manchester Railway. The fate of the unfortunate Huskisson who was run down by the 'Rocket' and mortally injured showed clearly enough that the new power was not to be trifled with. But the eager public who packed the first trains showed themselves incapable of estimating their speed or realizing its dangers and only learnt their lesson by experience. This lack of judgement was one of the most fruitful causes of the earliest accidents. Company by-laws forbidding passengers to travel on carriage roofs seem ridiculous today but it was quite otherwise then. Accustomed to the outside seats on stage coaches, passengers invaded the roof tops on the slightest provocation only to miss their footing or to have their brains dashed out against the arch of a bridge. Similarly, and with consequences equally dire, they would unhesitatingly leap off a train travelling at speed to retrieve a hat, blown off in an open or semi-open carriage. Such rash behaviour induced many of the early companies to lock their passengers into the compartments, a practice which would stand for ever condemned by the terrible train fire at Versailles.

It was not only the passenger who had to learn by trial and by errors frequently tragic in their consequence the unprecedented power and the potential danger of the new steam railways. The same applied to the Government of the country and to the railway companies themselves. Self-propelled vehicles of great weight covering long distances at high speed on rail-prescribed courses posed innumerable practical and operational problems which were quite without precedent. In spite of their trials, tribulations and disasters, we may envy the first railwaymen for they were the heroes of a revolutionary technical adventure unique in human history. Hitherto it had been accepted as axiomatic that any highway, whether it was a turnpike, a canal or a horse tramway, should be open to all on payment of tolls fixed by statute. Indeed, it was held that for the owners of such highways themselves to act as carriers upon them would be unfair to the private trader and it was for this reason that the canal companies were legally debarred from operating their own fleet of boats. The Liverpool & Manchester Railway was authorized by Parliament upon a similar basis, but fortunately it was soon recognized that at least the new Company must be exclusively responsible for the provision of motive power. The alternative would certainly have been chaos. Imagination boggles at the thought of a number of 'by-traders', canal fashion, each working their own trains over the same stretch of line. One result of this compromise between the old principle and the new power was the private owner wagon which survived until our railways were nationalized. But in other ways the old conception of the freedom of the highway died hard. It was only gradually that operational methods which would make a modern railwayman's hair stand on end gave place to the iron discipline of the absolute block system, dividing the line into a series of 'train-tight' compartments that only one train may occupy at one time. At first, trains, or especially light engines, had a way of appearing where or when they were least expected. Favoured individuals were granted the privilege of a train to themselves in which they roamed the railway conducting obscure experiments. On occasions of crisis or for purposes of inspection, engineers would commandeer a locomotive from the shed as light-heartedly as they would take a horse from the stable and drive themselves away, sometimes on the wrong road. If a train failed to appear at the expected time it was generally assumed that the engine had broken down and a relief was sent out to meet it.

One of the most tiresome and menacing of the early experimentalists was Doctor Dionysius Lardner, a character strongly reminiscent of 'Beachcomber's' Doctor Strabismus. That he enjoyed for a time a great reputation as a railway expert was due to the fact that he was one of the first masters of the art of blinding the layman with science, but that he was able to impose upon the railway companies themselves is more mysterious. Speaking against Brunel's proposal to construct the Box Tunnel on the main line of the Great Western Railway with a continuous gradient of 1 in 100, the Doctor pronounced that if the brakes of a descending train were to fail as it entered the tunnel it would emerge at a speed of 120 miles per hour, a velocity at which no passenger could breathe. Brunel pointed out that the Doctor had failed to take into account either frictional or wind resistance and that the speed would in fact be only fifty-six miles per hour. But the savant's self-esteem remained unshaken. With an inconsistency surprising in view of this first gaffe, we next find him pontificating against the broad gauge on the grounds of the increased 'atmospheric resistance' of the wider vehicles. It is obvious that a

man of the calibre of Isambard Brunel knew perfectly well
that Doctor Dionysius Lardner was a pompous fraud and yet
for some extraordinary reason the Great Western Company
gave him the use of an experimental train and the liberty of
their tracks. For the two months of September and October
1838 the Doctor's train was at large on the main line to the
extreme hazard of the regular services. It was asking for
trouble and, sure enough, it came. On September 26th George
Henry Gibbs, promoter and director of the Company wrote in
his diary: 'the eight o'clock train ran into the experimental
train and injured three of the carriages very much'. Did the
Doctor apologize? Did the Company order him off? Not a bit
of it. He seems to have assumed the rights of royalty and wrote
the Great Western board a furious letter which Gibbs described as 'very improper'. A month later the experimental
train was again involved in a collision. Fortunately, or perhaps
unfortunately from the Company's point of view, the sage was
not on board on this occasion and it was his unfortunate pupil
who paid the penalty. He was killed on the spot.

Even on the Great Western the privileges granted to
Dionysius were not unique. Professor Charles Babbage, the
inventor of the calculating machine and a friend of Brunel's,
was similarly favoured. Arriving at Paddington one morning
to take out his special train he was somewhat disconcerted
when he was told by an official that he should travel down on
the up line.

As this was an invasion of the usual regulations [he
writes], I inquired very minutely into the authority upon
which it rested. Being satisfied on this point, I desired him
to order out my train immediately. He returned with the
news that the fireman had neglected his duty, but that the
engine would be ready in less than a quarter of an hour. The
officer took pains to assure me that there was no danger on
whichever line we might travel as there could be no engine
but our own on either line until 5 o'clock in the evening. A

messenger arrived soon after to inform me that the obstructions had been removed, and that I could now pass upon the south, which was the proper line.

While we were conversing together, my ear, which had become peculiarly sensitive to the distant sound of an engine, told me that one was approaching. I mentioned it to the railway official. He did not hear it and said – 'Sir, it is impossible.' 'Whether possible or impossible,' I said, 'an engine is coming, and in a few minutes we shall see its steam.' The sound soon became evident to both, and our eyes were anxiously directed to the expected quarter. The white cloud of steam now faintly appeared in the distance. I soon perceived the line it occupied, and then turned to watch my companion's face. In a few minutes more I saw it slightly change, and he said – 'It is indeed on the north line.' Knowing it would stop at the engine house, I ran as fast as I could to that spot. I found a single engine, from which Brunel, covered with smoke and black had just descended. We shook hands, and I inquired what brought my friend here in such a plight. Brunel told me he had posted from Bristol to meet the only train at the farthest point of the rail then opened, but had missed it. 'Fortunately,' he said, 'I found this engine with its fire up, so I ordered it out, and have driven it the whole way up at the rate of 50 miles an hour.'

I then told him that but for the merest accident I should have met him on the same line at the rate of 40 miles, and that I had attached to my engine my experimental carriage and three wagons with 30 tons of iron. I inquired what course he would have pursued if he had perceived another engine meeting him upon his own line? Brunel said in such a case he would have put on all the steam he could command with a view to driving off the opposite engine by the superior velocity of his own.

Happily for the history of British railways, Brunel's suggested procedure in the event of imminent collision has never found favour. Its simultaneous adoption by two opposing engine crews would indeed be spectacular. I suspect that Isambard was pulling his friend's leg. After his experiences with the egregious Doctor Lardner he probably felt it was time that these experimentalists were scared off the Company's metals. That Brunel was aware of the dangers of haphazard working is revealed by two letters which he wrote to his colleague, Daniel Gooch the Locomotive Superintendent, in October 1840:

On Saturday I saw an engine on the line near the Scrubbs sent to look for the 3 o'clock train, in which I was and which was very late. This engine started after the 5 o'clock out and without any special orders from anyone in authority, but authorized by a general order which is issued, and returned on the wrong line. I cannot contemplate the dreadful results that might have happened, and there must be an immediate revision of our locomotive arrangements.

Again:

J. Hill brought the 'Cyclops' up on Monday in 27 minutes from Slough, following the short train into Paddington within three minutes. This work must be put a stop to effectually, and the Directors have determined to fine him ten shillings. I have spoken severely to him and will see him myself about the fine. I should wish the 'Cyclops' tried alone with the 3 o'clock up; it might do it.

Obviously the errant Hill was determined to demonstrate the superior capabilities of his steed, and in spite of the official frown he obviously succeeded.

These complaints of Brunel's had an immediate effect for on November 3rd the Great Western board approved the following rules for enginemen and firemen:

10. No engine must ever, on any account whatever, be moved from any of the stations on to the main line, except

when the engineman is proceeding in his turn and at the proper time to take his place in front of a train: or, when on the main line, he must never run beyond the limits which may be fixed at each station without a regular despatch-note, both as regards the time of starting and the place and time of returning.

11. The engines are never to run forward on the right-hand road, but always to move on the south road from Paddington towards Bristol, and on the north road from Bristol towards Paddington, except when specially ordered to do otherwise by the conductor of a train; and then the engineman must always ascertain from the conductor, and also satisfy himself, that the police have been made aware of the circumstances for the whole distance which he proposes to run; and he must proceed slowly and continue to sound his whistle by beats the whole time.

In such a fashion did experience dictate the first primitive safety precautions.

Recalling these earlier days of railways from the experience of thirty years, Daniel Gooch himself wrote in his diary:

When I look back upon this time, it is a marvel to me that we escaped serious accidents. It was no uncommon thing to take an engine out on the line to look for a late train that was expected, and many times have I seen the train coming and reversed the engine and run back out of its way as quickly as I could. What would be said of such a mode of proceeding now?

Gooch was probably thinking of an alarming experience which he had when the great Box Tunnel was first opened for traffic. He writes:

Only one line of rails was complete through the tunnel, and the trains had therefore to be worked on a single line. I undertook to accompany all the trains through the tunnel, and did so the first day and night, also the second day,

intending to be relieved when the mail came down on the
second night. At about 11 o'clock that night we had a very
narrow escape from a fearful accident. I was going up the
tunnel with the last up train when I fancied I saw some
green lights placed as they were in front of our train.[1] A
second's reflection convinced me it was the mail coming
down. I lost no time in reversing the engine I was on, and
running back to Box Station with my train as quickly as I
could, when the mail came down behind me. The policeman
at the top of the tunnel had made some blunder, and sent
the mails on when they arrived there. Had the tunnel not
been pretty clear of steam we must have met in full career,
and the smash would have been fearful, cutting short my
career also. But as though mishaps never come alone, when
I was taking my train up again, from some cause or other
the engine got off the rails in the tunnel, and I was detained
there all night before I got straight again.

Such were the experiences of the pioneers. It is indeed
marvellous that serious accidents so seldom occurred. There
were mishaps in plenty, often involving loss of life, but nothing which could be described as a major disaster occurred until
the Sonning accident of 1841. For this fortunate immunity the
infrequency of traffic, the light weight of the earliest locomotives and trains and their relatively low speed were undoubtedly partly responsible. So far was Brunel's thought
ahead of his time that when he was carrying out his first survey
of the line from London to Bristol he prophesied train speeds
of 100 miles an hour. It was just as well that his vision was not
too speedily realized. The total weight of a passenger train in
the earliest days seldom exceed 100 tons and was usually considerably less while the average running speed was between
twenty and thirty miles an hour. According to a paper read
before the Statistical Society in the spring of 1843 the fastest

[1] For many years all Great Western trains carried green headlights.
See Chapter 9: Norton Fitzwarren collision.

booked run on any English railway at that time was on the
Northern & Eastern Railway from London to Bishop's Stort-
ford at an average of thirty-six miles an hour exclusive of
stops. Next, and soon to outshine all its narrow gauge rivals,
was the broad gauge Great Western with an average of thirty-
three miles an hour over a greater distance. Sustained high
speed running such as Brunel envisaged was not possible
where the new embankments and cuttings were liable to sub-
sidences or slips and where locomotives could not run more
than twenty miles or so without stopping for water.

That minor misadventures, or hazards but narrowly
avoided, were accepted almost as a matter of course we may
infer from the writings of contemporaries. Thus a certain Mr
Bourne, a eulogist of railways, describes the awe inspiring
approach of a train in the usual fulsome terms and then con-
tinues:

> Suddenly, a wagon stands in the way, or a plank it may
> be has been left across the rails; a shrill, unearthly scream
> issues from the engine, piercing the ears of the offending
> workmen, and scarcely less alarming the innocent pas-
> sengers. Many a foolish head is popped out of the window,
> guards and brakesmen busily apply their drags, and the
> driver reverses the machinery of his engine, and exerts its
> utmost force, though in vain, to stop the motion. The whole
> mass fairly slides upon the rail with the momentum due to
> some sixty or seventy tons. Then comes the moment of
> suspense, when nothing remains to be done, and it is un-
> certain whether the obstacle will be removed in time. It is
> so; and the huge mass slides by with scarcely an inch to
> spare. Off go the brakes, round fly the wheels, the steam is
> again turned on, and the train rolls forward at its wonted
> speed, until smoothly and silently it glides into the ap-
> pointed stopping-place.

Uncomfortable and slow rail travel in those days may have
been, but it could seldom or never have been dull.

The persistent preference of the gentry for travelling in their own carriages added to the diversity of early rail travel and was another survival of the old tradition of the free highway. The carriages were mounted on flat trucks attached to the rear of the trains. On one occasion a gentleman who persisted in travelling down to Brighton in this fashion although advised not to do so was left marooned in the depths of Balcombe tunnel owing to the breakage of a coupling, shouting in vain after the disappearing train. It was not a very pleasant predicament, and when he heard the engine which had been sent to retrieve him approaching through the darkness, he imagined that his last hour had come. As the standard of comfort of the companies' first-class coaching stock improved so the gentry forsook their own carriages.

The first men to be practically responsible for railway safety were the Railway Police, men recruited by the companies and organized and modelled on the lines of the recently formed Metropolitan Police Force. On the first great trunk lines these men were usually sworn constables. That they were the forebears of the railway signalmen, is widely known, but at first they had many additional responsibilities which were soon to be delegated to other grades of railway servant. For example, the Great Western rules of 1841 defined their duties as follows:

The duties of the Police may be stated generally to consist in the preservation of order in all the stations and on the line of railway. They are to give and receive signals; to keep the line free from casual or wilful obstructions; to assist in case of accidents; to caution strangers of danger on the railway; to remove intruders of all descriptions; to superintend and manage the crosses or switches; to give notice of arrivals or departures; to direct persons into the entrance to the stations or sheds; to watch movements of embankments or cuttings; to inspect the rails and solidity of the timber; to guard and watch the company's premises; and to convey the

earliest information on every subject to their appointed
station or superior officer.

They were thus not only signalmen, pointsmen and policemen but station announcers, guides, permanent way inspectors
and messengers. Seldom can any policeman's lot have been
less happy, but fortunately their duties soon became more
specialized. Permanent way inspection ceased to be their responsibility, while special signal or 'switchmen' were
appointed whose rank and wages were above those of the
'common constable'.

Using flags and lamps, or later the first fixed signals, these
railway policemen regulated the passage of trains on the time
interval system, a method much less satisfactory and far more
dangerous than the space interval imposed by the block system. The early introduction of the electric telegraph did not
for some time overcome the faults and dangers of time interval
control. Only the more important stations along the line were
connected by telegraph, while the majority of the policemen
were incapable of working the instruments. Having no means
of communicating with his colleague at the next signalling
point along the line, a policeman could not know if a train had
broken down in the section ahead. He could only pass a following train forward after the stipulated time had elapsed and
hope for the best. Only too often his optimism was unjustified,
the leading train having come to a standstill along the line.

Locomotive failures due either to primitive design, to faulty
materials or to inexperienced footplate men were undoubtedly,
either directly or indirectly, the most frequent cause of accident in the early days. So unreliable were the first engines that
the traffic situation often became chaotic and would have defeated any system of train control let alone the primitive time
interval system. As an example, here is the record of only one
week's working on the North Midland Railway in 1843.

Jan 2nd. – No 48 engine, sent out to bring in a broken
horsebox; connecting rod broke, and that broke the cylinder

cover and otherwise seriously damaged the working gear.

Jan 3rd. – Before the goods train out of Leeds at 8 pm arrived at Masbro' – a distance of thirty-two miles – the driver was compelled to draw his fire out. He afterwards arrived at Derby six hours late. (This driver only worked a stationary engine before.) The eight o'clock into Derby overtook a coal train about three miles from Derby with four engines attached to it, the gatekeeper informing the alarmed and trembling passengers that it was only a coal train that had obstructed the line for five hours. The cause of employing so many engines was that three of them were sent out as pilots, one after the other, but unfortunately got so disabled themselves that they were unable to render the necessary assistance.

Jan 4th. – No 61 engine, running the coke train, broke down in Killamarsh cutting. No 44 engine, having just undergone a thorough repair, broke one of the cylinders and was otherwise much damaged. No 5 engine, running the mail train, broke the connecting rod.

Jan 5th. – No 11 engine, running the mail train out of Derby, broke down after running eight miles; with all the energy possible, it cannot be put into a proper state of repair for months. This caused a delay to the mail of two hours and twelve minutes into Leeds. No 9 engine damaged very much in the firebox. The 10.15 train into Derby broke down, and was unable to proceed till the 11.15 train came and brought both trains into Derby; damage serious.

Jan 6th. – The 3.15 train out of Derby broke down, and was taken into Leeds by the pilot engine; one hour fifty minutes late. An engine-driver (Moon is his name) proceeded immediately after a train full of passengers, overtook it, and pushed it before him just as he thought proper. The passenger train which leaves Leeds at 5.30 pm was standing at Barnsley Station when Edward Jenkins, driver of a luggage train, ran into it. The usual signals had been given to Jenkins, but from some cause or other were not observed.

3(a). The tragedy of Armagh, 12 June 1889: the high embankment strewn with the debris of the runaway coaches

3(b). High speed derailment: the wreck of the L & NWR West of England night mail on Shrewsbury curve, 15 October 1907

4(a) and (b) Quintinshill, 22 May
1915: the worst disaster in British
Railways history

4(c). The Hawes Junction disaster, Midland Railway, 24 December 1910: the
locomotives of the down Scotch Express and behind them the smouldering
remains of the burnt out train

There were only three carriages in the passenger train, and fortunately only one passenger. The carriages were all smashed to pieces, the head of the unfortunate passenger was cut completely off.

So unrelenting a series of misfortunes would be enough, one might suppose, to drive any locomotive or traffic super-intendent to drink or worse, but they were made of stern stuff these pioneers. The struggles of the early autocarists with their refractory horseless carriages were as nothing to the unre-corded and heroic feats performed by their forebears on the rail, working by the feeble flicker of tallow dips in rafty roundhouses. Then as always the railwayman's motto was 'the trains must go through', and, albeit irregularly, the trains *did* go through, even if it meant toiling for days and nights without sleep. That first week of January 1843 may have been a par-ticularly black one for the North Midland, but the most illus-trious of the old companies had similar experiences. Gooch wrote of his early locomotives on the Great Western:

> The 'North Star' and the six from the Vulcan Foundry Company were the only ones I could at all depend upon. The result was I had to begin in a measure to rebuild one half of the stock I had to work with. For many weeks my nights were spent in a carriage in the engine-house at Paddington, as repairs had to be done to the engines at night to get them to do their work next day.

Few passengers realized what crude and desperate ex-pedients were often resorted to in order to bring an engine into the platform: a cracked frame fitted with a crude temporary splint; handfuls of bran or oatmeal in the boiler to stop leaking tubes or seams; a large lump, or 'pill', as the enginemen called it, of tallow dropped down the blast pipe to lubricate the cylinders. Methods of lubrication were crude in the extreme and there was no reliable steam cylinder oil. It was a common practice for a fireman to administer one of these 'pills' while the train was in motion, crawling along the running plate to open the smoke-box door in peril of his life. No wonder there were mishaps and breakdowns.

In the event of an accident or a breakdown on the road it was the duty of the policeman (always assuming there was one on the spot) to run back a mile to protect it from oncoming traffic by showing a hand signal. Meanwhile if the adjoining line was obstructed also the crew were ordered to draw coals from their firebox and build a warning fire between the metals, a practice which must often have proved highly detrimental to the sleepers. But in 1841 E. A. Cowper's invention of the detonator which could be clipped on the rail to be exploded by the first wheel that touched it, soon put an end to these primitive practices. The detonator was a notable contribution to railway safety. It was rapidly adopted by all the railway companies and in fog or emergency it has been a good friend to railwaymen and passengers alike ever since. On the Great Western the policeman, instead of making his marathon mile run, was now ordered to place detonators in the rear of the disabled train, one at a distance of a quarter of a mile, one at a half and two at three-quarters of a mile. The same procedure holds good to this day except that the duty of protecting the train in the rear falls to the guard, while the fireman goes forward to notify the next signalman ahead, protecting the parallel road similarly if it be obstructed.

As this is not a treatise on railway signalling, a detailed description of the many early types of fixed signals which preceded the orthodox semaphore with which we are familiar would be out of place. Occasionally an individual signal might be worked remotely by a capstan, but as a rule they were at first controlled simply from the foot of the post on which they were mounted. They were not connected to any remote lever frame, nor were they interconnected with point levers or capstans, though the latter might be fitted with indicator discs which showed when they were set for the main line. The fault of most of these early signals was that their indications were

often highly ambiguous. This is especially true of the first
fixed signal on the Great Western Railway which was displayed only when the line was clear and gave no positive
danger indication. It was mounted outside Reading and consisted of a ball or disc which was hoisted up a pole by rope and
pulley like a high-water signal on a harbour jetty when the
station was clear for a train to enter. The fatal defect of this
signal is apparent in Daniel Gooch's 'Regulations' for March
1840, which contain a delightful Irishism: 'A Signal Ball will
be seen at the entrance to Reading Station when the Line is
right for the Train to go in. If the Ball is not visible the Train
must not pass it.'

Contemporary signals on other lines erred in the opposite
direction – they presented a positive danger indication but no
positive 'all clear'. In this respect the first signals designed by
Brunel were highly approved of by the Board of Trade because they were the first on any railway to give two positive
indications. They consisted of a large disc and a horizontal
cross-bar mounted at right angles to one another and per-
forated and slotted to reduce their wind resistance. They were
pivoted on the top of a post so that they could be turned
through ninety degrees. Presented to an oncoming train the
cross bar indicated 'stop' and the disc 'all clear'. So successful
were they that it was not until the end of the century that the
last of them disappeared from the Great Western system before the advance of the all-conquering semaphore. Another
type of signal, designed to indicate caution, which was evolved
by Brunel, proved far less satisfactory; in fact, it represents
one of that great man's singular aberrations. It consisted of red
and green flags mounted on a frame at the top of a pole so that
they could be furled and unfurled like a fan by means of ropes
and pulleys. These 'fantails' or 'kites', as the enginemen called
them, had a very brief career because they invariably blew
away in the first high wind.

Some of the earliest fixed signals were installed for the protection of road crossings which were a prolific cause of acci-

dents on the first railways. Here again the fatal inability of both men and animals to estimate and adapt themselves to the speed of the new trains was partly responsible. There is a railway legend, often repeated but never positively substantiated, that the locomotive whistle was evolved as a result of an accident at a crossing on the Leicester & Swannington – one of the earliest of railways which was destined to grow into the great Midland system. Whether it be authentic or not, the story is certainly circumstantial enough. It is that on May 4th, 1833, the locomotive 'Samson' ran down a market cart loaded with butter and eggs on a level crossing at Bagworth. As a result the manager of the line (Ashlin Bagster, subsequently first manager of the London & Birmingham Railway) suggested to George Stephenson whether it would not be practicable to provide his engines with a whistle which their steam could blow and so give a good warning of their approach. The 'Father of Railways', who had engineered the Leicester & Swannington, thought it an excellent idea and the first 'steam trumpet' was fashioned for the 'Samson' by a Leicester musical instrument maker.

The good fortune that Gooch marvelled at could not continue to favour the new railways indefinitely. Under such haphazard working arrangements it was inevitable that sooner or later some serious accident would occur. There is something ironical in the fact that the first major disaster should have occurred on the Great Western, a railway which, throughout its long history, maintained a safety record which was second to none. Moreover, it was caused by circumstances which the most modern safety devices could not have averted.

At 4.30 am on Christmas Eve, 1841, the regular down goods left Paddington for Bristol. The train consisted of the engine 'Hecla', a 2-4-0 of the 'Leo' class,[1] two third-class carriages, one six and the other four-wheeled, one covered parcels van and seventeen goods wagons. In the darkness of

[1] Built by Fenton, Murray and Jackson of Leeds and delivered April 1841.

the winter's morning in the deep defile of Sonning cutting, the 'Hecla' plunged into a 'slip'. Abnormally heavy rain had dislodged from the cutting side a great mound of earth which blocked the down road. The weight of the following goods wagons crushed the two third-class carriages against the engine and tender with the result that eight passengers lost their lives and seventeen were injured. Most of the casualties were workmen employed on the building of the new Houses of Parliament who were returning home for Christmas. The accident brought some ghoulish satisfaction to the Jeremiahs who saw their prophecies of death and destruction at last fulfilled. It also caused some jubilation among the hard-pressed coach proprietors who foresaw a revival of patronage from a frightened public.

Under the ancient Common Law of England prevailing at that time, any chattel which brought about the death of a man was *Deo Dandum* (to be given to God) and so liable to be forfeited to the Crown for pious uses. At the inquest on the victims of the disaster the jury laid a deodand of £1,000 on 'Hecla' and her train, payable by Crown Grant to the Lord of the Manor of Sonning. But the Board of Trade report exonerated the Company from all blame, and they successfully appealed against the claim which was reduced to a nominal sum. 'I do not imagine,' wrote the Inspector, Sir Frederic Smith, in his report, 'that any engineer would have thought it necessary to give the sides of this cutting a greater slope than two to one, and therefore there has been, in my opinion, no error in the construction.' The Company's treatment of its luckless third-class passengers, however, came in for stern and justifiable criticism. The wrecked coaches had no spring buffers. They were open-sided, exposing their wretched occupants to the bitter winter weather for the nine and a half hours which the goods train normally took to reach Bristol from London. The seats were mere planks only 18 inches from the floor and the coach sides and ends were only enclosed to a height of 2 feet. This meant that the passengers had no protection whatever in the event of accident and could easily be thrown out of the train even by a sudden start or stop. Moreover, the practice of running passenger vehicles such as these anywhere in a loaded goods train, let alone at the head of it where they were so extremely vulnerable, was strongly condemned. Upon further inquiry it was found that only the Great Western and the London & South Western Companies were guilty of this practice although the London & Birmingham, who consigned 'the lower orders' along with horses, cattle and empty wagons, were hardly less iniquitous.

Although the Great Western continued to convey third-class passengers by goods train for some years after, the carriages were fitted with spring buffers and higher sides and were never run next to the engine. It can safely be said that the Sonning accident began the movement for the reform of third-class travel. Three years after it happened, Gladstone's Railway Regulation Act was passed which compelled the railway companies to operate at least one third-class train daily in each direction over their lines. They were to stop at all stations, to run at a speed of not less than twelve miles an hour inclusive of stops and to carry passengers at a fare not exceeding a penny a mile in carriages adequately protected from the weather. Relics of these 'cheap trains' or 'Parliamentaries', as they were called, can still be found in the timetables and I know of at least one which is habitually referred to by the signalmen along its route as 'The Cheap'. Many years have gone by since it last carried passengers at a special fare, but tradition dies hard.

The Sonning accident had another result. It originated that fear of the leading coach on a passenger train which was increased by later disasters and which persists in some people to this day. It is not altogether unfounded, and in the days of wooden coaches and no continuous brakes it was very real. So much so that many companies made a practice of locking the doors of the two leading compartments against the public if there was no van or brake end intervening between them and the locomotive.

Although they were never funny for the people concerned most of the accidents of the pioneer days have that serio-comic quality which Buster Keaton so admirably exploited in his classic railway film *The General*: the overturned market cart at the crossing; the elegant gentleman marooned in his carriage in the tunnel; the driver reversing his engine in full career and 'exerting its utmost force to stop the motion'; Doctor Dionysius hopping with fury beside his wrecked special. But in the accident at Sonning on that dark December morning in 1841 there was no element of comedy. The railway was growing up. In February 1845 the Great Western directors announced that from March 10th onwards their best trains between Paddington and Exeter would cover the distance of 194 miles in five hours inclusive of stops. These, by a handsome margin, were the fastest trains in the world. They were also considerably heavier than the first dilatory caravans of rattling four-wheelers. The coming of the express train allowed little margin for error and the vagaries of youth must be forgotten for they could no longer be forgiven. The smallest breach of rule and discipline could now spell disaster of the most appalling kind.

2

DOUBLE LINE COLLISIONS OF EARLY DAYS

Cowlairs – Burnley – Aynho – Welwyn – Clayton Tunnel – Kentish Town – Tamworth – Brockley Whins – Kirtlebridge – Bo'ness Junction

T H E   S C I E N C E of railway safety has today reached a pitch of perfection undreamed of in the early days with which this chapter deals. It is perfection achieved at the price of a complexity of mechanical and electrical equipment which baffles the layman. Yet in fact it represents only the elaboration of the three simple basic principles upon which the safe working of railways was founded. These are: first, the interlocking of points and signals to prevent any possibility of conflicting movement or indication; second, the use of suitable 'block' telegraph instruments to enable signalmen to preserve an absolute space interval between successive trains; third, a form of brake which could not only be applied instantly by driver or guard to every wheel of a passenger train, but which would also apply itself in the event of a train becoming divided. Today, as we shall see in later chapters, these three vital requirements have merged into one another. The block system can automatically control the movement of signals, while a signal at 'caution' can automatically apply the brakes of a train. But during the period with which we are here concerned these three safeguards either did not exist at all or had been applied only on a few lines or in very rudimentary and inadequate forms. Had they been in operation, none of the accidents to be described in this chapter would have occurred.

Throughout the sixties, seventies and eighties successive Railway Inspecting Officers urged the adoption of these safety precautions upon the railway companies (not all very willing to listen) with such tireless and undaunted persistence that 'lock, block and brake' became a kind of theme song of the Board of Trade. The Regulation of Railways Act of 1873 required all the companies to submit annual returns showing the progress they were making with the installation of interlocking gear and block working, but it was not until 1889 that block working and continuous brakes were made compulsory by law. It speaks volumes for the success of the policy of persuasion that by this time the end was already within sight of achievement.

The old methods of railway working – independently controlled points and signals, the time interval system and manual brakes – proved surprisingly satisfactory so long as the traffic was light. But as the railway network spread so each new line brought its quota to the great trunk routes which became increasingly congested. The old system could not cope with this congestion, and to keep the trains moving railwaymen were forced to take risks and to ignore old precautionary working rules. The situation amounted to a race between the rapidly growing volume of traffic and the installation of the new safety equipment. For over two decades the traffic won until, in the seventies, Government and public alike became alarmed by the lamentable number of serious accidents. The Act of 1873 was an outcome of that concern, and after 1880 the position began to improve.

The first semaphore signal of the type with which we are familiar was copied from naval signalling practice and was installed on the London & Croydon Railway by Charles Hutton Gregory in 1841. Two years later this same Gregory installed a central lever frame for points and signals at Bricklayer's Arms Junction which incorporated the first crude form of wired interlocking. This was improved upon by John Saxby in 1856 and by Austin Chambers at Kentish Town Junction in 1859. The modern form of completely positive tappet interlocking lever frame was perfected by the brothers Stevens in 1870.

The principle of the space interval or 'block' system of train operation was first suggested by W. F. Cooke of Cooke and

Wheatstone, the pioneers of telegraphy, but the two foremost inventors of block telegraph instruments were Charles Spagnoletti and Edward Tyer, both of whom began their work as young men in the fifties. Spagnoletti was only twenty-three when he was appointed telegraph superintendent of the Great Western Railway in 1855. Disc block instruments of his invention were first installed on the Metropolitan Railway in 1864. In the two following years they were introduced on the Great Western between Bristol and New Passage and on the up main line between Goring and Pangbourne. Edward Tyer's needle block instruments also date back to the sixties, and he finally perfected his system in 1874.

The numerous efforts to improve the braking power of trains culminated in the famous brake trials organized at Newark in 1875 by the Commission on Railway Accidents, when the different systems were put to the test. The result was a convincing victory for the Westinghouse and vacuum systems and in 1878 an Act was passed which compelled all railway companies to submit bi-annual returns showing the progress they were making in equipping their rolling stock with these continuous brakes.

If these three vital safeguards were in existence in the seventies, the darkest decade in the records of railway safety, why, we may well ask, was not their adoption made compulsory long before 1889? Why, except in the case of newly constructed lines, was the Board of Trade for so long empowered only to recommend and persuade and not to compel? Such questions were raised by the popular Press at the time and they have been asked again in this century in connection with more modern safety devices such as Automatic Train Control. Indeed, whenever a serious railway disaster has occurred which some known safety appliance might have prevented, the railways have been pilloried by the public for their failure to install it. Such criticism has often proved salutary but it is hardly fair. It fails to take into account the labour and money which is involved in the universal application of even the smallest item of new equipment. As early as 1870 the railway companies of Great Britain owned over 15,000 route miles of track. The installation of complete interlocking and block working equipment over such a system was a vast undertaking. The wonder is not that it took so long but that it was accomplished so soon. The Railways Inspection Department of the Board of Trade appreciated the size of the job, but the public did not. Not that all the railway companies were conscientious by any means. There were rich and powerful companies who turned a deaf ear to the inspecting officers' 'lock, block and brake' refrain. But there are black sheep in every fold and changes of management often brought about swift and startling reformations, a reprobate among railways suddenly blossoming forth as a model to its astonished neighbours.

In the fifties two bad accidents occurred which were a portent of the future. For in both cases the old system of railway working was subjected to the strain of an abnormal traffic demand and was found wanting. The first happened at Cowlairs on August 1st, 1850. Three enormous trains were being run by the Scottish Central Railway from Perth and other stations to Glasgow on the occasion of the Highland Agricultural Society's show. They were running at a five minute time interval. Despite the fact that the second of these trains, which was in charge of a driver named Cardwell, consisted of no less than thirty-five coaches it became grossly overcrowded and passengers swarmed on to the roofs. The situation was plainly out of hand. Harrison, the Locomotive Superintendent, who was travelling on the footplate with Cardwell, tried without success to persuade them to come down. There was a complete impasse, the roof-squatting passengers refusing to budge and the railway staff refusing to start the train until they did so. This was finally resolved by attaching some open sheep trucks with hurdle sides to the rear of the train into which the recalcitrant passengers scrambled. The long train then moved off.

The line from Perth falls into Glasgow by the steep Cowlairs incline where cable haulage was employed for so many years. It was the practice at this time for all descending trains to stop at a ticket platform at the top of this incline and for the locomotive to be detached and to run round to the rear of its train which then descended under the control of the brakesmen. There were two crossovers which enabled locomotives to rejoin their correct road when performing this manoeuvre. When the first train pulled up at Cowlairs it was so long that it blocked the first crossover and before the driver could make use of the second crossing farther down the line Cardwell arrived with his train and blocked that one also. The two trains now extended their combined length for a considerable distance down the line but apparently their crews were much too absorbed in discussing how best to deal with the situation to think of protecting them in the rear. In fact, of course, where the only protection was a five minute interval such a consideration was of the first importance. Driver Cardwell was asked to set back so as to clear the second crossover. As he was doing so the engine of the third train, running tender first, crashed into his rear, demolishing the flimsy sheep trucks like so much matchwood. Many of their more agile occupants were able to jump over the hurdle sides to safety, but five were caught and killed and a number seriously injured.

The inspector found that the accident was entirely due to the fact that the second train had not been promptly protected in the rear and he strongly criticized the Company's rule on this subject. This stated that: 'Guards and brakesmen are responsible that the proper signals are made in fogs and in all accidents and detentions on the road according to regulations; but if in these cases a difference of opinion should arise as to what is the proper course to pursue the engineman shall decide.' This, commented the inspector, 'encouraged discussion at a time when every moment is of value'.

In 1852 the Lancashire & Yorkshire station at Burnley was the one platform terminus of a single line branch. There were, however, two through roads in addition which continued past the terminus to the East Lancashire Company's sidings. The following plan of the station layout will make clear the circumstances of the accident:

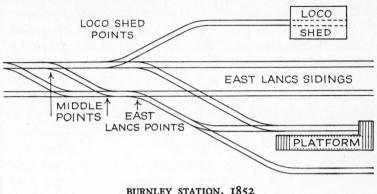

BURNLEY STATION, 1852

The station was not signalled, nor were the points remotely controlled. The 'East Lancs' points, as they were called, were weighted to lie open to the platform line, that is to say they had to be held over in order to admit a train to the East Lancashire sidings. Traffic on the branch was normally light and the station platform could only accommodate a six coach train. But on the day in question two school excursion trains of most prodigious size were dispatched from Burnley to York and Goole. One consisted of forty-five and the other of thirty-five vehicles, both were double-headed and, because the station could not accommodate them, they were loaded and sent off from the East Lancs sidings. When they returned that night it was decided to adopt the following procedure: The trains would be stopped short of the crossover known as the 'middle points', the locomotives uncoupled and drawn ahead and the coaches allowed to run on the falling gradient over the crossover and into the East Lancs' sidings. The first train to return was satisfactorily dealt with in this way, but when the second arrived things went sadly wrong. In the first place the station was hopelessly understaffed that night. There were only two men on duty, Parker, a porter, and Grant, a night watchman, and because they were quite unable to cope with the situation they had called in two obliging friends to help them who were nothing whatever to do with the railway. One was James Crabtree, a calico printer by trade, and the other a blacksmith named Tom Bridge who lived near by. When the first (York) train returned, Tom had collected the tickets in his hat. When the Goole train arrived and stopped as agreed above the middle points, Parker hurried up to it telling Crabtree to look after the 'East Lancs' points. But Crabtree decided he ought to help Parker and Grant so he called out to the blacksmith: 'Tom, hold these points while I go up the line.' Tom obliged. He was holding the points over as he had been told when one of the engines which had been detached from the train came slowly towards him down the parallel track and her driver called out, 'Turn me into the shed.' Anxious to help, the blacksmith let go his lever and stepped across to the shed points. Immediately, the weighted 'East Lancs' points clicked over and before Tom could get back to them the long, crowded rake of coaches went rumbling down into the short bay platform where they crashed into the buffer stops. Although it was not travelling very fast, the weight of the train was such that the damage was considerable and three children and a teacher were killed and a great number injured. The Board of Trade inspector pointed out that damage and casualties would have been less had not the buffers over-ridden each other because they were of unequal height above rail level. He urged that buffer heights should be standardized. Needless to add, he also made some scathing remarks about the Company's staffing arrangements which made it necessary to recruit amateurs to help. The Burnley accident enables us to understand why, in 1858, the Board recommended all railway companies to group point levers together in the most convenient position and 'as close as possible under the hand of the person working them' and that 'the signals should be connected with the points so as to be worked in conjunction with them'.[1] It was the first step in the direction of the interlocking lever frame.

The time interval system of train working placed a great burden of responsibility on engine crews, for there was always a grave risk of rear collisions such as occurred at Cowlairs, especially when we remember that in those days locomotives were much more liable to break down or to stall on a gradient. The safety of passengers then depended upon the vigilance of the enginemen and the promptitude with which the guard of a stalled train protected it in the rear. The latter often found himself in a terrible predicament. According to the rule, as soon as his train came to an involuntary stand he should run back down the line laying detonators at the prescribed intervals. But if he did so, more often than not his driver would succeed in getting his train on the move again and he would be left behind. So he would await advice from his engine crew or go forward himself to meet the fireman and such delay was often fatal, so perilously short was the time interval.

So long as station clocks observed 'local time' the system was a farce. Trains went forward by guess and by God where local time could vary as much as fifteen minutes between one town and another. It was the Board of Trade inspector, Captain Melhuish, who suggested, in his first report in 1840, that station clocks should all keep London time and so originated what became known as 'railway time'. Yet for some years station clocks continued to be somewhat erratic. A passenger train which ran into the rear of a goods train which had stalled in a tunnel near Bootle on the East Lancashire Railway in 1849 had been dispatched from Bootle only three and a half minutes behind it. In explaining this perilous proceeding to the inspector afterwards, a witness candidly admitted that the Bootle station clock 'went wildly'.

In 1851 there was a similar, but much more serious accident on the Chester & Warrington Junction Railway when a train broke down in Frodsham tunnel and six lives were lost in two

[1] See Appendix 2.

following collisions. Then, in 1853, came Ireland's first major railway disaster at Straffan on the Cork–Dublin main line of the Great Southern & Western Railway in County Kildare. In this case it was a passenger train from Cork to Dublin which broke down. The crew neglected until too late to protect the train in the rear with the result that a following freight train crashed into the back of it causing sixteen deaths.

On October 20th, 1852, there occurred a following collision at Aynho, near Banbury, which, though happily not attended by any fatal results, is worth recounting for two reasons. First it was a typical example of the kind of accident which happened only too frequently at this period. Secondly, it occurred on the occasion of the opening of the Great Western's broad gauge route to Birmingham. It was an ill-starred beginning to that broad gauge invasion of the Midlands which had been so hotly fought for and which was to be so short-lived. Just after 9 am a special train of ten coaches filled with Great Western directors and officials, their families and friends, pulled out of Paddington. Resplendent at its head was that legendary and magnificent 8-foot single 'Lord of the Isles' with Daniel Gooch himself on the footplate. The locomotive had but lately returned from the Great Exhibition where, in the words of the accident inspector, 'it's huge proportions and fine workmanship had been so much admired'. The party planned to run to Birmingham and then to return to Leamington for one of those protracted orgies of eating and toasting which invariably accompanied the opening of new lines of railway. Unfortunately the Oxford & Rugby Railway, as it had hitherto been called, had not woken up to the fact that greatness had been thrust upon it; that it was no longer a bucolic cross-country line where time was of little account but had become a section of an important main route. Its signalling and traffic arrangements had not been altered, while it is obvious that whoever was responsible for arranging the timings of the special at Paddington was quite unaware of its dilatory habits. While the glittering 'Lord of the Isles' was speeding westwards from

Paddington the 9.27 mixed train for Banbury left Didcot thirteen minutes late. In the two years that it had been running this shocking train had never once been known to run to time and this morning was no exception. Regardless of the express which was so rapidly bearing down upon it, the 'mixed' pottered along as usual, stopping every now and again to carry out desultory shunting operations. It stopped to shunt off three wagons at Abingdon Road, dropped three more at Oxford and then picked up some others including a van loaded with cheese and parcels for distribution at various stations north. It dropped off two more wagons at Heyford and then trundled on to Aynho where it arrived thirty-eight minutes late. The special passed Heyford crossing only six minutes behind the 'mixed'. The usual GWR warning signals had not yet been erected at the crossing but the 'policeman' who was stationed there made no attempt to warn the special by hand signal. On the gentle curve approaching Aynho, a thousand yards from the station, there stood a disused signal. It had been installed to protect a temporary siding and had been left there showing *All Right*. The crew on the special, unfamiliar with the road, thought it gave them a clear run through and put on steam. The guard of the 'mixed' was unloading cheeses from the van and the station staff at Aynho were preparing to unhitch a couple of wagons from the rear when upon this pleasant and leisurely rural scene there burst in swift and awful majesty the 'Lord of the Isles' running at over fifty miles an hour. For the only time in its disreputable career the mixed train moved very smartly, so smartly indeed that a coupling parted and she left her tail of wagons behind as a kind of defensive rearguard. But she was too late. 'Lord of the Isles' fell upon the wagons, demolished one of them and catapulted the rest forward into the rear of the retreating train.

Discreditable though this accident was, it demonstrated the extraordinary safety and stability of Brunel's 7-foot gauge. The special was travelling at high speed and on any narrow gauge line such a violent collision would almost certainly have figured in the list of major disasters. Yet at Aynho both trains remained intact upon the metals and only six passengers in the 'mixed' complained of slight injury. The only casualties were the smashed wagons and 'Lord of the Isles' which broke her front buffer beam and was derailed by a broken wagon axle. The sequel was ignominious. The engine of the 'mixed' drew her train on to Banbury and then returned to rescue the stranded special which had meanwhile been man-handled over a crossover clear of the wreckage. Another locomotive which was telegraphed for from Birmingham was derailed en route with the consequence that the special never reached Birmingham at all. It was the somewhat breathless engine of the 'mixed' which eventually drew the distinguished but rather shaken and disillusioned company into Leamington for their belated banquet.

Today we regard with patronizing amusement the acute trepidation which the passage of railway tunnels inspired in the bosom of the Victorian railway traveller and his often reiterated pleas that all long tunnels should be artificially lit. But his fears were by no means unfounded, so long as the time interval system prevailed. If a train broke down in the open, even if there was no time to protect it adequately, at least there remained a sporting chance that the crew of a following train would see it and be able to pull up in time. But if a train stopped in the smoke filled darkness of a tunnel where visibility was almost nil, there was no such hope. Moreover, of every kind of railway accident that can befall, a serious collision in a tunnel is the most to be feared. It creates a scene of nightmare horror. In the confined space the wreckage is hideously compressed together and if fire breaks out the tunnel and its ventilation shafts become furnace flues. Rescue work is hampered by the darkness, and cranes and other heavy wrecking gear cannot be used. Wreckage must be dragged by main force to the tunnel mouths before it can be lifted and cleared from the lines. And unfortunately the Frodsham accident was not unique but was the first of a series. There were serious collisions in tunnels at Blackheath in December 1864, at Welwyn in June 1866 and at Canonbury in 1881 where no less than four trains were involved.

Because the Welwyn accident involved goods trains there was fortunately little loss of life – two railwaymen only – but from the point of view of damage to engines and rolling stock it was one of the most destructive in railway history. It occurred in Welwyn North tunnel at a time when this part of the Great Northern main line was terribly congested with traffic. It remains to this day a difficult section to work with its four roads strangled by the two-track bottlenecks of the tunnels, but at this date St Pancras station had not been opened and the line was carrying Midland traffic as well, by virtue of running powers, between Hitchin and King's Cross. On the night of June 9th, 1866, the engine of a down Great Northern goods train burst a tube and came to a standstill in the tunnel. A few minutes later a following Midland goods crashed into the rear, blocking both roads with the wreckage of shattered wagons. Before anyone became aware that anything was wrong an up express perishable goods train laden with Scottish meat for Smithfield thundered into the tunnel and ploughed into the debris. The accident took place immediately beneath a ventilation shaft, and the wreckage, tightly packed from rail level to tunnel roof, took fire from the coals of one of the engines. The three trains were totally consumed. All that night and all through the next day the ventilation shaft belched flames, smoke and the smell of roasting meat over the surrounding countryside.

It was because of the peculiar danger and dread of tunnel collisions that some of the first crude installations of block or space interval working by electric telegraph were provided to safeguard tunnel sections. The first to be protected in this way was Clayton tunnel on the London, Brighton & South Coast Railway where single needle instruments were installed as early as 1841. But on Sunday, August 25th, 1861, they failed to avert a most appalling catastrophe, the worst, at that time, which had ever occurred on any British railway.

On this fine Sunday morning of August, three heavy trains left Brighton bound for Victoria. The first was a fortnightly excursion from Portsmouth consisting of sixteen coaches, the second a Brighton excursion of seventeen vehicles and the third a regular train of twelve coaches. With the exception of the Clayton tunnel section the line was worked on the time interval system, the minimum permissible interval according to rule being five minutes which was slender enough in all conscience. But a comparison between the booked departure times of these trains from Brighton, the times at which they were alleged by the stationmaster to have started and their actual times of departure as determined at the inquiry shows with how perilously narrow a margin of safety the traffic on a busy main line could be conducted at this period. The times were as follows:

| | Times | | |
Train	Advertised	Stationmaster	Actual
PORTSMOUTH EX.	8.5	8.22	8.28
BRIGHTON EX.	8.15	8.27	8.31
BRIGHTON ORD.	8.30	8.36	8.35

From Lovers' Walk Junction at the end of Brighton yard to Clayton Tunnel South, a distance of four and a half miles, the line rises steadily at 1 in 264 while visibility is much restricted by curves, cuttings and bridges and by the 700-yard Patcham tunnel. Up this section the heavy trains laboured one after another towards the long tunnel under the chalk downs, separated from each other only by three and four minutes.

Signalman Henry Killick was on duty at Clayton Tunnel South that day. Sunday marked the change over from day to night duty when it was his practice to work a continuous shift of twenty-four hours instead of the regulation eighteen in order to get one clear day off per week. In his little cabin was a clock, an alarm bell, a single needle telegraph instrument with which he could communicate with his colleague, Brown, at Clayton Tunnel North and a handwheel which worked an up distant signal 350 yards down the line. Killick was also provided with red and white signal flags. The telegraph instrument normally indicated a neutral zero and only showed whether the tunnel was clear or occupied so long as the signalman held the appropriate key. The distant signal was of a type called Whitworth's patent which was then much favoured on the Brighton line. By means of a treadle on the rail and weights on the wire it returned automatically to danger as a train ran past it, but if the train pressed the treadle and the signal failed to respond it rang the alarm bell in the cabin.

When the first train, the Portsmouth excursion, passed Killick and was swallowed up in the long tunnel the automatic signal failed to work. The alarm bell rang, but if Killick noticed it he did not immediately respond. In any case he had to send the 'train in tunnel' signal to Brown. When he did turn to attend to it he saw to his dismay that the Brighton excursion had already passed the defective signal and was rapidly bearing down upon him. He snatched up his red danger flag and broke it out just as the engine of the Brighton train dived into the tunnel. Again he gave Brown the 'train in tunnel' signal, and then paused for a few moments in desperate anxiety and indecision. Had the Portsmouth train cleared the tunnel safely? Had the driver of the second train seen his red flag and stopped in the tunnel or had he continued? He signalled to Brown 'Is tunnel clear?' and at that moment the Portsmouth train burst out of the northern portal and clattered past Brown's cabin. If Brown had received Killick's second signal he had either forgotten or confused it. He signalled back 'Tunnel clear'. With a sigh of relief Killick took in his red flag and unfurled his white just as the third, the ordinary train, approached. Driver Gregory, who had shut off at the distant, immediately opened his regulator, waved acknowledgement to Killick and passed swiftly into the darkness.

Just as his engine ran into the tunnel, Driver Scott of the second train had glimpsed for the fraction of a second the flicker of a red flag from Killick's box. Immediately he shut off steam, and opened his sanders while his fireman screwed down brakes. But such was the weight of his train that it was half a mile inside the tunnel before he brought it to a standstill. Something must be amiss with the 'Pompey' ahead, he decided, and he began cautiously to set back with the object of finding out from Killick what was wrong. The rear of his train was about 250 yards from the mouth of the tunnel when Gregory's engine collided with it with such violence that, having been running backward, the whole train was propelled forwards for 50 yards. The detonation of this terrible impact reverberated through the darkness. The guard in the rear of the Brighton excursion leapt for his life as his van was smashed to pieces. Having demolished it, Gregory's engine ploughed into the hind coach, rearing itself upon it until its chimney struck the roof of the tunnel 24 feet above and was knocked off. In the mangled wreckage beneath its driving wheels, burned with hot coals and scalded by steam escaping from broken pipes, twenty-one people died most horribly. In all, twenty-three passengers lost their lives in the Clayton Tunnel disaster and no less than 176 were seriously injured.

At this time the Board of Trade were doing their utmost to urge the adoption of the block system so that the occurrence of such a catastrophe upon a section of line so controlled was a serious blow. It placed a weapon in the hands of the traditionalists who opposed 'new fangled devices' and to counter it copies of Captain Tyler's report on the accident, which was exceptionally detailed and lengthy, were sent to 189 railway companies. He found much to criticize and condemn. In the first place he censured the station staff at Brighton for dispatching trains at such short intervals over a difficult section where an effective method of block working should certainly be introduced without delay. It was disgraceful that a man in so responsible a position as Signalman Killick should be compelled to work for twenty-four hours at a stretch in order to earn one day of rest a week. He considered the Whitworth patent signal most unsatisfactory. There had been other occasions, he had found, when signals of this kind had failed to respond to the treadle and any automatic arrangement of this kind which was proved unreliable was more dangerous than a simple manual device. He strongly criticized the type of telegraph instruments used for the protection of the tunnel. The fact that their needles normally registered zero meant that the signalmen using them must needs commit to memory the signals they transmitted and on occasions such as this when trains followed quickly upon one another the risk of confusion and error was very great. Electric block instruments should retain a positive indication to show whether the section they governed was clear or occupied. Bad equipment such as this, he concluded, tended to compromise the installation of good equipment.

Captain Tyler then embarked upon a lengthy discourse on block working in general which is of great interest by reason of the light it sheds on the safety arrangements prevailing at this particular moment of railway history. Tyler took as his desirable model the South Eastern Railway where the absolute block system had been worked for some years using Tyer single needle two position instruments for each line of rails and single beat bells with different toned gongs to denote, offer and accept the trains from cabin to cabin. In their two positions the Tyer instruments showed 'Line Clear' and 'Line Blocked'. The South Eastern was, indeed, working the system which is still in use today on some lines. By contrast the London & North Western and the Great Northern Railways were operating peculiar forms of 'permissive' block systems over their main lines between Euston and Rugby and between King's Cross and Hitchin. The North Western had telegraph stations two miles apart in which trains were entered on a slate when they were accepted and crossed off as they passed. Each station was equipped with three position block instruments for each line of rails which indicated thus:

Line
Obstructed

Train on   Line
Line   Clear

But the block was not absolute. Only on 'Line Obstructed' was a train brought to a stand. On the 'Train on Line' indication a following train was allowed to proceed at reduced speed under caution signals.

On the Great Northern only one instrument was used for both lines of rails. It read thus:

Line Clear

Up Line   Down Line

Captain Tyler considered this system dangerous and defective though he had to admit that in the telegraph offices record books of train movement were efficiently kept and he commended the practice of giving an 'Is line clear?' signal on train approach. Yet here again the block was not absolute, trains being allowed to proceed at fifteen miles per hour under caution signals into an occupied section. Both the companies declared that without this 'permissive' system they could not pass the traffic over these busy main lines. To this Captain Tyler retorted that if traffic had become so great that an absolute block could not be observed on sections only two miles long then it was high time such Companies laid additional lines. An absolute block, separate instruments for each line of rails and a third set for communication, this, he said, was the system to aim for.

What was the effect of this lengthy homily upon the Brighton Company? One might suppose that after such a disaster it would find them in a somewhat chastened mood and disposed to listen to such words of wisdom. Not a bit of it.

The London, Brighton & South Coast Railway knew better. They were at this time numbered among the black sheep that no persuasion could bring into the fold. They knew that old ways were best whatever interfering Government officials might say about costly and complicated gadgets. The chill and formal reply to his report which Captain Tyler received from the secretary Frederick Slight is typical of the attitude which the inspectors had to oppose in their fight for 'interlocking and block working'. Reading it we seem to hear no forgotten secretary but the cold, ghostly voice of John Chester Craven, that most formidable martinet among locomotive superintendents.

My board feel bound to state frankly that they have not seen reason to alter the views which they have so long entertained on this subject, and they still fear that the telegraphic system of working recommended by the Board of Trade will, by transferring much responsibility from the engine drivers, augment rather than diminish the risk of accident. Indeed they think it is open to grave doubt whether the circumstances of the serious collision in question do not, when fairly considered, tend to prove that the increasing practice of multiplying signals, and thus lessening the responsibility of the engine driver who is in charge of the motive power, and whose own life is at stake, has not resulted in reducing rather than increasing the safety of railway locomotion.

Yet Tyler won a small but significant victory. The Brighton Company condescendingly agreed to give the block system 'a fair trial' between Brighton and Hassock's Gate. It was the thin end of the wedge.

Only a week after the Clayton Tunnel accident there was another disastrous collision at Kentish Town on the Hampstead Junction Railway which would not have occurred if the points at the station had been centrally controlled and interlocked with signals. The railway was at this time staffed by the North Western but worked by the North London Company.

On the afternoon of September 2nd a ballast train passed through Kentish Town station on the up line and set back into a siding on the up side to unload ballast for some new coal sidings which were being laid out. It had emptied and was ready to depart when the 6.35 pm regular up passenger train ran through. It was North Western practice at this time to attach a target to the rear of the last coach of a train if a second part or a special train was following. But the 6.35 carried no target and the men in charge of the ballast train did not know that a special excursion train for railway employees was following it. At 7 pm the regular signalman, Fessey, went off duty leaving a lad of nineteen named Raynor in charge. Meanwhile, the empty ballast train pulled out of the siding on to the up line. The engine was then detached and ran round its train via the down line. It had been coupled up and was pulling its train forward over the crossover on to the down line when the excursion appeared at speed and crashed into it. Three coaches broke away and ran down an embankment. Sixteen lives were lost. Raynor's signals showed clear for the excursion and it seems likely that owing to the dusk and the curve of the line he mistook the position of the ballast train when he lowered his signals and thought it was standing on the down line.

By 1870 some progress had been made with interlocking, but even on the great main lines the arrangements were incomplete, rudimentary and dangerous. This was revealed by the wreck of the up Irish Mail at Tamworth on the night of September 4th, 1870. The attached simple diagram will help to explain the arrangements at Tamworth at that time and also the circumstances of the accident.

It will be noticed that the platform roads were loops clear of the fast running lines and that the points controlling them were worked from two cabins hidden from each other by the station buildings and the Midland railway bridge. Each signalman had under his control distant, outer home and inner home signals for the up and down lines respectively but of these only the inner homes were interlocked with the loop points. All the others were free. The two sets of points marked A which controlled the exit from the up platform at the south end of the station were interlocked to protect the fast line from conflicting movement. In other words, if the points were set for a through train the platform road points were automatically set for a siding which ended in a dead end. Near this dead end was an engine house which pumped water from the River Tame into a small reservoir for locomotive purposes. Telegraph apparatus had just been installed in the signal boxes but was not yet operating so that the signalmen received no advice of approaching trains.

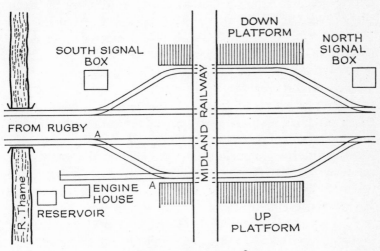

TAMWORTH STATION, 1870

On this night the Irish Mail had been delayed by the late arrival of the steamer at Holyhead and it was thirteen minutes behind time when it approached Tamworth at speed at 4.9 am. Distant and outer home signals both showed clear and the unfortunate driver kept his regulator open quite unaware of the most deadly trap which had unwittingly been prepared for him for fully sixteen minutes before his arrival.

James Higgins in the south box had been expecting the Mail and had set his road accordingly which meant that the up platform line was open to the siding. Signalman Evans in the north box, however, had become confused because his watch had stopped. He was expecting a goods train, he said, and had the road set for the up platform. Even when he saw headlights approaching fast he still did not realize it was the Mail but thought it was a light engine. The driver may have seen that the loop home signal was off and the main on but such a warning came far too late. The Mail rocked over the crossover and thundered through the up platform with sparks flying from the wheels. It is just possible that even at this eleventh hour Signalman Evans might have averted disaster by resetting his road and bringing the Mail back on to the main. But by cruel mischance his attention was distracted by a down goods train which was at that instant passing his box and he did not see what was happening. The engine of the Mail crashed through the stop block at the end of the siding and landed on its wheels in the middle of the river. A coach and a postal van piled up in the reservoir and ten passengers and two sorters had an unexpected early morning bathe. One passenger and the unfortunate engineman were killed and a guard very seriously injured. The accident would have been much worse had not the train been fitted with Fay's patent continuous brakes which reduced its speed from fifty miles an hour to ten at the moment of collision. They might, Captain Tyler thought, have saved it altogether had not the rail been very greasy at the time. He pointed out the dangers arising from lack of information about train movement and the obvious defects of the signalling and interlocking arrangements.

Another bad accident on the North Western main line at Harrow in November – a rear collision in fog between the five o'clock Liverpool and Manchester express and a goods train – called forth more criticism of the 'permissive' block system and the close interval between trains which it allowed. To provide the regulation ten minute clearance the heavy goods train had been allowed only sixteen minutes to run the five and a half miles to Harrow and then shunt to clear the express. The shunting operation was delayed by the breakage of a wagon coupling and the train had just been re-united when the express, a train of nineteen vehicles drawn by two engines, crashed into the rear. The signals were at danger but were overrun in the fog. Porter White of Harrow ran back waving a red lamp and laying detonators but only got 300 yards before the express bore down upon him. There were seven deaths including Driver Shelvey on the leading engine who was criticized for driving too fast in view of the bad visibility.

The seventies were indeed a black decade in railway history. They began with the Newark disaster in June 1870 and ended with the fall of the Tay Bridge in December of 1879. And between the Harrow accident in November and the end of the year there were three more serious accidents, Brockley Whins, Stairfoot and Marshmoor crossing, of which the two last-named are dealt with in other chapters.

Brockley Whins on the North Eastern line between Sunderland and Gateshead and the junction for branches to South Shields and Washington was a very peculiar station in 1870, and its layout was of a kind unlikely to appeal to Board of Trade inspectors. It presented only one platform face to the main up line. This meant that in order to call at the station, down stopping trains must needs cross over to the up line. There was no interlocking gear whatever at the station at the time of the accident. The crossover which admitted down trains to the platform had originally been equipped with weighted levers so that it normally lay open for through running. But this arrangement had been done away with and, instead, the two points had been connected by rodding to a single lever, unweighted, in a small pointsman's cabin. On the day in question the pointsman had admitted a down passenger train over the crossover points to the platform and had then forgotten to reset them. As a result a down coal train met an up express in violent head-on collision in the middle of the crossover. The goods was travelling at fifteen miles an hour at the time and the express at thirty. The driver and fireman on the goods jumped for their lives at the last moment, but the engine crew and the guard of the express were numbered among the five who perished. Fifty-seven passengers were injured. The coroner's jury found that the accident was due to the negligence of the pointsman and criticized the fact that he had someone with him in his cabin to distract his attention.

The inspector, Colonel Yolland, had some particularly pungent remarks to make in his report on this accident, not only about the North Eastern Railway Company but about coroner's juries. He pointed out that the shunter who had come to the pointsman's cabin to advise about train movements had a perfect right to be there and that the jury's verdict was misleading.

This verdict [said Yolland] and the subsequent remarks supply further confirmation, if any were needed, of the fact that coroner's inquests, as generally conducted, are singularly ill calculated to ascertain the real causes of railway accidents; but they are supposed to be sometimes serviceable, as in this instance, to the railway companies, in concealing the mismanagement of the Company from the public.

He then turned a baleful eye upon the North Eastern.

I find [he said] the Company's management wholly to blame for the accident. It is fifteen years since I first drew attention to the danger of allowing facing points to be moved by the heedless action of pointsmen.

It was fourteen years since means had been devised to remedy this danger and the inspectors had insisted on their use on new lines for upwards of ten years 'in the face of the most strenuous opposition on the part of important railway companies'. The North Eastern's attention had been already drawn to this matter by Captain Tyler as long ago as 1863. The Company's excuse was that the layout at Brockley Whins was due for complete alteration. If this was so, he asked, why had the points in position been altered when the older weighted arrangement was manifestly safer?

So devastating an argument was unanswerable. Indeed the long battle for 'interlocking and block working' was going well. But before victory was won there were to be two more major disasters, both in Scotland, due to the absence of these essential safeguards. The first occurred at Kirtlebridge on the Caledonian main line on October 2nd, 1872, and the second on the Edinburgh to Glasgow line of the North British at Manuel (Bo'ness Junction) on January 27th, 1874. In both cases expresses ran into shunting goods trains.

The train involved in the Kirtlebridge disaster was the 9 pm night Scotch express from Euston. It had been delayed on the North Western by the derailment of a wagon at Grayrigg and left Carlisle at 7.50 am, one hour and fifty minutes late. It consisted of eighteen vehicles drawn by two locomotives. At Solway Junction, just north of Kirtlebridge, a new layout was fully interlocked, but at Kirtlebridge itself there was no interlocking, nor was the line worked on the block system. At 7.55 am a goods train arrived at Kirtlebridge and began to shunt. The intention was to drop off some wagons in sidings on the down side and then to cross over to the up line to clear the down for the express. The crossover points were not controlled by the signalman but by ground levers and they were over 300 yards away from his box. Those in charge of the shunting operations failed to keep the signalman informed about their manoeuvres; nor did he receive any advice by telegraph concerning the whereabouts of the express. Despite the local rule that the signals should be kept at danger until they were whistled 'off' by an approaching train, the down signals were showing clear.

Having completed its shunting operations on the down side, the goods locomotive crossed over to the up line leaving the down main line clear. It then pulled a long rake of wagons out of a siding and proceeded to push them down the up line with the object of clearing a set of points in the rear. It was at this juncture that the Kirtlebridge stationmaster made two fatal mistakes. He momentarily forgot that the belated express had not yet passed and he mistook the purpose of the shunting movement. Believing there was more shunting to be done on the down side he threw over the crossing points and so diverted the wagons on to the down line. As he did so the express appeared, running at forty miles an hour, and a fearful collision ensued. The leading locomotive finished up on its side on the up line facing the way it had come, while its tender was flung on to the down platform where it came to rest standing on its wheels. The train engine remained on the rails with its tender and the wreckage of the three leading coaches reared against it. Eleven passengers and one engineman died and the wretched stationmaster was charged with culpable homicide. Happily he was acquitted and, as in the case of the Brockley Whins accident, Captain Tyler's report stressed the fact that the disaster was due primarily, not to the errors of the railway staff, but to the system of working which allowed them to happen. Once again 'interlocking and block working' was the answer.

Manuel is a name with unlucky railway associations. On October 13th, 1862, fifteen lives were lost in a head-on collision in a deep cutting between Manuel and Winchburgh during temporary single line working. And on a subsequent occasion a driver was scalded to death there when the coupling rod of his engine broke and pierced the side of the firebox. On this January day of 1874 the disaster of Kirtlebridge was repeated in almost every detail at Manuel. And the tragedy in this case was heightened by the fact that the absolute block system was in process of installation at the time and was brought into use only ten days after the accident. There was no telegraph system in operation and no interlocking.

The train concerned in this disaster was an East Coast night Scotch express which was divided at Edinburgh. The first portion for Glasgow was due to leave Edinburgh at 6.30 am and the second for Perth five minutes later. On this occasion the train was late and the first portion ran past Bo'ness Junction box just beyond Manuel station at 7.10 on the down (Glasgow) line. Five minutes before this a goods train had arrived in Bo'ness up sidings from Causeway End via the Bo'ness Low Junction curve. Now Rule 229 of the Company stated that all goods trains must shunt clear not less than fifteen minutes before an express was *due*. The Perth express was due at 7.7 and allowing for late running it could be expected to pass at 7.15. Yet no sooner had the Glasgow portion gone through than this goods train was shunted across on to the down main line. It was explained at the inquiry that owing to the traffic to be handled it had become quite impossible to carry out Rule 229, but even so it was a movement of such perilous folly that there is reason to believe the suggestion that owing to their late running the station staff confused the two trains, thought the first had previously passed and mistook the Glasgow for the Perth. Be this as it may, the goods train proceeded to fly shunt some wagons into Bo'ness south sidings with the signalman, Gordon, and the guard, Anderson, holding over the points while an inspector, Cummings, superintended the operation. While this was going on there is some doubt as to the position of the down main line signals. Manuel station distant, which was nearly three-quarters of a mile away and controlled from the station cabin, was certainly at clear. At the inquiry Cummings insisted that he had not forgotten the Perth express. He alleged that when shunting began he said to Gordon, 'Be quick, the express is due,' and that Gordon replied, 'It's all right, my signals are on.' Yet in the light of what followed it would seem that in fact Gordon's signals were off, that he only set them to danger when it was too late and that Cummings knew it. For the goods had shunted its first rake of wagons and was setting back for a second time when Cummings heard the roar of the approaching express and at once called out to Gordon, 'Here's the express; see what we have done; give them your red.'

Gordon, it seems certain, at once rushed to his levers and threw them back to danger.

Fireman Sutherland on the express was firing as the train approached the junction and did not see the signals, but it is probable that the Bo'ness inner repeater, only 450 yards from the point of collision, flew to danger just as the express approached. For his driver, Robert Allan, suddenly shouted, 'Brakes! Brakes! that is a red, but it is too late,' opened his whistle and flung over his reversing lever. Allan knew the position of those outer signals, but these were the last words he ever spoke. The engine of the express was running tender first, and in the collision which followed the wretched man was buried in coal up to his neck and crushed against the searing backplate of the firebox. Such was the violence of the collision that a road bridge near the point of impact was so badly damaged that it had to be demolished. Sixteen passengers perished in the leading Caledonian third-class coach which was smashed to pieces and in the following coaches twenty-eight more were injured. Only the last two vehicles of the express, an East Coast Joint Stock composite coach and a van, survived practically undamaged.

When, at the inquiry, Colonel Yolland criticized the practice of allowing locomotives to run tender first on express trains, Thomas Wheatley, the North British Locomotive Superintendent, explained that the Caledonian objected to North British engines running over their metals to Greenhill to turn and that congestion was such that engines were often delayed two hours in the process. A new turntable was under construction at Larbert which would relieve the situation. Like the block telegraph, it was an improvement which came too late to save Driver Allan.

Whatever the precise rights and wrongs of the Manuel disaster may have been, the moral was the same: 'interlocking and block working'. Had the block telegraph system been working Gordon could not have remained unaware of the approach of the express. Had there been interlocking between points and signals the position of the junction signals would not have been in doubt. With the points open to the south sidings for the goods to shunt, they could not have failed to show DANGER. On such congested lines as that between Edinburgh and Glasgow it had become obvious that the old system of train working was no longer practicable without the gravest danger. Its day was done.

3

BLOW-UPS AND BREAKDOWNS

Boiler Explosions – Tyre Failures – Hatfield – Shipton –
Cowie Viaduct – Llantrissant – Weedon – Penistone –
Unstable Locomotives – Doublebois – Tavistock – Charles-
town Curve – Sevenoaks

NOT SO long ago an express from Liverpool to Euston became derailed just south of Weedon station, and the subsequent inquiry showed that faulty fitting of the bogie wheel
axle boxes on the locomotive was the cause of the disaster.
Serious accidents of this kind caused solely by some mechanical defect or material failure in the locomotive or its train are
becoming increasingly rare. Better materials capable of with-
standing higher stresses, better equipment for material testing
and a rigid system of inspection have between them greatly
reduced these risks. Nevertheless, the flawed or fatigued part
or the fitter's error must sometimes elude the most vigilant
scrutiny. For this reason failures on the road still occur from
time to time, but they seldom lead to serious consequences
unless there is negligence in other quarters. A train halted in
mid-section is today perfectly protected by the block system
provided the rules are properly observed.

In the old days of the time interval system the broken-down
train was much more of a menace. Moreover, such breakdowns
were more frequent and were often, as in the case of the
Weedon accident, disastrous in themselves. One type of failure
which occurred all too often when railways were young but
which is now very rare was the boiler explosion. Nowadays
when we take our seats in the express it never occurs to us to
wonder whether the boiler of our locomotive will burst before
we reach our destination. But there was a time when it was
always a possibility although happily for the passengers' peace
of mind they did not realize it. Boilers were often only in-

frequently and cursorily examined, while to make matters worse the Salter type safety valves fitted at that time were all too easily tampered with as I know from personal experience.

Many years ago I helped an old driver to pull up some trees with the aid of a cable traction engine. The engine was nearly as old as he was and was fitted with Salter safety valves. The cable was run out, attached to a tree, and the engine pulled. If the tree refused to budge, the old man merely screwed down the knurled nut of the safety valve and then waited, placidly puffing at a stubby pipe, until steam pressure was sufficient to overcome stubborn tree roots. I watched this proceeding from a distance. So it was on the railway until that king of Crewe, John Ramsbottom, delivered us from evil by inventing a valve which the most ingenious engineman could not alter. It was a very notable contribution to railway safety. That handy nut on the Salter valve was far too great a temptation to men whose engines possessed little reserve of power and were often grossly overloaded.

In the quiet of Bromsgrove churchyard lie the remains of Driver William Scaife and Fireman Rutherford of the Birmingham & Gloucester Railway. Locomotives are carved on the headstones of their graves, while Driver Scaife's bears a touching inscription. Both were killed when the boiler of their engine exploded in Bromsgrove station on November 10th, 1840. We do not *know* whether they had tampered with the safety valve, but the fact that the disaster occurred at the foot of the celebrated Lickey incline is highly suggestive. Incidentally, the locomotive involved was an experimental one named 'Eclipse' and not, as the tombstones depict, one of the curious engines built for this railway by the American Norris in Philadelphia.

One fine June evening in 1849 the broad gauge goods engine 'Goliah'[1] of the 'Hercules' class was approaching the

[1] The spelling of broad gauge engine names was often peculiar. It would seem that orders were sometimes given orally to the unscholarly makers of nameplates at Swindon, who then did their best with such

foot of the Hemerdon incline on the South Devon Railway when the crown of the firebox collapsed. Fortunately in this case the crew escaped with their lives. The Board of Trade inspector recovered the safety valves from the wreckage and had them tested. He found that they lifted at 150 lb per square inch, more than double the working pressure of 70 lb. Not unnaturally, he had something to say on the subject to the locomotive department of the Great Western Railway, who provided the South Devon motive power, and as a result the following edict went forth:

Notice to Enginemen and Firemen
Paddington, July 5th, 1849

A serious accident having occurred on the South Devon Railway in consequence of the roof of the firebox giving way, the enginemen and firemen are desired strictly to observe the following order: The engineman must once every week *himself* examine both his safety valves and ascertain that they are in proper working order, and that the spring valve is not screwed down to a pressure beyond 75 lb on the square inch in the old engines, and 100 lb in the engines built at Swindon.... Both enginemen and firemen are strictly forbidden on any account to *hold down* the lever-valve after it is screwed to the proper pressure, or at any time to press the boilers beyond the pressures allowed by this order.

(Signed) Daniel Gooch

Unfortunately it was not a case of 'other companies please copy', for in the very next year a London & Birmingham locomotive exploded with great violence at Wolverton. The engine was standing in the yard and had been blowing off for some time until a labourer, disliking the noise of the escaping steam, silenced it by the simple expedient of screwing down the safety valves. By a kind of rough justice the costive locomotive

---

curious results as 'Lagoon' for Laocoon'. Another engine of this class was named 'Sampson'.

retaliated by slicing off one of his unduly sensitive ears with a flying fragment.

The hard lessons of experience and the introduction of the Ramsbottom valve reduced the number of accidents due to excessive pressure, but year after year the Board of Trade returns continued to record spectacular explosions. They were caused, almost invariably, by defects which would have been disclosed by frequent and thorough inspection. But motive power departments appear to have adopted a policy of *laissez-faire* where boilers were concerned and ignorance was bliss in those days until corroded plates could stand no more.

Nothing seemed to be amiss with the down Irish Mail on the night of July 8th, 1861, when it ran smartly in to the platform at Rugby dead on time. Yet station staff, engine crew and passengers alike would surely have taken very rapid evasive action had they known that the lower plates of the boiler barrel on the locomotive, one of the 'Bloomer' class built by Sharp Bros of Manchester in 1851, had become so corroded that they were only a sixteenth of an inch thick. Such a state of affairs conjures up a terrifying vision of that boiler 'breathing' like an inflated paper bag under its concealing lagging. The train had left Rugby and was just approaching Easenhall bridge near Newbold Revel when the boiler barrel failed and there was a terrific explosion. It is doubtful whether any locomotive in history has ever disintegrated quite so quickly into so many small pieces. Part of the boiler hit the parapet of the bridge and fell back upon the tender; one of the driving wheels blew off and also crashed into the bridge; the crank axle broke; part of the framing and motion was flung on to the up line while fragments of tubes, boiler lagging and sheeting, feed-pipes and handrails littered both sides of Easenhall cutting for a considerable distance. The unlucky fireman was killed, but otherwise everyone had very remarkable escapes considering that the train was travelling at nearly forty miles an hour at the time. The driver was blown off the footplate on to the side of the cutting but miraculously survived and in the following coaches, which remained upright, only a postal sorter and the leading guard complained of slight injuries. The consequences might have been more serious had not the three leading vehicles of the train consisted of two postal vans and a guard's composite. Three years before, the engine had been re-tubed, but no one had noticed the corrosion of the barrel.

It was precisely the same defect that caused the broad gauge single 'Perseus' to blow up in Westbourne Park shed in November 1862, but in this case the boiler had not been examined at all for seven years. The explosion killed two cleaners and a 'lighter up'; part of the boiler weighing 15 cwt was blown through the roof and landed in the carriage sidings 100 yards away while the engine itself was flung 30 feet.

The year 1864 was marked by three particularly destructive explosions on three different railways. On May 5th a Midland six-coupled goods engine, No 356 built by Kitson and Co., had worked a train from Leeds to Colne and was getting ready to return. Her driver and fireman were oiling round in Colne yard when the boiler blew up. The driver was killed instantly and his fireman badly injured; an old woman lying in bed in a cottage a quarter of a mile away was hit on the leg by a piece of plate which fell through the roof and substantial portions of No 356 were still being recovered from the surrounding countryside a fortnight later. In this case not only was the boiler in doubtful condition but the pressure had been officially raised from 120 to 140 lb, a move which the accident inspector, Captain Tyler, described as unwise. Meanwhile on the ninth of the same month another six-coupled goods engine, No 138 of the Great Northern, succeeded in demolishing the best part of Bishop's Road station on the Metropolitan line. She had brought in the 9.5 am passenger train from Farringdon Street and her driver had just received the 'right away' when she exploded. The station roof was blown off, the footbridge collapsed, a glass screen fell on the remains of the engine and a passenger in another train was injured. The driver was found in a dazed condition, as well he might be, covered in mud and

minus his cap which was recovered later from the Great
Western yard. It was the same story. No 138 had been built by
Hawthorns of Newcastle in 1850, and examination of the bits
and pieces revealed that her barrel plates were little thicker
than an egg-shell.

The third explosion of this series caused equally substantial
damage at Leominster on the Shrewsbury & Hereford joint
line. The train concerned was the 1.25 am goods from Hereford and the engine a little 2–4–0, No 108, built by Hicks of
Bolton. The locomotive was standing in the station and the
driver, luckily for him, had walked back down the platform to
ask a pointsman for permission to start. 'It wants two or three
minutes to your time,' said the pointsman, and at that instant
the boiler went up, completely demolishing a small goods shed
and subjecting the station house to a heavy bombardment
much to the alarm of the stationmaster and his family who
were fortunately sleeping at the back of the building. Subsequent investigation showed that a recent overhaul of the engine carried out by the Vulcan Foundry had included a defective and most peculiar piece of boiler repair work. The
barrel had been patched and strengthened by means of a
circular hoop of wrought iron as though it were a leaky
cask.

Each year brought reports of similar boiler failures which, if
recounted, would become as tedious in repetition as the bomb
stories of the last war. Suffice it to say that after 1870 the
number of explosions on English railways began to decline
steadily. It was realized that high pressure steam was not to be
trifled with; that a locomotive boiler was not a glorified steam
kettle but held in leash a terribly destructive power. Boiler
inspections became more frequent and more thorough and tests
more exacting. Whereas a hydraulic test only 20 or 30 lb
above normal working pressure had been considered sufficient,
an excess of 100 lb became the rule. One Board of Trade
inspector went so far as to suggest that even so severe a
hydraulic test was not good enough and that boilers should be

given such a test under steam in a specially protected siding, but needless to say this alarming idea was not adopted.

Another reason for the improvement was the revolution in boilermaking technique which developments in the iron and steel industry brought about. The Siemens Martin and Bessemer processes of steel making, employed in conjunction with larger rolling mills, produced steel plates which were both bigger and stronger than the old wrought iron plates which boilermakers had used hitherto. The new steel boilers had fewer seams and a greater margin of safety than the iron boilers which they gradually replaced. By the same token, the improvement of permanent way dates from this period, the longer and tougher steel rails taking the place of the old 21-foot iron rails to make possible that smooth high-speed running which we take for granted.

Only one latter day boiler explosion may be mentioned before we leave this subject because it shows that no boiler however strong and well maintained and no safety valve however carefully designed and 'locked' can be proof against human fallibility. It occurred in Cardiff Shed on the Rhymney Railway in 1909. The engine concerned was No 97, one of a numerous class of outside-framed six-coupled tank engines. Many readers will be familiar with the old chestnut about the amateur fireman during the general strike who, when his attention was drawn by an inspector to the low steam pressure recorded on the gauge brightly replied that the needle was on its 'second time round'. In the case of No 97 this really happened. The driver who took over the engine went to the shed foreman with the complaint that he could not get the injectors to work and that the steam pressure gauge was not recording. Had he observed the gauge more closely he might have noticed that the needle was the wrong side of the zero stop. In other words it had been 'right round the clock'. A fitter who had been repairing the Ramsbottom safety valves had reassembled them in such a way that the valves could not open. The boiler exploded with such violence that the locomotive was completely destroyed, while of the men working in the shed at the time three were killed and three more badly injured.

Although less spectacular than boiler explosions in their immediate result, fractures of wheels, wheel tyres or axles, either of locomotives or rolling stock, can have much more disastrous consequences. They have also occurred much more frequently. The cause of such fractures may be either some unsuspected flaw in the metal or crystallization and cracking due to fatigue. Here again better materials and better methods of testing have brought about progressive improvement, although it is only very recently that such failures – one of the most frequent and stubborn of railway troubles – have been reduced to negligible proportions by new ultrasonic methods of detecting unseen flaws. Previously such perilous defects could elude the most minute scrutiny until disaster occurred.

The champions of Brunel's 7-foot gauge always argued that a wider gauge meant greater stability and safety and this contention was certainly borne out by an accident which occurred on the Great Western main line at Southall in 1847, soon after the Broad Gauge expresses to Exeter had begun to fly. It was a most extraordinary affair. The locomotive 'Queen' of the Prince class, then newly delivered from Swindon, was approaching Southall at speed with the up Exeter express when the tyre of one of the 7-foot single driving wheels broke into fragments which flew through the air to bombard a down goods which was passing at that moment. One broken section killed two drovers who were accompanying cattle while another derailed the goods. The stage seemed to be set for a major disaster, for the express was running on to the Wharncliffe Viaduct over the Brent. Yet not only was the goods derailed away from the express, but 'Queen' held the rails. She ran over the viaduct and was pulled up in Hanwell station. Here the driver took stock of the damage and then drove his train on into Paddington minus the tyre.

Six years later a similar breakage on the narrow gauge Lancashire & Yorkshire Railway at Dixenfold had much more serious consequences. Running at forty-five miles an hour, the locomotive slewed broadside across the metals, the three leading coaches of the train were wrecked and five passengers were killed in addition to the driver of the engine.

Again, on February 20th, 1860, the same thing happened on the Eastern Counties Railway. Seven lives were lost when a leading wheel tyre on the locomotive broke as a train was running through Tottenham station and derailment followed. For unpunctuality, discomfort and general inefficiency the Eastern Counties Railway at that time was unrivalled even by the much maligned Chatham & Dover, and in this case the Company did not escape censure. 'The deceased,' the coroner's jury declared, 'met with their deaths from the breaking of the tyre of one of the leading wheels of the engine, in consequence of the defective weld; and had proper caution and vigilance been used the same might have been detected.' Needless to say, railway wheel tyres are no longer welded. They consist of continuous rings of cast steel which are shrunk on to the wheels.

Not only fatigue but extreme cold can weaken metal by altering its molecular structure. For instance, in very cold weather the smiths in a heavy forge will not use steam hammers until they have warmed their heads or 'tups' by surrounding them with pieces of red hot scrap metal. I have seen a hammer head 6 inches in diameter that had not been properly 'thawed' break off as cleanly as if it had been cut with a knife. On the railway this effect of extreme cold is aggravated by the additional stresses of a 'hard road', as railwaymen call it; a permanent way without resilience owing to the frost in the ground. Such conditions caused a disaster on the main line of the Great Northern in the darkness of a bitter December evening in 1870.

The driver of the 4.25 pm train from King's Cross to Peterborough noticed an uneasy oscillation as he passed over Marshmoor level crossing, two miles south of Hatfield. Peering back to see if anything was wrong he discovered to his alarm that he had lost his train. Pulling up at Redhall Box, three-quarters of a mile beyond the crossing, he began to set back cautiously, preceded by his fireman on foot showing a red hand-signal. Before they reached the crossing, however, they were met by a white-faced guard who told them there had been a disaster whereupon the driver again reversed his engine and made with all speed to Hatfield to warn oncoming traffic and summon help. What had happened was this. As the train was approaching the crossing the tyre of the left hand leading wheel of the van at the front of the train broke and almost immediately the wheel itself began to disintegrate. The coupling between the van and the locomotive parted and the former, followed by the two leading coaches, ran off the rails and into the roadway, demolishing a wall and the crossing posts and gates as they went and crushing to death the mother and sister of a signalman who were standing in the roadway. In addition to these unfortunate women, six passengers were killed in the two coaches which were completely destroyed. The accident inspector criticized the method of tyre fixing and recommended, not for the first time, the use of Mansell composite wheels on passenger rolling stock on account of their greater safety and resilience.

The luck which had attended the Great Western on the occasion of the broad gauge mishap at Southall did not hold on the narrow gauge at Shipton on Christmas Eve, 1874, where a broken wheel tyre caused the worst disaster in the whole history of that Company. And once again, be it noted, the accident occurred in extremely cold weather. Owing to the Christmas holiday, traffic was exceptionally heavy and the ten o'clock narrow gauge fast train from Paddington to Birkenhead consisted of fourteen packed coaches drawn by the Armstrong 7-foot single No 478 assisted by a pilot. The latter was due to come off at Oxford, but when the train arrived there half an hour late, Garlick, the district loco foreman, advised stationmaster Gibbs that No 478 would never haul so heavy a load over Hatton Bank, north of Leamington, without assistance. No 386, a second 7-footer stationed at Oxford, was therefore put on. At the same time, to accommodate the waiting Oxford passengers, an extra coach was added immediately behind the train engine, a lad connecting up the Harrison cord communication which passed along the right-hand eaves of the coach roofs and operated a warning gong to attract the driver's attention in an emergency. Oxford must have been short of rolling stock that day, for this additional vehicle was an antiquated little four-wheeler which had been built by Wright and Sons of Saltley for the Newport, Abergavenny & Hereford Railway in 1855.

The train pulled out of Oxford and was soon running through Kidlington station (then called Woodstock Road) at a speed which was later estimated at forty miles an hour. A quarter of a mile south of a bridge over the Cherwell a small piece of the tyre on the right-hand leading wheel of the little four-wheeled coach broke away. This fragment was subsequently found and from this point forward the history of the disaster – the disintegration of the tyre and wheel and the derailment of the coach – was plainly written on the permanent way. The first to realize that something was wrong was Driver Richard on the train engine. Glancing back from his position on the right of the footplate he saw a fountain of snow and ballast flying up from behind the tender. A few moments later his fireman saw a man lean from a compartment window, wave his arms and cry 'Whoa! Whoa!' He also noticed that the clapper of the alarm gong was moving though not sufficiently to sound the gong. By this time the train was about 50 yards south of the bridge which crosses the Oxford Canal between Shipton-on-Cherwell and Hampton Gay, and it was at this point that Driver Richard made a pardonable but fatal mistake. He opened his deep-toned alarm whistle and signalled for brakes. Before the guards in the rear had had time to respond both drivers shut off steam and reversed their engines while both firemen screwed down their tender brakes. The effect was immediate and appalling. The little four-wheeler which, although off the road, had been held upright by the pull of the couplings was instantly overwhelmed and reduced to matchwood by the momentum of the heavy train behind. Couplings parted and nine of the following coaches tumbled pell mell to destruction over the side of the canal bridge. Three more coaches were derailed but remained upright and of the whole train only the two locomotives and the last two vehicles stood upon the rails quite unharmed. In the wreckage that lay piled on both banks of the frozen canal no less than thirty-four passengers died and sixty-five were badly injured. Faced with so sudden and overwhelming a catastrophe the train crew now acted with most commendable presence of mind. As the line was not worked on the block system the danger of further disaster was very great but the rear guard, accompanied by two passengers, immediately ran back down the line and reached Woodstock Road in time to warn the stopping passenger train ('The Cheap') which was scheduled to follow the express. Meanwhile the pilot engine was uncoupled and ran forward to Kidlington station to stop up traffic and summon help.

Colonel Yolland, the Board of Trade inspector who conducted the inquiry into the Shipton disaster, made some strong criticisms in his report. In the first place he had found that the tyres of the ill-fated four-wheeler were secured to the wheels by four countersunk rivets through the rims, an archaic form of construction which the Company had agreed to discard as dangerous as long ago as 1855. Yet the vehicle had been re-tyred in the same fashion in 1868. Once again the inspector urged the introduction of Mansell wheels. The cord communication had failed to work in this emergency and it was apparent that the youth who had reconnected it at Oxford had failed to test it properly as he should have done.

It may be mentioned here in parenthesis that this system of external cord communication, which was invented by T. E. Harrison of the North Eastern Railway, was the subject of a complete change of opinion on the part of the Board of Trade inspecting officers – a very rare occurrence. On the strong recommendation of the railway companies it was approved by the Board in 1859, but on January 1st, 1873, this approval was revoked on the grounds of 'a constant failure to communicate'. On the non-corridor stock of the day, some reliable form of emergency communication was essential, and the Harrison system was not only undependable but inaccessible. Credit for introducing the present internal cord system connected to the vacuum brake goes to the Manchester, Sheffield & Lincolnshire Railway. Their device was fully approved by the Board in 1893 although the Harrison cord lingered on until 1898 when it was absolutely condemned.

In addition to criticizing the cord communication, Colonel Yolland found that the train was deficient in brake power and wrongly marshalled with vehicles coupled both in front of and behind the brake vans. Most important of all was the action of the enginemen. Had they merely shut off steam and allowed the rear guards time to apply their brakes it was unlikely that any disaster would have occurred. The Colonel did not attach much blame to the drivers for acting as they did; he severely criticized the Company for their failure to give their staff any guidance as to how they should act in such an emergency. As a result of this criticism the following new rule was made which, with subsequent amendments to bring it up to date, found a permanent place in the Great Western Railway Rule Book:

If any of the vehicles be off the rails, the brakes in the rear must be instantly applied, in order that by keeping the couplings tight the disabled vehicles may be kept up and out of the way of the vehicles behind until the force of the latter is exhausted, it being desirable that the front portion of the train should be brought slowly to a stand. The application of the front brakes might result in further damage, and great care must be exercised in their application. In all cases the application of brakes behind a disabled vehicle, or the application by the Guard of the continuous brake at the rear of the train, will be attended with advantage, and rear

Guards of trains fitted with the continuous brake must apply the continuous brake as well as the hand brake.

This is a good example of the lessons learned from railway accidents and the reforms they initiate. Except when an occasional train rumbles past, Shipton-in-Cherwell is a very quiet and peaceful spot today. Shipton church gazes down from a gentle slope at its reflection in the still surface of the Oxford Canal while opposite, alone in the wide, willow-bordered Cherwell meadows, the church of Hampton Gay stands beside its ruined manor house. No one would suppose that it was once the scene of a terrible calamity which earned a permanent memorial in the working rules of a great railway company.

Many years later, on October 3rd, 1927, a somewhat similar accident occurred on the LMS at Cowie viaduct near Stonehaven which might have had even more disastrous results than Shipton had it not been for continuous brakes. Even so it was one of the narrowest escapes from serious catastrophe that has ever been recorded. As the 7.50 pm Aberdeen to Glasgow and Euston express, consisting of thirteen coaches drawn by two locomotives, approached the high viaduct the brake reservoir on the train engine came adrift, dropped in the 'four-foot' and fouled the train with the result that the four leading coaches were derailed. The train was travelling at speed and owing to the darkness, vital seconds may have elapsed before the engine crews realized what was amiss. This and the fact that the couplings held probably saved the day for had the rear of the train overrun the derailed front portion as had occurred at Shipton it would undoubtedly have gone over the edge of the viaduct. As it was, the fourth vehicle, a Pullman dining car, carried away a considerable length of the parapet which crashed into the valley below. Another fortunate thing was that by the time the train was stopped it was clear of the viaduct. Otherwise the passengers who clambered, somewhat shaken, from the damaged coaches might have fallen to their deaths before they could be warned.

Since the Shipton accident there has occurred only one major disaster on a British railway due to the breakage of a tyre. This was the Lytham accident on the LMS in 1924 when fourteen passengers lost their lives in the derailment which followed the breakage of a tyre on the locomotive. Casualties in this case would not have been so high had not fire broken out in the gaslit coaches. Although better materials and better methods of testing have combined to minimize this risk today we still hear from our seat in the express the reassuring ring of the wheel tapper's hammer as he goes on his round of our train.

The accident on Cowie viaduct was not the only example of a serious derailment caused by a part of the locomotive coming adrift and fouling the train. Early in railway history, on August 3rd, 1852, the ashpan fell off the engine of the 9.15 am train from Rugby to Birmingham near Hampton station. The leading van and the second-class coach behind it were derailed and ran into the path of a Leamington train killing two passengers and injuring several more. Much more serious was the accident at Llantrissant on the Taff Vale Railway on August 12th, 1893. The engine concerned was No 173, one of that Company's smart 4–4–2 tank locomotives, and the cause was a hidden flaw in one of the heavy T links by which her underhung springs were suspended. This link broke as No 173 was running down the bank from Merthyr to Cardiff with a passenger train and the spring dropped until one of the spring buckles hit a chair on the permanent way. Immediately the spring broke away from the engine and fouled the wheels of the leading van. The whole train was derailed and the first six vehicles ran down an embankment. Thirteen lives were lost. Among minor railways, the Taff Vale was unlucky, for it suffered two other major accidents, both at Pontypridd, in 1878 and 1911.

Curiously enough it was at Weedon, the scene of the recent accident to which I referred at the beginning of this chapter, that there occurred on August 14th, 1915, the most unfortunate and luckless disaster of this kind. Because of the loss of a taper pin smaller than a pencil the down Irish Mail was derailed, ten passengers were killed and sixty-four passengers and staff were injured. The pin fell off the engine of a train which was travelling on the up line. Its purpose was to lock the screwed collar which retained the offside coupling rod on its crankpin. The pin having dropped out the collar unthreaded itself and the coupling rod then came off the crank pin, struck one of the sleepers of the up line and pushed the track out of alignment just as the Irish Mail was approaching at speed. Seldom has so trivial a defect caused so terrible a result. The accident inspector made the sensible suggestion that the collars in question should in future have left- and right-hand threads so that even if their locking pins were lost they would not tend to unscrew themselves in this way.

Accidents due to axle failure have often been more serious than those caused by defective tyres because immediate derailment is the more certain. It was the breakage of a wagon axle on a goods train at Newark in June 1870 that led to the loss of eighteen lives. The derailed wagons fouled the down line and before it could be warned an excursion train from King's Cross ran into the wreckage. Even more disastrous was the accident which occurred at Hazlehead, between Woodhead tunnel and Penistone on the main line of the Manchester, Sheffield & Lincolnshire Railway (later to become the Great Central) on July 16th, 1884.

The 12.30 express from Manchester had cleared Woodhead and was gathering speed on the favouring gradients beside the headwaters of the Don under Thurlstone Moors. Driver Cawood had a clear road. The signalman at Hazlehead box watched the train pass under his windows and on to the Bullhouse curve and then turned to his levers. In the few seconds that it took him to throw his signals 'on' behind the express disaster struck. When he looked again all he saw of the train was the locomotive and a horse-box, which was marshalled next to it, lurching to a standstill. The following coaches had run down the steep embankment on the outside of the curve and lay in indescribable confusion, some in a country lane and some in a field, some smashed to pieces and others resting on their roofs. Amidst the confusion and the cries an incongruous sound was heard. A cock which had been released from a box in the guard's van was celebrating a false and terrible dawn by crowing lustily. The cause of this disaster, which cost twenty-four lives, was an undetected flaw in the crank axle of the inside cylinder four-coupled engine. Cawood stated that as he entered the curve the locomotive suddenly developed a peculiarly uneasy motion which made it evident that something was wrong but that before he was able to react to the situation he heard a crack which was obviously the final fracture of the axle. No doubt the effect of this collapse was to spread the road under the train. The horse-box was derailed but the coupling between it and the engine tender took the strain whereas that in the rear of the horse-box unfortunately did not.

By the strangest of coincidences a second accident occurred in the neighbourhood of Penistone only six months later and this, too, was caused by an axle failure. In this case it was the axle of a private-owner goods wagon which broke. It formed one of a train of empties which was being worked from Ardwick and by great ill fortune the breakage occurred at the moment when an excursion train from Rotherham and Sheffield to Liverpool was passing on the adjacent track. The light derailed wagon struck the engine of the passenger train, was hurled back but rebounded again and this time tore the side out of the fourth coach and derailed it. The rest of the train piled up against it. Four passengers were killed and forty-five injured. This second Penistone accident took place on New Year's Day, 1885, and, as in the case of the disasters at Hatfield and Shipton, the effects of extreme cold may have contributed to the failure of the axle. Nevertheless, although once again no blame was laid upon the Company, the Board of Trade inspector, Major Marindin, recommended a more thorough and systematic examination of all rolling stock, particularly private-owner vehicles.

Despite the fact that the Manchester, Sheffield & Lincolnshire Company were exonerated, these two accidents on their main line undoubtedly did them much harm. The coincidence was a gift for the superstitiously inclined. The bleak and desolate surroundings of the Pennine moors probably helped the legend that Penistone was an ill-fated spot, and for some time afterwards nervous passengers tended to avoid the line, crossing the Pennines by other routes.

The Manchester, Sheffield & Lincolnshire seem to have been dogged by misfortune just at this period for the disastrous collision at Hexthorpe occurred less than two years after the second Penistone accident. The driver of an express from Manchester to Hull overran signals and crashed into the rear of a race special which was standing at Hexthorpe ticket platform, killing twenty-five people. This accident was remarkable for the fact that all the employees of the Company offered to forgo a day's wages in order to defray the costs of the disaster. It was an example of the tremendous *esprit de corps* and loyalty which pervaded all ranks of the old companies and which sounds, alas, like a fairy story today. Needless to add, the MS & L directors declined the offer with thanks, saying that they did not consider it consistent with their duty to tax to such an extent those who lived by the sweat of their brow.

Considering the comparative rarity of serious railway accidents it is a curious fact that the coincidence of Penistone is by no means unique. Other places, for no good reason, have been the scene of more than one bad accident: Tamworth and Weedon on the North Western; Welwyn on the Great Northern; Little Salkeld and Ais Gill on the Midland; Manuel Junction on the North British; Norton Fitzwarren on the Great Western. All these are unlucky names in railway history and others could be added to the list.

Apart from any specific defect developing on the road, derailments have occurred which have been attributed, at least in part, to the design of the locomotive involved. In September, 1893, for example, the Great Western express engine, 'Wigmore Castle' became derailed in Box tunnel, fortunately without any catastrophic results. She was one of a class of thirty narrow gauge[1] 7-foot single drivers with a 2–2–2 wheel arrangement designed by William Dean and built at Swindon in the two previous years. The weight of these engines – 44 tons – was considerable for a six-wheeler and it was thought that the excessive load on the leading wheels was a contributory cause of the derailment. At any rate, as a result of 'Wigmore Castle's' misbehaviour the whole class was withdrawn from service and fitted with a four-wheeled leading bogie under suitably extended frames. The difference in the appearance of these engines before and after treatment is a most striking example of the dictum that 'beauty is fitness expressed'. As originally built the locomotive *looks* front heavy and therefore wrong in proportion. It seems to be sitting up and begging for that forward extension which made the Dean bogie single one of the most beautiful machines ever built.

Champions of the old Great Northern Railway will at this point assert the superior symmetry of the 8-foot single drivers of Patrick Stirling. Arguments of this kind are a matter of personal taste and insoluble. The fact is that there was something uniquely graceful about the proportions of the bogie single wheeler express engine such as we shall never see upon rails again. To choose between three such graces as the Dean and Stirling singles and those designed by S. W. Johnson for the Midland would indeed call for the judgement of Paris. Yet, as we have seen, the first was evolved by trial and error while even Patrick Stirling nodded. On the day before the great man died, No 1006, one of the last and largest of his famous singles, was derailed at St Neots and two lives were lost. A permanent way fault was directly responsible, but the inspector commented upon the abnormally heavy axle loading of the locomotive – nearly 20 tons on the driving axle. This St

[1] A few were built as broad gauge convertibles.

Neots accident occurred on November 10th, 1895. In the following March No 1003, another engine of the same class, was derailed at Little Bytham with an up express from Leeds and again two lives were lost. This time there was no excuse and the six engines of this type were rebuilt at Doncaster in such a way that the driving axle loading was suitably reduced.

'Wigmore Castle' was not the only design of William Dean's which misbehaved. A series of twenty 0–4–2 tank engines built at Swindon in 1887–8 had a much more chequered career than the stately singles. They were an odd design – an unusually long rigid wheelbase and a peculiar rear pony truck with outside axle boxes which were unguided by any hornblocks on the frames. This combination proved unstable and the locomotives were apt to sway alarmingly at high speed. To overcome this trouble Dean replaced the two rear wheels by a very short outside framed bogie with Mansell wooden wheels so that the engines became 0–4–4s and in this form they were sent to the west country immediately after the abolition of the Broad Gauge to work express traffic over the main line west of Newton Abbot. But it was soon evident that the new bogies had not cured the trouble. On April 16th, 1895, two of these engines, Nos 3521, the first of the class, and 3548, were heading the 5 pm down passenger train from Plymouth. While running at fifty miles an hour on a curve between Doublebois and Bodmin Road both engines left the metals. The pilot turned over against the side of the cutting while the train engine finished up broadside across both tracks and several of the leading coaches were badly damaged. It was subsequently found that the alignment of the permanent way in the vicinity had been seriously affected by the passage of the preceding train – the down 'Cornishman' – drawn by two engines of the same class. The inspector, Major Anderson, in his report, condemned the locomotives as being quite unsuited for express passenger working. Once more they returned to Swindon where this time they underwent so radical a transformation that they were scarcely recognizable when they next emerged. They were, in fact, rebuilt back to front; the cylinders were remounted at what had previously been the rear of the frames, and the boilers were turned round with the result that the erstwhile 0–4–4 tank engines became 4–4–0 tender engines. After this drastic surgery they were reformed characters, sober and hard-working members of the Great Western stud, the last of which survived until 1934.

After Doublebois, Major Anderson not only condemned the locomotives involved but he also expressed the opinion that tank engines of this type with heavily loaded coupled wheels leading were unsuitable for fast working. Several railway companies who had used 0–4–4 tank engines on express duties for a long period with complete success considered that it was somewhat sweeping to disparage a whole class because of the misdemeanour of one particular example. However, three years later, on March 6th, 1898, another accident occurred in the west country which suggested that there might be some truth in the gallant Major's strictures after all.

The Great Western's neighbour and historic rival, the London & South Western, also employed 0–4–4 tank engines, designed by Dugald Drummond, for express working between Exeter and Plymouth. On the date in question one of these engines left the road at high speed on a curve near Tavistock while working a down express. It was a spectacular accident though casualties were mercifully light. Once again the inspector, this time Lieut-Colonel Yorke, criticized the locomotive, although he also had some unkind things to say about the state of the permanent way at the point of derailment. He considered that an engine with a weight of 16 tons on the leading axle was not suitable for express service. What the great Dugald had to say about this is not recorded, but all these Drummond tanks were withdrawn from the west and relegated to suburban work in the London area. Here they performed yeoman service for many years, although it is interesting to remark that it was one of this same class which was concerned in the serious derailment at Raynes Park so late as 1933. In this case, however, there was an indisputable permanent way defect. An inspector and ganger were at fault in carrying out track lifting operations without first obtaining possession or ensuring that proper restrictions were imposed. Nevertheless, it may be that a locomotive of different type would not have taken such a violent objection to that unstable section of rail. Accident records certainly tend to show that, all other conditions being equal, tank engines are less stable and therefore more sensitive to permanent way faults than tender engines and that for this reason they are less suitable for sustained high speed running.

This fact was proved by the serious derailment of an entire train on Charlestown Curve near Hebden Bridge on the Lancashire & Yorkshire Railway in 1912. The 2–4–2 radial tank engine which was drawing the 2.25 pm express from Manchester to Leeds quite literally burst the rails asunder on a curve of 30 chains radius. The inspector, Colonel Druitt, considered that while the 45 mph speed restriction which the Company had enforced at Charlestown might be perfectly suitable for bogie express engines it was too high for locomotives of this type which, in his opinion, were unsuitable for duties of this kind. It was one of the first cases where an inspector recommended the fitting of speed recorders to locomotives.

The instability of the tank engine was again revealed by the disastrous derailment near Sevenoaks in 1927. On August 24th, the Southern Railway's afternoon express from Cannon Street to Deal left London in charge of the six-coupled tank engine No 800 of the 'River' class. In the light of after events, several passengers stated that from time to time the train seemed to roll excessively. One of them said that the motion was so uneasy that when he went to the lavatory to wash his hands most of the water shot out of the basin on to the floor. On a straight road the train would steady up, but on a fast curve the rolling would recommence. As the train ran through Pollhill tunnel near Sevenoaks at an estimated speed of sixty miles an hour the rocking became alarmingly violent and as it emerged into the deep chalk cutting beyond the fireman said that he heard a knocking noise. Although he did not realize it at that instant it was the sound of wheel flanges striking the chairs of the permanent way. The locomotive was off the road. Had the cutting been an open one clear of obstructions all might yet have been well, for the steep cutting sides would have prevented the heavy engine from running badly amok and the train might have been drawn safely to a standstill. Unfortunately, however, the cutting is spanned by a high bridge which is known locally as the dark arch, and by the time the train reached this point the engine had slewed to such an angle that the side of the cab struck the bridge pier. It then slewed farther and turned over on its side across the cutting, the leading coaches piling up against it. Thirteen passengers were killed and there was a heavy toll of injury. An odd freak of the accident was that a number of passengers who were quite uninjured had their shoes torn off. They recovered them from the wreckage with laces still tied although their feet were unhurt.

As soon as they received the report of the accident the Southern Railway Company immediately withdrew all their 'River' class engines from service, an action which caused quite a public sensation at the time. It was found on examination that 250 yards from the mouth of Pollhill tunnel the flange of the nearside leading coupled wheel of No 800 had mounted the rail. The mark of the flange was visible on the running surface of the rail for a distance of 23 feet before it dropped over and the knocking sound which the fireman noticed began as the wheels rode over the chairs. Other drivers testified to the unsteadiness of the 'River' class engines and it was disclosed that on a previous occasion there had been a derailment at speed. In this case the engine had miraculously re-railed itself, but telltale flange marks had been noticed on the sleepers afterwards. It was held that the springing of the engine was too hard. Also that a high centre of gravity, aggravated by the tendency of the water in the side tanks to surge, caused the engines to roll to a dangerous degree at high speeds, so much so that in this case the nearside wheels had lifted. The 'Rivers' had their side tanks removed and reappeared as tender engines in which form they gave no further trouble. All the same, it would be a mistake to condemn too sweepingly the 'River' class locomotive in its original form. In the course of experiments, which were carried out after the accident and before conversion, one of the 'Rivers' was tried out on the old Great Northern main line out of King's Cross and ran at a speed of eighty-five miles an hour without developing any dangerous roll. Yet on her own road the motion became violent at a mile a minute. Indifferent permanent way was thus partly responsible, and we may say that, like Dugald Drummond's tank engines, the 'Rivers' were a track-sensitive rather than a defective design.

4

BRIDGE FAILURES – STORM AND TEMPEST

Dee Bridge – Tay Bridge – Norwood – Carr Bridge – Owencarrow – Little Salkeld – Killingworth – Abbot's Ripton – Elliot Junction

O N T H E night of January 20th, 1846, heavy rain caused the River Medway to rise in furious spate and soon after midnight the floodwaters carried away part of a timber trestle bridge carrying the South Eastern Railway over a backwater between Tonbridge and Penshurst stations. As a result the engine, tender and leading wagons of an up night goods train fell through the gap. The fireman managed to extricate his injured driver from the wreckage and drag him ashore, but the latter died soon after.

This, so far as I can discover, was the first serious accident due to a bridge failure on a British railway. When we consider the exceptional stresses of storm and flood to which bridges are sometimes subjected and remember also that railway bridges had to carry loads which were unprecedented at the time they were built, the rarity of such accidents reflects great credit on the railway engineers. Where they built in masonry or wrought iron their work stands fast to this day under far heavier loads than they ever envisaged. This is true of Brunel's famous flat arch brick bridge over the Thames at Maidenhead, the collapse of which under the weight of the first puny locomotives was confidently predicted. But when the railways were built the Siemens-Martin and Bessemer processes of steel making, which revolutionized civil as well as mechanical engineering technique, had not been perfected and wrought iron was very costly so that engineers perforce used other materials: the less durable timber or the brittle and treacherous cast iron.

Nowadays we do not associate the high timber trestle with

this country but with American railroads in the days of bulbous spark arresting chimneys and huge oil headlights. Only railway historians and an older generation remember Brunel's slender timber viaducts which were once so familiar a feature of the landscape of the West of England, particularly in Cornwall. On the Cornwall Railway main line between Plymouth and Truro alone there were thirty-four of them with a total length of four miles, those at Liskeard and St Pinnock being 150 feet high. In old photographs these airy cat's-cradles of wooden trusses, some supported on masonry piers, some on wooden piles, look so fragile that we feel they must surely have been the scene of disasters similar to that on the Medway bridge. Cornishmen did regard them with some misgiving at first and a certain reluctance to travel over the Cornwall Railway was manifest when it was opened. An unfortunate accident which occurred only two days after the opening did not help matters. The down evening train from Plymouth became derailed on the approach to the Grove viaduct near St Germans with the result that the locomotive 'Elk' and the two leading coaches fell 30 feet into the creek below, the engine sinking into the mud, wheels uppermost. The driver, fireman and guard were killed but the fourteen occupants of the two coaches miraculously escaped serious injury. This mishap was hardly calculated to inspire confidence although the viaduct itself was in no way to blame. In fact these frail looking structures were never the scene of any serious accident. In 1852 and again in 1868 the Penzance timber viaduct was partially destroyed by heavy seas, but with this exception they all proved the soundness of their design and construction before they were either rebuilt in more durable materials or replaced by embankments. The last considerable timber trestle which I can recall carried the Criggion branch of the Shropshire & Montgomeryshire Railway over the Severn at Melverley. Now that has been replaced, and none too soon, for it became so dilapidated that I felt some trepidation when I last crossed it on a platelayer's trolley.

It was a little over a year after the Medway accident that a second and much more serious bridge failure occurred, this time to a cast iron structure. The Shrewsbury & Chester Railway, soon to become a part of the Great Western system, was opened for traffic in the autumn of 1846. This new line obtained access to Chester via a junction at Saltney with the Chester & Holyhead Railway. The latter had been engineered by Robert Stephenson and included, between the junction and Chester, a bridge over the Dee. This consisted of three oblique 98-foot spans of cast-iron girders resting on stone piers. Only six months after the opening of the Shrewsbury line the driver of the 6.15 pm train from Chester to Ruabon heard a peculiar noise accompanied by unusual vibration as his engine ran on to the third (Saltney) span of the Dee bridge. Suspecting that something was amiss, he opened his regulator, in an effort to get his train clear but the next instant the girders collapsed. The engine just managed to reach solid ground before the disaster occurred, but her driver had one of the narrowest escapes in railway history, for the tender was derailed and became detached from the engine, while the unfortunate fireman who was on the tender was jerked off into the river and killed. A guard and two coachmen who were travelling in the leading van were killed instantly, one other passenger died afterwards and sixteen were injured, a casualty list remarkably light considering that the whole train fell with the girder. The accident was remarkable also for the courage and presence of mind displayed by the driver. He immediately drove his locomotive, minus tender, on to Saltney Junction where he gave the alarm, crossed over to the down road and then recrossed the bridge by the remaining girders in order to warn up traffic and summon help from Chester. To trust himself to that treacherous bridge immediately after such an unnerving experience – according to contemporary accounts the noise of the crash was heard half a mile away – was an act of heroism in the highest tradition of the railway service.

The report on the accident submitted to the coroner by Captain Simmons, the Inspector-General of Railways, must have been a bitter pill for the great Robert Stephenson. It condemned the bridge girders as too weak and the whole principle of construction as unsound. This report caused a considerable stir in railway circles and for the first time the use of cast iron in railway bridges was seriously questioned.

The Dee bridge disaster was the first railway accident I ever heard about. The present bridge is provided with a footwalk which is connected to the Roodee below and the road above by wooden stairways that provide an ideal train watching vantage and here, as a very small boy, I was for ever dragging my reluctant nurse. It was a thrill, fearful yet delightful, to stand on the bridge and feel it tremble under my feet as a train thundered over. For the disaster impressed itself indelibly on local memory and I was regaled, seventy years after the event, with graphic accounts of how a train once plunged into those muddy waters which I could see between the planks of the footwalk.

Although the memory of the Dee bridge failure may still live locally, it was effectually erased from national consciousness thirty-two years later by the most tragic and dramatic of all accidents of this kind – the fall of the first Tay Bridge on the night of December 28th, 1879. No other railway accident in history has ever made so deep or lasting an impression on the public. Subsequent accidents have taken as heavy or even a heavier toll of human life and have caused a great stir for a time only to be forgotten outside the immediate locality except among railwaymen. But to millions of people who take not the smallest interest in railways the words 'Tay Bridge' still have an ominous ring. The story of that disaster has been told more often and at greater length than any other episode in railway history but these accounts rarely mention the immediate cause of the failure.

Of the two great railway routes to the north of England the Great Northern and North Eastern alliance had a decided advantage over their rival the London & North Western.

Their line was at once more direct and more easily graded. But once they had handed the traffic over to the care of their Scottish partner, the North British, this advantage was lost. North of Edinburgh the deep inlets of the Firths of Forth and Tay cut the line of route. Twice the unfortunate traveller by the east coast route to Dundee and stations north to Aberdeen must needs exchange the comparative warmth and comfort of his compartment for a small ferry boat which wallowed slowly and sickeningly across these storm-swept firths. It was inevitable that such a state of affairs should sooner or later be remedied and in 1871 a contract for the construction of a bridge over the Tay to the design of Thomas Bouch was let to Messrs De Bergh and Company. After three years work, however, the contract was transferred to Messrs Hopkins, Gilkes and Company of Middlesbrough who took over much of their predecessors' plant including the foundry which had been established at Wormit near the south end of the bridge and where much of the ironwork was cast. Bouch's original design was for a single line lattice girder bridge supported on brick piers, each span to be 200 feet. This design had assumed a rock foundation, but soon after construction commenced, Bouch found that he had been misled by the preliminary borings and that the bed of the Tay was not so solid as he had supposed. After fourteen piers had been constructed in brick, he decided to reduce the weight on the pier foundations by using cast-iron columns. At the same time the main spans were increased to 245 feet with the exception of two of 227 feet.

Each of the new piers consisted of a circular masonry base 27 feet in diameter on to which were bolted six cast-iron columns in hexagonal formation. These columns were cast in sections which were flanged and bolted together and filled with concrete. To these column flanges were also secured by lugs, gibs and cotters, the tie bars which provided cross and lateral bracing. The lattice girders were 27 feet high, their upper booms being braced by struts and diagonals. In order to pro-

5(a). The destructive power of head-on collision, Abermule, 26 January 1921. The twisted frame of one locomotive is reared on end while its boiler lies in the foreground

5(b). Gale victim: the train which was blown off Owencarrow Viaduct on the L & LSR Burtonport Extension, Co. Donegal, 30 January 1925

6(a). Ditton Junction, 17 September 1912: L & NWR 'Precedent' Class locomotive re-railed after the disaster showing how the boiler barrel sheared from
the firebox

6(b). 'Greek meets Greek' (Paragon Station, Hull)

vide maximum headway for shipping the bridge was built on a gradually rising gradient from pier 85 at the south end as far as pier 41, and over this portion the rails were laid on top of the girders. From pier 41 to pier 28 extended what were always referred to as the high girders, their lower booms being on a level with the upper booms of the rest of the bridge so that the rails were laid within them instead of on top. By thus raising the girders over the shipping channel the bridge allowed a navigable headway of 88 feet above high water level at its summit. From this summit the line fell much more steeply towards the north shore, the gradient of 1 in 130 stiffening to 1 in 74 over the last four spans. The high girders were constructed in three continuous sections as follows: five spans of 245 feet each; four spans, two of 245 feet and two of 227 feet; four spans of 245 feet. Between each of these three sections was an expansion joint, each had a fixed bearing on one pier and rested on roller bearings on all the others.

This immense bridge, by far the longest in the world at that time, was completed in 1878 and was then inspected, prior to its official opening, by the Board of Trade inspector, Major-General Hutchinson. During the tests which were then carried out six locomotives, each weighing 73 tons, were coupled together and run over the bridge at a speed of forty miles an hour. The inspector then expressed his approval, but he proceeded to qualify it by making two statements which, in the light of after events, were of great significance.

'It is not desirable,' said Hutchinson, 'that trains should run over the bridge at a high rate of speed and I recommend that a limit of twenty-five miles an hour be imposed.' 'I should wish,' he went on, 'to have an opportunity of observing the effects of a high wind when a train of carriages is running over the bridge.' Little did he realize as he wrote these words how terrible that effect would be and in how short a time it would be revealed.

By a people intoxicated with material progress and achievement, the great bridge was acclaimed as a masterpiece of engineering skill. Queen Victoria crossed it soon after it was opened to the accompaniment of a salute of guns and forthwith knighted a triumphant Bouch who was now busily at work upon a bridge to span the Forth.

On that stormy and tragic last Sunday of 1879 travellers by the afternoon service from Edinburgh to Dundee had to suffer the usual discomforts of the Forth Ferry between Granton and Burntisland, for Bouch's second bridge had so far made little progress. It was blowing a full gale up the Firth, and the crossing was more than usually unpleasant. The train which awaited them at Burntisland was the return working of the Sunday Mail from Dundee. The few Sunday trains which ran in Scotland at that time were generally so dilatory and discreditable that the more observant passengers may have been surprised to see so impressive a locomotive heading their train. She was No 224, one of two inside cylinder 4–4–0 express engines, designed by Thomas Wheatley and built in 1871, which were the very first examples of a type soon to become common on every British railway. The explanation of her presence was that she was spare engine at Dundee at the time and had taken the place of the regular engine, a little 0–4–2 Drummond tank 'Ladybank', which had broken down.

It was seven o'clock when the train reached St Fort station on the approach to the Tay Bridge and by this time the fury of the storm had increased. As was customary, the tickets of the Dundee passengers were collected at St Fort and then the train moved off, Driver Mitchell picking up the staff for the single line section at St Fort box as he passed on to the bridge. Such was the force of the wind that after delivering the staff signalman Barclay had to crawl back to his cabin on all fours. After he had sent the 'Train entering section' signal to his colleague on the north shore, Barclay and a surfaceman named John Watt stood by the window of the box watching the tail lights of the train as they dwindled over the girders. They did so because, when the previous train had crossed at 6.5 pm Barclay had noticed sparks flying from its wheels. It afterwards transpired that Shand, the guard of this train, had also observed this. He had applied his brake and showed a red light forward which the engine crew failed to see. On arriving at Dundee he had examined his train but could find nothing wrong. Now Barclay again saw the same phenomenon and was pointing it out to Watt when a sudden violent gust of wind shook the cabin. At the same moment both men saw a sudden brilliant flash of light followed by total darkness; tail-lights, sparks and flash all instantly vanishing. Barclay tested his block instruments and found that they were dead. He and Watt then attempted to go out along the bridge but were driven back by the force of the wind. They next went down to the shore of the Firth. As they stood there the moon momentarily broke through the flying cloud wrack and by its fitful light they saw to their horror that all the high girders had gone.

A number of other people became simultaneously aware that something was dreadfully wrong. Barclay's colleague at the northern end of the bridge wondered why the expected train did not appear, while the villagers of Newport were puzzled and concerned, to discover that their water supply had failed. It was piped over the bridge from Dundee. Close to the main spans of the bridge the training ship *Mars* lay at moorings – the same ship which, only a few months previously, had fired a salute as Queen Victoria's royal train crossed the bridge. A sailor on deck watch followed the lights of the train as it moved out over the girders until the sudden blast which had shaken Barclay's signal cabin made him turn his head for a moment. When he looked again there was a gap in the bridge and no sign of the train. Yet he had heard no sound above the roar of the wind.

A man named Maxwell was also watching the lights of the train from the window of his house on Magdalen Green by the northern shore. When the great gust swept up the Firth he saw what he described as three separate streams of fire falling from the bridge. But evidently this did not appear to him particu-

larly alarming for he said afterwards that he thought the fireman must be cleaning his fire and throwing down red hot
clinker. It was the disappearance of the train lights which
puzzled him and made him focus a telescope on the bridge to
discover, like the others, that the main spans had gone. Maxwell hurried off to Dundee station where officials and people
waiting to meet the train were already concerned by its non-
arrival. His story caused much consternation and Foreman
Kerr with Stewart, a waiting-room attendant, decided to go
out along the bridge to investigate. Such was the fury of the
storm that this was no light undertaking. Both men were
drenched by flying spray and had the utmost difficulty in keeping their feet, but they returned to the station with the news
that the bridge was certainly down.

Now none of these people had actually seen the fate of the
train. Barclay, Watts and Maxwell probably did so but they
were not certain at the time. On both sides of the Firth it was
known that the bridge was down but communication between
the two shores had been broken. Those on the south side hoped
that the train had cleared the bridge before it collapsed while
those on the north believed that the train had stopped in time
and had set back to St Fort. Kerr and Stewart's statement that
they had seen a red light between the girders beyond the gap
caused hopes to run high in Dundee. What light it was that
these men saw never seems to have been positively established.
It may have been a St Fort signal light or more probably it
was the port light of some ship in the Firth below. It was
certainly no train light that they saw. Hopes in Dundee began
to fade when two reports came through from Broughty Ferry.
One said that mail bags had been washed ashore there and
another that a fisherman had recovered a carriage ventilator
and a destination board lettered DUNDEE AND BURNTISLAND
from the sea at Tayport. Finally at ten o'clock the Tay ferry
steamer managed to struggle across the Firth from Newport to
Dundee to establish beyond doubt the certainty of catastrophe.
The steamer put out again in the slender hope that it might

pick up some survivors but owing to the storm her skipper dare not approach too closely the stumps of the piers and the mass of twisted girders which in places protruded from the broken water between them. From pier 28 to pier 41 the whole of the three great sections of the high girders had fallen and from the Dundee end of the gap water was cascading down from the burst water main.

With the fate of the train established there remained the melancholy task of finding out how many passengers she carried. The rumour went round that 300 tickets had been collected on the train at St Fort but this was happily proved false. It had arisen from the fact that the tickets of the seventy-five who formed the actual complement of the doomed train were placed in a box along with those which had been collected on the previous day. The final estimate was arrived at by an elaborate check on the tickets issued from as far afield as King's Cross.

The cause of the disaster was established when a diver was sent down as soon as the weather served. He found the train lying within the southern portion of the wrecked girders and it became clear from this that the train had not, as some had suspected, plunged into a gap already torn in the bridge by the storm, but that the girders had been unable to withstand the increased pressure exerted by the gale on the surface of the train with the result that both had collapsed together. It was due to this fact that she was to some extent protected in her fall by the cage of broken girders that locomotive No 224 owed that remarkable freedom from damage which was one of the strangest features of the disaster. The same was true of her train with the exception of the last two vehicles which were badly damaged. The locomotive remained submerged for three months and when salvage operations were begun in the following April she displayed a marked reluctance to leave the Tay. First a chain parted as she was being raised and again two days later, when she had been brought to the surface and was being towed to the south shore between two salvage craft, the tackle broke so that she sank to the bottom for the third time. She had lost her chimney, cab and dome casing, and her footplating was buckled, but when she was finally recovered she was run on her own wheels to Glasgow for overhaul. No 224 was the only survivor of the disaster and a remarkably hardy one. She worked east coast expresses until 1907 when the coming of the famous North British Reid 'Atlantics' relegated her to more menial duties. For many years no driver would work her across the Tay, but eventually the taboo was broken. On December 28th, 1908, the twenty-ninth anniversary of the disaster, she worked the same Sunday night down mail to Dundee over the new Tay Bridge. She was not scrapped until 1919.

The victims of the Tay Bridge disaster met an instantaneous death. The most truly tragic figure was that of poor Sir Thomas Bouch who would have suffered much less had he gone down in the wreck. For never has an engineer endured so swift and pitiless an eclipse of fortune. The sensation caused by the fall of his bridge has no parallel in railway annals and is comparable only with that occasioned by the loss of the *Titanic* many years later. Concern was widespread and speculation as to the cause of the disaster was rife. Of all this poor Sir Thomas became the scapegoat. At the inquiry the engineer put forward his own theory which was that the rear part of the train had been blown off the rails and had fouled the high girders when it came to them, bringing them down as a complete section from the expansion joint on pier 41 forwards. In support of this contention he drew attention to the sparks which were seen before the collapse and to the damage which the two rear coaches had sustained. This theory was rejected. It was held that the girders had fallen first at their northern end and that the damage to the rear of the train could not have been caused in this way. As sparks had been seen to come from the previous train which had crossed the bridge, it seems unlikely that they were produced by derailment. What did cause this phenomenon? On this question the experts are strangely silent. Was it, perhaps, due to the wheels on the leeward side bearing heavily against the outer guard rails owing to the force of the wind?

The experts who formed a committee of inquiry, Messrs Yolland, Barlow and Rothery, came to the conclusion that the immediate cause of the disaster was the failure of the bracing ties and the cast iron lugs to which they were secured. They found by calculation that the former provided little more than half the strength required to resist the maximum pressure which a cross wind could exert when a train was on the girders. The total weight of the bracing ties used was only 413 tons out of a total of 10,518 tons of metal work which went into the bridge, a proportion totally inadequate. It had emerged at the inquiry that as early as September 1878, very soon after the bridge was opened, the ties had worked themselves loose. Henry Noble, who had been left in sole charge of the maintenance of the bridge, was taking some soundings from a boat near the piers when he heard the ties chattering as the train passed over. Without informing Bouch or the railway company he had ordered packing to be inserted in the gibs and cotters which maintained the ties in tension. It was thought that the ties had become loosened, not only by the stresses set up by previous storms, but by the excessive speed of trains over the bridge. Contrary to General Hutchinson's recommendation, trains descended the steep gradient at the northern end of the bridge so fast that a number of Dundee passengers became alarmed and refused to travel over the bridge in the down direction. As to the defective lugs on the piers to which the ties were secured, this was due to bad workmanship and lack of proper supervision over their casting at the Wormit Foundry.

The construction of the piers themselves came in for severe criticism. They were a makeshift modification of an original design which had assumed a rock base – 'a very grave mistake', said the committee; the bridge should have been redesigned when it was found that the solid base did not exist. The final summing up spelt ruin and disgrace for the unfortunate engineer.

> We find [they said] that the bridge was badly designed, badly constructed and badly maintained and that its downfall was due to inherent defects in the structure which must sooner or later have brought it down. For these defects both in design, construction and maintenance Sir Thomas Bouch is in our opinion mainly to blame.

This damning verdict not only ruined Bouch but also provoked criticism of the Board of Trade and, in particular, of General Hutchinson. If the bridge was so defective, why then had the General passed it as fit for public service? This raised the familiar question as to the extent of the supervision and control which the Government should exercise. In reply to this criticism the Board of Trade said that beyond ensuring that the public were reasonably safeguarded they must assume that the designers and engineers of new works were competent and responsible men. If they did not proceed upon such an assumption, then there was no alternative other than that Government officials should supervise design and construction throughout. This, it was rightly considered, would mean a highly undesirable division of responsibility. It was the opinion of the Government that General Hutchinson had acted perfectly correctly. He had subjected the bridge to a severe test and passed it for traffic. But he had also recommended a speed restriction and questioned the effects of a high wind upon the structure. That these wise and far sighted observations had been disregarded was not the responsibility of the Government but of the engineer. This conception of individual responsibility was the bedrock of Victorian greatness and achievement. That it must also carry with it the risk of failure complete and inescapable was never more clearly revealed than by the tragic downfall of Sir Thomas Bouch.

The magnitude of the Tay Bridge catastrophe makes subsequent bridge failures pale into insignificance. Yet one of them, though it caused no loss of life, had very important consequences. In May 1891 a bridge carrying the Brighton line over Portland Road near Norwood Junction collapsed as an up train passed over it. Fortunately for the passengers the train, although derailed, cleared the bridge instead of crashing into the road below. Only the last vehicle, the guard's brake, hung for a while precariously suspended above the gap and then fell. Only a few passengers complained of injury in what might so easily have been a very serious disaster. The report of the Board of Trade inspector, Major-General Hutchinson, showed that once again the cause of the accident was the failure of a cast-iron girder.

> The cast-iron girder which failed on this occasion [he wrote] had been in its place for about thirty-one years, and during the whole of this time had had concealed in the interior of the web and in the outer part of the lower flange a very serious flaw, abstracting at least one-fourth from the strength of the girder. This flaw was invisible even to careful inspection, nor was it visible when the girder was cast. . . .

He then gave his opinion that even had the girder been perfectly sound its margin of safety was insufficient for the weight of the locomotives now using the line, and finally he urged the replacement of cast by wrought iron or steel girders on bridges throughout the railway system. This report and recommendation had far-reaching results. The Brighton company requested their consulting engineer, Sir John Fowler, to examine and report upon all their bridges. In his reply, Sir John advised the reconstruction of twenty bridges within twelve months and of a further sixty thereafter. Other companies followed the example of the London, Brighton & South Coast. On the Midland alone the Chairman, Sir Ernest Paget, called for an expenditure of £85,000 on the rebuilding of 181 cast-iron bridges. Thus the railways learnt their lesson and new and stronger structures have ensured that there would be no repetition of the early failures.

Occasionally, as the disastrous washouts on the East Coast Route between Berwick and Cockburnspath in 1948 revealed, a freak storm can play havoc with the stoutest structure. Destructive flooding of this kind is peculiar to hill country where exceptional rainfall on some high moorland watershed may convert an insignificant stream into a raging torrent in less than an hour. Thus it was a great storm on the Lammermuirs which did such damage in 1948 by turning the docile and diminutive Eye Water into a destructive monster. For similar reasons the old Cambrian Railway had its troubles on its route through the mountains of central Wales between Moat Lane and Machynlleth. On one occasion a sudden flood undermined the approach embankment to the bridge over the Severn at Caersws during the night, causing the wreck of an early morning goods train and the death of the engine crew. On another a bridge at Pontdolgoch was swept away and a crowded passenger train was halted in the nick of time. But it was the Highland Railway that suffered the most unlucky flood disaster. Local railwaymen know by experience the places where trouble is likely to occur under stress of exceptional weather; suitable precautions are taken and traffic is usually warned in time. But at Carr Bridge on the Highland main line the flood waters struck so unexpectedly, so swiftly and at such a fatal moment that no amount of vigilance could have averted the disastrous result. Of all the accidents mentioned in this book, that at Carr Bridge conforms most closely to the definition of an 'Act of God'.

No line of railway in Britain traverses a country grander or more romantic than the Highland Railway's Grampian route from Perth to Inverness. The names along the line have become so charged by the tragic history of the Highland Clans, with the memories of Montrose or of Charles Stuart, that when they are strung together they have the power of an incantation: Pitlochry, Blair Atholl, Drumochter, Aviemore, Boat o' Garten, Dava Moor, Forres.... But the Victorian traveller was often in no mood to appreciate their romance.

Northbound before the days of sleeping cars he reached the
Highland after a night of extreme discomfort and little sleep
in a train which, more often than not, had abandoned all pre-
tence of time-keeping. Then, even if there were no snow blocks,
the slow journey over that tortuous, heavily graded single line
seemed interminable. To paraphrase Chesterton, if it was not a
merry road it was certainly a mazy one, for to travel from
Aviemore to Inverness via Forres was almost as bad as going
to Birmingham by way of Beachy Head. The Highland Company at last contrived to mend matters and in 1898 they
opened a new direct route to Inverness via Carr Bridge, Moy,
Daviot and Culloden Moor which was no less than twenty-five
and three-quarter miles shorter than the old main line. Climbing to a height of 1,300 feet at Slochd Summit and crossing
the Findhorn and the Nairn by towering viaducts, it was a
heroic feat of engineering, especially when we remember that,
by English standards, the Highland was a small and impover-
ished concern. All the works on this new line were massively
constructed, for its engineers were under no illusions about the
weather in the Highlands.

Yet on June 15th, 1914, circumstances conspired to defeat
them. At about noon on this sultry summer day a terrific storm
broke over the Grampians and the Monadhliaths which culminated at two o'clock in a cloudburst on the high moors
above Carr Bridge. All the burns came roaring down their
glens in sudden tremendous spate. The railway bridges withstood this onslaught, but the Baddengorm, the stream most
affected by the storm, completely carried away the old stone
road bridge which stood on the upstream side of the railway.
The debris formed an effective dam across the narrow glen so
that the floodwaters formed a sizeable lake. As the torrent
continued to pour down from the moors above, it was obviously only a question of time before this dam must fail.
Meanwhile, all unaware of this fearful trap which had been set
for it a little way up the line, the 10 am train from Glasgow to
Inverness ran into Carr Bridge station. Fate could not have

dealt more hardly with the Highland Railway that day for just as the train pulled away from the station and approached the Baddengorm bridge, the trap was sprung. Those who saw the results of the appalling flood disaster at Lynmouth in 1952 will not need to be reminded of the terrifying power which water can at such times assume. When the dam broke a wall of water, tearing down trees and tossing up 2-ton boulders like pebbles, fell upon the bridge as the train of six coaches passed on to it. The engine had just cleared the bridge when it began to subside at the northern end with the result that the tender and the two leading coaches became derailed. Speed was slow on this long pull up to Slochd Mhuic and the train was quickly brought to a standstill. The two derailed coaches were now clear of the bridge, the next three stood wholly or partially upon it, while the rearmost was still on the south approach embankment. It is small blame to the driver that he did not immediately grasp the peril of the situation. Even had he done so it is highly improbable that he could, in the last few seconds that remained, have dragged his crippled train to safety. As it was he climbed down from the footplate and walked back across the bridge to notify his guard of the derailment. He had an extraordinarily lucky escape from almost certain death for no sooner had he reached the other side than the bridge collapsed and was swept away. Fortunately the power of the brakes and the parting of couplings prevented the whole train from following it, but the third and fifth coaches reared up on end while the unlucky fourth fell fairly into the torrent and disappeared in a maelstrom of flying boulders and debris. No coach in railway history has ever disintegrated more rapidly and completely. Its bodywork was reduced to matchwood and tatters of upholstery which were swept far down the burn into the Dulnan and thence into the Spey. When the spate subsided as quickly as it had risen few traces of it remained. The passengers in the upended coaches luckily escaped with minor injuries; the question was how many people had been travelling in the one ill-fated vehicle. Again, as in the case of the

Tay Bridge disaster, rumour was rife. At first it was thought that Sir Oliver Lodge was among the victims, but the case bearing his name which was found in the wreckage was claimed by a niece of his who was in another part of the train. Mercifully the train was unusually empty that day and only five bodies were subsequently recovered from the bed of the burn. The bridge was completely demolished but by a remarkable feat of engineering on the part of the Highland contractor, Sir Robert MacAlpine, a new bridge was completed and opened for traffic three weeks after the accident.

As was demonstrated on the Tay Bridge, the powers of the air can be as terrifying as those of floodwater. It seems almost inconceivable that the force of the wind could be great enough to overthrow anything so weighty as a railway train, yet in 1903 a terrific gale, sweeping up Morecambe Bay from the south-west at over 100 miles an hour, derailed a train of ten coaches on the Furness Railway as it was crossing the long viaduct over the Leven estuary. But it was the narrow gauge railways which run (or ran, for two are gone now) into the farthest west of Ireland that suffered most from the fury of such storms. For along that savage western coastline there is no shelter from the great Atlantic gales; like Valkyries they ride unchecked over the bogs and stony fields where even stunted thorns can find no roothold. In the wild winter of 1898–9 three Irish trains were blown off the metals, one on the Tralee & Dingle Railway in West Kerry with the loss of one passenger and two on the same day near Quilty on the West Clare line. After the West Clare accidents an anemometer was installed at Quilty to measure the wind velocity and some of the rolling stock, both passenger and freight, were 'ballasted' with concrete slabs placed, in the passenger coaches, under the seats. A rule was made that the stationmaster at Quilty should send out a warning when wind velocity exceeded sixty miles an hour whereupon all unballasted stock must be detached from the trains. If the velocity reached eighty miles an hour all traffic must stop.

The worst accident of this kind occurred in January 1925, on the Burtonport Extension of the Londonderry & Lough Swilly Railway. For nearly fifty miles from Letterkenny to Burtonport this thin ribbon of steel encircled the highlands of north Donegal: Glendowan, Muckish, Sleive Snacht and the strange volcanic peak of Errigal. Two glens, Laheen and Veagh, bisect these highlands from southwest to northeast as the Great Glen divides the Highlands of Scotland. North of Lough Veagh, at the mouth of the glen the mountains fall away and the Owencarrow river flows down to Glen Lough through a shallow valley, its floor a bog, its slopes a treeless waste more stone than turf. It must be one of the most desolate and windswept places in all Ireland. The southwesterlies thunder through the central glens while the westerlies sweep down upon this lowland from the Muckish Gap under the saddle of the mountain. Coming down from its summit at Barnes Gap, the Burtonport Extension crossed this valley by the Owencarrow Viaduct, the largest engineering work on the line. Fortunately it was little more than 30 feet high, but it was none the less an impressive structure 380 yards long. On January 30th, 1925, it was blowing a full gale through the valley as a Burtonport train ran down from the gap and on to the viaduct. The three six-wheeled coaches were lifted off the rails by the terrific force of the wind and flung against the parapet. This held them for a few yards but then they broke through. Very fortunately this break through occurred near the one point on the viaduct where a very short and steep section of rock embankment forms the transition from stone arches to girders on piers. But for this all three coaches would almost certainly have fallen the full height of the viaduct and the accident would have been even more serious. As it was one coach came to rest at a drunken angle half on and half off the viaduct, the next turned over on its side while the third turned upside down and lay suspended in mid-air. It was in this coach that the casualties occurred. Its roof was torn off and its luckless occupants decanted into the valley below. As a result of this disaster similar rules were enforced to those on the West Clare line, a wind gauge being installed at Dunfanaghy Road station.

There have been many occasions when abnormal weather conditions – excessive rainfall or severe frost followed by a sudden thaw – have caused slips in deep cuttings. At such times the permanent way men are on the alert, and more often than not lengthmen have discovered them in time to warn traffic. On a few sections which are particularly liable to slips or rock falls, wires are now stretched along both sides of the track and convey a warning to the signal boxes at each end of the section if they are broken or deflected by falls. Sometimes, however, disasters similar to that in Sonning cutting have occurred when by ill fortune there had been a bad slip immediately ahead of a train. Such an accident occurred on the afternoon of January 19th, 1918, on the Settle–Carlisle section of the Midland. Just as the 8.50 am St Pancras to Glasgow express was running into the Long Meg cutting between Little Salkeld and Lazonby a heavy slip occurred as a result of a sudden thaw which completely blocked both roads immediately ahead of the train. Only five minutes earlier a platelayer had walked past the spot and seen nothing amiss. The driver had no chance to reduce speed. The engine ploughed into the heavy mass of clay at nearly sixty miles an hour; then it heeled over on to its side and the two leading coaches were telescoped against the tender. Seven passengers were killed in these coaches, but fortunately there was no fire or casualties might have been much heavier. The locomotive involved in this accident was surprisingly little damaged. She was No 1010, one of the famous Midland compounds and by a strange double coincidence she was involved in another accident at the same place fifteen years later. Hauling the Thames–Forth Express on July 10th, 1933, she ran into a shunting goods train at Little Salkeld. From the casualty point of view this second accident was less serious, but this time the unlucky locomotive was much more extensively damaged, one of her outside cylinders being torn completely away.

The Settle–Carlisle section, the last of the great main lines to be built, suffers more from the weather than any other railway in England. A prodigious feat of civil engineering, the great cuttings, viaducts and tunnels which carry the rails along the high backbone of England feel the full fury of the Pennine winters: gales which whip away ill-secured wagon sheets, blizzards which choke the cuttings with snow, frosts which hang curtains of icicles from the tunnel ventilation shafts and days of cold rain that turn solid clay to soft and treacherous quagmire. Such a rainstorm falling over Wold Fell might have led to a repetition of the disaster in Long Meg cutting had it not been for a keenly observant driver. He noticed as he passed that the ground was bulging ominously in the deep defile north of Dent Head signal box and gave the alarm. Scarcely had he done so when there was a tremendous fall which completely blocked the line for weeks. Single line working was in force at Dent Head for six months after while a massive concrete retaining wall was constructed.

When I was a boy I knew an old railwayman by the name of Andrew Agg who had seen many years of service on the Settle and Carlisle, first as a porter and then as signalman. With his grizzled beard and bushy eyebrows, he was every inch the Victorian railwayman as we see him portrayed in so many contemporary illustrations. He had retired when I knew him to a little cottage in the Cotswolds close beside a Great Western halt where he acted as honorary stationmaster, meeting each train, lighting the oil lamps each evening at dusk and putting them out after the last train. For although in Andrew's opinion there was only one railway company – the Midland – railways were in his blood and he could not keep away from them. He was my Ancient Mariner. It was one of the long looked forward to delights of school holidays to be able to slip away and visit old Andrew; to sit in his tiny living-room where potted geraniums (he used to grow them in his signal box once, he said) excluded half the light and listen spellbound to his tales

7. Sevenoaks, 24 August 1927: Southern Railway 'River' Class locomotive after the accident

8(a). After the Welwyn collision of 15 June 1935. LNER 'K3' Class locomotive No. 4009 and the twisted remains of the rear coach of the Newcastle express

8(b). Fire: the two coaches of the Birmingham–Glasgow express blazing furiously on Beattock Summit, 8 June 1950

of storm and tempest on the high Pennines. He had been stationed at Hawes Junction (now called Garsdale) when the famous turntable incident occurred and I first heard that classic railway story from his own lips. A locomotive was being turned on the table at Hawes when the wind took charge of it. No doubt it was that mysterious Helm wind which blows with such freakish fury out of a helmet of cloud upon the moors in the neighbourhood of Eden Dale. Anyway that engine rumbled sedately round and round and defied all the efforts of its crew to stop it until someone hit upon the happy thought of shovelling some cinders into the turntable pit. After that they built a stockade round the runaway turntable. Another of Andrew's yarns told of a platelayer who was once blown over the parapet of Ribblehead Viaduct, through the arch below and back over the parapet on the other side. This, however, was too much even for my youthful gullibility though I was much too polite to say so.

Snow was the subject of most of Andrew's tales, for on that line it is the railwayman's greatest natural enemy. So it is upon the Highland line on Drumochter, Slochd and Dava Moor or at Fairy Hillocks and Forsinard on the line to the farthest north where, in spite of snow fences, blizzards can bring trains to a standstill and, in a few hours, bury them completely under many feet of snow. But such snowblocks cannot fairly be called accidents whereas snow can positively increase the risk of accident by clogging points and signal installations, bringing down telegraph wires and generally disorganizing traffic operation.

In the great age of railways your chief mechanical engineer was no push-button tycoon who did his engineering by deputy and telephone. As kings once led their troops in battle, so the engineer was often to be found beside his men when there was a crisis on the line. Thus it was that when a fierce blizzard blocked the East Coast Route north of Newcastle in 1889, Wilson Worsdell of the North Eastern himself went out in the cabin of a snow plough propelled by four engines and had an extremely narrow escape from death. Because the first part of the down 'Flying Scotsman' had been snow blocked at Long-hirst, north of Morpeth, the second part was stopped at Morpeth and sent back to Newcastle on the up road. The blizzard was still raging with the result that this second part also became snowbound at Annitsford near Killingworth. The snow plough, travelling correctly on the down road, reached the stranded train whereupon it was decided that the plough should return to the nearest crossover, which was at Killing-worth, and then come back, clearing the up road in order to free the express. All this took place in darkness and driving snow which would make it difficult for the plough crews to see the headlights of the express when they approached it. So it was agreed that they would shut off steam and apply brakes when they reached an overbridge which lay just ahead of the snowbound train. This manoeuvre was successfully carried out except that, either because the rail was icy or the four engine crews failed to act in concert, they did not stop in time and the plough hit the engine of the express. Although it was only moving slowly, the weight behind it was such that its scoop lifted the locomotive clean off the rails. It came to rest with its front framing propped on the chimney top of the leading plough engine. In the shattered plough cabin underneath were Wilson Worsdell, a friend of his, two other North Eastern officials and a local journalist. Little hope was entertained for any of them and the rescue operation was a highly delicate one for fear the tilted locomotive would slide back from its pre-carious perch and complete the demolition of the cabin. After two hours work the reporter and the two officials were rescued miraculously unhurt, but the chief mechanical engineer and his friend had been less fortunate. Worsdell was found lying seriously injured under a pile of heavy jacks and snatch blocks while his companion had been trapped under the cabin stove and was terribly burned. The engineer recovered but his friend did not.

On the evening of Friday, January 21st, 1876, a terrific

snowstorm accompanied by a northeasterly gale swept across a narrow belt of eastern and middle England. All those who experienced it agreed that they had never seen snow fall so thickly or in such large flakes. Moreover, because the temperature of the ground was much below that of the air, it froze as it fell till telegraph wires became hawsers of ice two inches thick. It was in such conditions of bitter winter darkness and blinding storm that there was played on the Great Northern main line a drama which culminated in the Abbots Ripton disaster.

We must imagine a heavy coal train of thirty-seven wagons rumbling slowly southwards from Peterborough, her driver Joseph Bray and his fireman peering for signals through puckered eyes round the cab side sheets for the spectacle glasses were blinded with snow. Behind them, twenty minutes away, running to time and at full speed was the up Flying Scotsman. The signalman at Holme had been instructed to shunt the goods to let the Scotsman pass so he had set his signals to danger. To his astonishment he saw the goods run past his box and he immediately reported to his stationmaster that the train was running against signals. The signal boxes south of Holme were Conington, Wood Walton and Abbots Ripton but the first two were not in telegraphic communication with Holme. The Holme signalman therefore telegraphed to Charles Johnson at Abbots Ripton and instructed him to shunt the goods. Meanwhile Joseph Bray was continuing on his way unaware of the fact that the Scotsman was rapidly overhauling him. At Holme the express was sixteen minutes behind him, at Conington thirteen minutes and at Wood Walton nine minutes. Bray and his fireman saw only white 'all clear' lights until they approached Abbots Ripton where they saw a red lamp waved from the box. Expecting to be shunted, they were travelling slowly and were able to pull up at the box. Bray shouted, 'What's up, Bobbie?'[1] and Johnson called down, 'Siding! Shove them back, the Scotsman's standing at Wood Walton.'

[1] Note that our nickname for a policeman was still being applied to railway signalmen.

It must have been at this moment that Signalman Rose at Wood Walton saw with dismay the Scotch express fly past his box although all his levers were 'on'. Driver Bray began to back his heavy train into the siding. Six wagons were still on the main line when the express suddenly burst through the curtain of snow and pitched into them in a sidelong collision which flung the locomotive on to its right side with the tender lying across the down main line and the leading coaches piled against it. Like Bray, the enginemen of the Scotsman had seen no danger signals. Fireman Falkinder declared afterwards that he had seen both the Wood Walton signals and the Abbots Ripton distant showing clear white lights. He then put some coal on his fire and looked up to see the obstruction close ahead. He remembered shouting to Driver Catley, 'Whoa! here's some wagons,' and then the crash came. Guard Hunt on the goods train was the first to see the approaching express for his van was well down the siding and he described how he saw it pass at full speed with steam on within his train's length of destruction.

The staff at Abbots Ripton made immediate efforts to protect the two blocked lines. The foreman platelayer ran southwards along the down line laying detonators. At 6.45 pm, only one minute after the collision, Signalman Johnson was trying to get through to Huntingdon signal box to give warning and summon assistance. Repeatedly he signalled 'SP', 'SP' (the code for 'urgent and important') on his telegraph but received no acknowledgement. After trying for eight minutes he sent the 'obstruction danger' five beat bell signal to Stukeley cabin, the next block post two and a half miles south. The engine of the goods train was undamaged by the collision and Driver Bray acted with great promptitude and presence of mind. He uncoupled his engine, ordered his fireman to go forward with detonators to protect the down line (not knowing that the platelayer was doing likewise) and sent a relief clerk, Usher, up to the box to obtain permission for him to proceed south. Usher shouted back, 'All right for you to go,' and Bray set off with his guard Hunt on the right of the footplate waving a red lamp.

While these dramatic events were taking place, Driver Will Wilson was speeding northwards through the storm with the 5.30 pm express, King's Cross to Leeds, quite unaware of the frantic efforts which were being made to warn him of the danger ahead. He ran into the snow between Tempsford and St Neots. It was blowing strong from the northeast, he said, and he had never known worse conditions in all his time on the footplate. When we recall the apology for a cab which Great Northern express locomotives carried in the seventies we may imagine what those conditions must have been like. But Will Wilson was made of stern stuff and a driver to whom punctuality was a point of honour. 'I was trying all I could to keep time,' he said afterwards. Signalman Johnson had been sending out his desperate and unavailing 'urgent and important' message for four vital minutes when Wilson thundered through Huntingdon at full speed in a flurry of flying snow at 6.49, only four minutes late on schedule. Although neither side realized it at the time, each second counted now in the race between the northbound express and the men of Abbots Ripton who were trying to save it. The next hope was Stukeley, but again Johnson's warning came too late. The train had just swept past Stukeley cabin under clear signals when the bell rang five beats. Hope now centred upon the efforts of the foreman platelayer. He had placed detonators by the Abbots Ripton down distant signal 1100 yards from the scene of the accident, had run on and was just about to place another when the express bore down upon him running at over fifty miles an hour and he had to step back with the warning detonator still in his hand. It was not until Wilson's engine exploded the detonators at the distant signal that he shut off steam, reversed and whistled for brakes. Immediately afterwards he caught a glimpse of a red lamp waving and heard another engine whistling. This was Hunt and Bray on the goods engine. Guard Hunt had seen the express approaching. He waved his lamp wildly and shouted to Bray, 'For God's sake, Joe, blow up, here's a train coming up.' Wilson had been travelling fast on a falling gradient over rails slippery with ice and snow. He could not now pull up in time. To the accompaniment of the flash and fusillade of exploding detonators, the train slid helplessly and was still travelling at from fifteen to twenty miles an hour when Wilson's engine struck the tender of the Scotch express, cut through it and fell over on its nearside, the following coaches adding to the pile of wreckage heaped upon both tracks. Fourteen lives were lost, most of the casualties occurring in this second collision.

It had now become obvious that there was something very wrong with the signals. Signalman Johnson had all his levers 'on' to protect both lines, but Joseph Simpson, the guard of the Leeds express, described how, after the second collision, he walked along the down line towards Peterborough until he met an up express from Manchester and Leeds. It was proceeding slowly, having already been warned by someone whose footprints he saw in the snow ahead of him. When he climbed on to the footplate her driver, whom he knew, drew his attention to the up home signal. 'Joe,' he said, 'look at that signal, what do you call it – showing red or white?' Simpson acknowledged that it was showing clear. It was indeed the case that Bray had been misled and Catley and Falkinder on the Scotsman lured to destruction by false and fatal 'all clear' signals. The Great Northern signals of this date were of the slotted type in which, when pulled to clear, the arm fell into a slot in the signal post. This had become so clogged with snow, driven by the gale and then frozen solid, that the balance weights would not return the arms to danger, the latter not being balanced themselves. To make matters worse, some of the signal wires were covered with three inches of ice. Joshua Pallinder, a signal fitter, told at the inquiry how he had to hack the ice off the Abbots Ripton signals to release the arms from the slotted posts, how he had to tie a 36-lb rail chair to the balance weight of the up distant before it would return. Even when he had freed the arm of the down distant at Wood Walton it automatically dropped back to 'all clear' because of the weight of the frozen snow on the long signal wire.

The conclusions of the Board of Trade inspector, Captain Tyler, are of the greatest interest and had a permanent influence on railway practice. He pointed out how both collisions might have been avoided in spite of the appalling weather conditions. In the first place, in such weather fogmen should have been stationed at signals with detonators, though he appreciated that the storm came on suddenly at a time when the men had just gone to their teas after a hard day's work. But at the same time he censured the stationmaster at Holme for taking no action whatever when his signalman there reported to him that the up goods had run through his signals although he knew that the Scotsman was following. Had he promptly taken proper precautions the express could have been stopped and cautioned at Holme and the first collision averted.

Turning to the second collision he observed that Signalman Johnson at Abbots Ripton might have succeeded in stopping the Leeds express if he had immediately sent the 'obstruction danger' signal to Stukeley instead of first trying, for that vital eight minutes, to get in touch with Huntingdon. But he thought the most culpable of all was the signalman at Huntingdon who, although he denied it, had clearly ignored Johnson's urgent signal and had not, indeed, acknowledged it until 7.5 pm. He questioned the wisdom of allowing trains to run at such high speeds in such weather conditions and criticized the stopping power of the down express. He also condemned the block system as it was then operated by the Great Northern. He pointed out that even had conditions been perfectly normal there was nothing to prevent the signalman at Abbots Ripton from accepting the Scotch express up to his home signal while the goods train was still shunting only 68 yards ahead. He cited two collisions on the Midland Railway where 'the space interval had been reduced to the thickness of the signal post' and concluded that 'the block system so worked becomes a snare and a delusion'.

At this time it was common practice for all signals to show clear as their normal indication, that is to say they were only raised to danger when required to protect a train. This explains why they became frozen in the clear position. Captain Tyler suggested that in future the opposite should prevail. His recommendation was adopted, and to this day all railway signals show 'danger' and are only cleared to allow a train to pass. The accident had another far reaching result. The Company rapidly abandoned their slotted post signals and replaced them by the centrally balanced semaphore type falling clear away from the post which became so characteristic a feature of the Great Northern Railway.

This example of the Great Northern Railway was not followed by other companies for many years and it was not until 1892 that balanced signal arms which would automatically fly to danger if disconnected became a positive requirement of the Board of Trade. Meanwhile many rod operated signals which could fall 'off' if the linkage failed still continued in use. Another thing which seems odd to us today was the persistent use of white as an 'all clear' light at night. One might have thought that an indication so liable to confusion with other lights that it was necessary to screen the lamps used in signal boxes would have been abandoned at an early date. Yet white all clear lights persisted until the end of the century and it was only in the 1892 requirements of the Board that the green 'all clear' indication was insisted upon, white to be used only for the tell-tale backlight of a signal when at danger. In the same year the interlocking of distant with home signals was enforced. It was at this time, too, that the Board of Trade managed to prevail upon the railway companies to arrange their signals in a uniform manner on brackets or gantries. Hitherto, on multi-track lines or at junctions, some companies arranged signals applying to different lines one above the other on the same post, the semaphores reading from the left from the top downwards. Such arrangements seem to us now highly confusing and fraught with peril. Another aid to easier identification – the use of yellow as a distant caution indication – was not introduced, with the exception of the District Railway, until 1925.

The Abbots Ripton disaster taught railwaymen many lessons, yet, when all was said and done, the 'white devil' of the storm was the real villain of the piece. 'The most subtle ingenuity,' wrote Captain Tyler, 'could hardly devise means more misleading or more certain of success, for luring the engine drivers, with their precious human freight, forward to inevitable destruction.'[1]

Thirty years after Abbots Ripton there occurred, again on the East Coast Route, the worst snow disaster of all. The scene was Elliot Junction on the North British and Caledonian joint line just south of Arbroath, and the date was December 28th, 1906, the twenty-seventh anniversary of the Tay Bridge catastrophe. The worst snowstorm Forfar had experienced for many years, accompanied by a violent wind and keen frost, had created conditions of chaos. The 7.35 am express from Edinburgh struggled into Arbroath over an hour late and there terminated, for just north of St Vigean's Junction all lines had become hopelessly blocked by drifts. Meanwhile a double-headed goods train of forty-one wagons, proceeding south, ran into a snow drift near Dowrie Siding, one mile south of Elliot Junction, and broke into three portions. The engines continued for some distance before the break was discovered. Driver Boyd on the leading engine then decided to go on to Easthaven, cross to the down line, return to Elliot, cross over once more to the up line and then propel the rear portions of the train on to Easthaven. This proceeding took longer than he

[1] The circumstances of the Abbots Ripton accident have probably been the subject of a greater controversy than has attended any other major disaster. The foregoing account is based exclusively on the evidence given at the Inquiry and on Captain Tyler's subsequent Report.

expected for he found that the points at Easthaven had become blocked and he had to go forward to Carnoustie before he could cross. When he finally reached his objective and began to propel the wagons they became derailed almost immediately and in consequence temporary single line working had to be introduced between Elliot Junction and Easthaven. To make this confusion worse confounded, the snow, freezing on the wires, brought down the telegraph lines and put the block system out of action.

Under these appalling conditions the staff at Arbroath were struggling to remarshall the snowbound trains and get stranded passengers away to the south. Shortly after three o'clock in the afternoon they managed to get a local train on to the down platform line. Its four leading coaches were off the platform under the Keptie Street bridge, but fifty passengers scrambled thankfully into the five carriages in the rear. The train then made the short run to Elliot Junction, arriving there at 3.19 pm. Here it was forced to wait until Inspector Souter, who was acting as pilotman over the single line section, returned on foot from Easthaven. Meanwhile Arbroath had got the stranded Edinburgh express ready to return to the south. But they had not been able to get Driver Gourlay's engine on to the turntable so he was forced to run tender first. Because the block telegraph was out of action, the old time interval system had to be introduced, and the train, now no longer an express but calling at all stations to Dundee, left fifteen minutes after the local. Grant, the Arbroath stationmaster, warned Gourlay and his front guard, Kinnear, to proceed with great caution and keep a good look out for the train ahead. The latter part of this advice was easier said than carried out, for Kinnear's look-out window became instantly covered by driving snow, while the plight of the engine crew, running tender first through a raging blizzard, may well be imagined. At Arbroath South Box, less than a mile and a half from Elliot Junction, Gourlay was stopped and again cautioned.

Carnegie, the Elliot stationmaster, had just decided that he would get the passengers out of the waiting local train and draw it forward clear of the platform when the second train appeared through the driving snow, running at a speed which was afterwards estimated at thirty miles an hour, and crashed into the rear of the stationary local. The last three coaches were completely demolished. Gourlay's engine mounted their wreckage and turned over on top of the debris, its driving wheels revolving furiously for ten minutes until John Ogilvie, the driver of the local, managed to crawl into the cab and shut the regulator. He also managed to free Gourlay who was buried in coal. But his fireman was dead and so were twenty-one passengers in the wrecked coaches.

Although Gourlay maintained that the Elliot Junction home signal had given him a false 'clear', it was observed after the accident that the arm was only drooping ten degrees owing to the snow on the wire. In any event, Gourlay's speed was reckless under the conditions prevailing, and evidence at the inquiry showed that he had unwisely accepted 'something to keep the cold out' from waiting passengers before leaving Arbroath. The unfortunate man was sentenced to five months' imprisonment for manslaughter, but the sentence was rightly remitted. For, apart from the appalling weather, the inquiry had revealed that the general organization of the joint line left much to be desired. In the first place the inspector, Major Pringle, had some scathing comments to make about the wagon derailment which, by delaying the local train, was an indirect cause of the disaster. Driver Boyd's idea of propelling goods wagons through snow drifts with no one to assist him but his fireman and a guard was sheer folly, and a derailment was inevitable. Even then, serious delays might have been avoided and the local would not have been kept standing if Inspector Souter had been provided with a pilot engine instead of having to walk between Easthaven and Elliot Junction. No attempt was made, after communications broke down, to keep staff in touch with each other by messenger. Arbroath was not aware until evening that single line working was in force south of Elliot or Gourlay might have been warned. Easthaven did not hear of the accident until 6 pm and it was 11 pm before the news reached North British headquarters in Edinburgh. The joint staff had no equipment for dealing with accidents, not even heavy jacks, and it was not until the early hours of the following morning that the breakdown train arrived.

The Colonel strongly condemned the practice of tender first running, especially in such weather. After considering all the evidence he said: 'My opinion is that if an attempt had been made to get Gourlay's engine turned, the operation could have been carried out.' While it was true that Gourlay had acted rashly, he should not have had to rely on signals in such weather. In extreme conditions of this kind traffic should have been controlled by hand signals and detonators, all fixed signals being lashed to danger. Yet in spite of the emergency created by this terrible storm, not a single extra man had been called out.

As was the case at Abbots Ripton, snow was the real villain of the Elliot Junction disaster but, as Colonel Pringle's report showed, only because it subjected the railway organization to a strain which it was quite unfitted to bear.

5

OTHER MEN'S RESPONSIBILITIES PERMANENT WAY FAULTS AND RUNAWAY LOCOMOTIVES

Wellingborough – Rednal – Staplehurst – Witham – New-market Arch – Runaway Locomotives

ON SEPTEMBER 2nd, 1898, a luggage trolley was left standing on a gradient in a passage at right angles to the platform at Wellingborough station on the Midland main line. Just as the 7.15 pm St Pancras to Manchester dining-car express was due to pass, the trolley ran away, tipped off the platform edge and fell across the down fast line. A postman and a station inspector made a heroic attempt to pull it clear but in vain. The express bore down upon them at full speed and they had to jump for their lives. The engine struck the trolley and the leading bogie was derailed. It travelled on until the bogie fouled a diamond crossover at the north end of the station where derailment became complete. The engine broke away from its tender and finished up lying on its side facing the way it had come. The three leading coaches passed between the engine and tender, the first capsizing on the up line and the second, a twelve-wheeler, being completely wrecked. Five passengers and both enginemen lost their lives. The moral of this – and of many another accident – is that safety on the railway does not depend on enginemen and signalmen alone but that railwaymen of every grade from porters to permanent way staff carry a share of responsibility.

The responsibilities of permanent way men are particularly heavy, for the maintenance of a busy main line in a fit state for fast running calls for unceasing care and vigilance at all times and in all weathers. A constant watch must be kept for cracked or broken rails, for track distortion and mis-alignment or 'pumping' sleepers which require packing. The fishplates and their bolts which secure one rail to another must be periodically removed and oiled. For a certain amount of movement must be permitted at each joint to allow for rail expansion in abnormally hot weather. Serious derailments due to track distortion have occurred in heat waves where rail joints have not been sufficiently flexible. Over and above all this it is the responsibility of the permanent way department to ensure that traffic is adequately warned, slowed down or stopped while their work is in progress. Nowadays the most meticulous precautions are observed in this respect, but it was not always so. By a strange coincidence on June 7th and 9th, 1865, two disasters occurred owing to the inefficient protection of permanent way work.

The first of these accidents happened at Rednal on the Great Western line between Chester and Shrewsbury where a permanent way gang were lifting and packing the up line 600 yards north of Rednal station on the 1 in 132 gradient which falls from Whittington. Near the top of this incline and 1100 yards away they had set up a green flag on a rough pole as a caution indication. At 12.29 pm, over an hour late, an excursion train from Birkenhead left Chester for Shrewsbury. It consisted of twenty-eight coaches and two brake vans, and four more coaches were added at Gobowen. This mammoth train was hauled by two locomotives, No 5, a 2–4–0 with five-foot coupled wheels, as pilot with Driver Anderton in charge, and No 72, an engine of similar type but with six-foot wheels manned by a driver named Evans. When the train passed Whittington and began to gather speed on the gradient, Anderton did not see the warning flag; indeed, when he lay dying after the accident he continued to maintain that there was no flag. Yet Evans on the train engine said he saw it and that he 'touched his whistle' with the object of attracting Anderton's attention. But the latter did not shut off steam until he sighted the men working on the track. Anderton thereupon sounded first his shrill whistle and then his brake whistle, calling for tender brake to his fireman, David Griffiths. By then it was far

too late to check so heavy a train. As they ran past the point
where the men were working, Griffiths felt the engine drop; 'it
shook tremendously,' he said, and he could hear a grinding
noise against the rails which continued until they reached
Rednal station, still endeavouring to pull up. What had happened was that the leading wheels of Anderton's engine had
jumped the rails at the point where the track was unsupported.
All might yet have been well had it been possible to pull up
the train short of Rednal station, but here the derailed wheels
struck the check rail of a set of points and No 5 ran off the
road on the nearside and turned over. The train engine, which
had so far kept to the rails, struck the tender of the pilot and
ploughed its way across the down line. Such was the weight of
the following train that the four leading coaches were completely destroyed and eleven others badly damaged. In addition to Driver Anderton, Evans' fireman and eleven passengers
were killed and thirty injured.

As Colonel Rich pointed out in his report, there were contributory causes for this disaster. The braking power available
was totally inadequate for so great a train, while the load on
the leading axle of No 5 was excessive. But the primary cause
of the accident was the inadequate protection of the permanent
way work. It was not enough, said Colonel Rich, to rely solely
upon the visual warning of flags or lamps; they must be
supplemented by the audible warning of detonators.

The gang who were working at Staplehurst two days later
had been issued with detonators, but they failed to use them
according to rule and the responsibility for the disaster which
followed lay heavily upon John Benge, the foreman in charge
of the work. The Beult viaduct on the South Eastern Railway
main line near Staplehurst was a very modest structure. It
carried the line a mere ten feet above a muddy stream and
consisted of a series of cast iron trough girders resting on brick
piers. The work in hand was the replacement of the longi-
tudinal timber baulks which lay in the girders and upon which
the rails were laid. It was being carried out between trains and

no mention of it appeared in the monthly service timetables. The work had proceeded smoothly and by the afternoon of June 9th only one of the thirty-two baulks on the viaduct had still to be changed. John Benge planned to do this between the passing of an up train at 2.51 and a down train at 4.15. John Wiles, a platelayer's labourer was protecting the up line. According to rule it was his duty to place one fog signal on the rail every 250 yards from the viaduct up to an extreme distance of 1,000 yards where he was to place two 10 yards apart and station himself with a red flag. But Benge had posted him at the tenth telegraph pole from the bridge which was only 554 yards away. Wiles was supplied with only two detonators and was told not to use them unless it was foggy. It was a bright and sunny afternoon.

It is obvious that John Benge and his leading carpenter were so sure of their ability to carry out their work between trains that they had come to look upon the business of protection as a mere formality. Beult was not the first bridge they had dealt with in similar fashion and the whole job had gone like clockwork until now when it was practically completed. But on this last afternoon John Benge made a fatal mistake. There was one train in the Company's timetable which did not run to a fixed schedule. This was the Folkestone Boat Express which was known as the 'tidal' because its timing varied with the tides which governed the arrival of the Folkestone Packets. These daily times were shown in Benge's working timetable but he misread it. He believed that the boat train was not due at Headcorn until 5.20 whereas in fact it was due at 3.15. The leading carpenter had also been issued with a copy of the timetable but he had dropped his on the rail where it had been destroyed by a passing train so he could not correct his foreman's error. Disaster was in these circumstances a foregone conclusion.

The new timber baulks had been set in position but two 21-foot lengths of rail had still to be replaced when the express approached running at fifty miles an hour. Her driver acted promptly as soon as he saw Wiles's red flag, but in so short a distance he could not hope to bring his train of thirteen vehicles to a stand. The leading van and the first two coaches were fitted with Cremar's patent brakes, but unfortunately the guard in charge did not himself see Wiles's frantic signal and in response to the brake whistle he first put on his ordinary screw brake. Not until half the critical distance had been covered did he realize the urgency and apply the patent brakes. By that time the engine was practically upon the bridge, and before the eyes of the horrified gang a scene of frightful destruction ensued. Extraordinary to relate, the locomotive, its tender and the leading brake van actually succeeded in crossing the rail-less gap on the timber baulks, but the following train was less fortunate. The strain was too much for the cast iron girders beneath. The offside girder collapsed as the tender and van passed over. The first coach came to rest hanging at a perilous angle supported by the van coupling, but the next five fell through the gap into the muddy bed of the stream where they lay in a confusion of splintered wreckage, one standing on its end and another on its roof. Ten passengers in these coaches perished and forty-nine were injured.

The travellers in the leading coach – so commonly shunned by nervous passengers – were in this case more fortunate than their fellows in the rear. Among them was Charles Dickens. He was reading through the manuscript of *Our Mutual Friend* when the accident occurred, and he alluded to his experience in a Postscript which he added to that book.

On Friday, the ninth of June in the present year [he wrote] Mr and Mrs Boffin (in their manuscript dress of receiving Mr and Mrs Lammle at breakfast) were on the South Eastern Railway with me, in a terribly destructive accident. When I had done what I could to help others, I climbed back into my carriage – nearly turned over a viaduct, and caught aslant upon the turn – to extricate the worthy couple. They were much soiled, but otherwise unhurt. .... I remember with devout thankfulness that I can never be much nearer parting company with my readers for ever than I was then, until there shall be written against my life the two words with which I have this day closed this book – The End.

That end, unfortunately, was not far off. Although Dickens escaped physical injury his terrifying experience seriously affected his nervous system with results which became apparent later. 'I am curiously weak,' he wrote, 'weak as if I were recovering from a long illness. I begin to feel it more in my head. I sleep well and eat well; but I write half a dozen words and turn faint and sick.' It was some time before he could bring himself to travel by rail again and when he did so he preferred slow trains.

A perfect conviction against the senses, that the carriage is down on one side (and generally that is the left, and *not* the side on which the carriage in the accident really went over) comes upon me with anything like speed, and is inexpressibly distressing.

It is true to say that Dickens never fully recovered from the after effects of Staplehurst, and on June 9th, 1870 – the fifth anniversary of the disaster – the great man died in his fifty-eighth year. We cannot estimate the loss which English literature sustained as a result of John Benge's tragic mistake. Certainly he deprived us of the solution to *The Mystery of Edwin Drood.*

On September 1st, 1905, a very spectacular high speed derailment occurred at Witham on the Great Eastern main line between London and Colchester. The 9.27 am express from Liverpool Street to Cromer was approaching Witham station at nearly seventy miles an hour when, with the exception of the locomotive and tender, the entire train of fourteen vehicles became derailed as it was passing over a trailing crossover. The first three broke loose from the train and from each other and came to rest at different points beyond the station. One of these, a first-class coach, caught fire owing to escaping gas. The next five vehicles fouled the down island platform. One completely demolished the porters' and ticket collectors' rooms, killing an unfortunate porter in the process. Another was flung upside down and its bodywork was smashed to fragments, eight occupants being instantly killed.

Two platelayers, Arthur Newman and Morris Pavelin, were working on the crossover at the time under the direction of Foreman Platelayer Robert Pryke. But all three men assured Colonel Von Donop at the subsequent inquiry that they were merely clearing the ballast away from the knuckle timber at the 'V' of the crossing prior to repacking it and had done nothing to impair the stability of the road. When the inquiry closed there appeared to be nothing positive to account for the disaster except the high speed of the train. Indeed the Witham accident is often cited to this day as the first of that extraordinary series of high speed derailments which form the subject of another chapter. But six weeks after the accident additional evidence came to light in peculiar and somewhat suspicious circumstances. It was of such importance that Colonel Von Donop reopened the inquiry and re-examined a number of witnesses.

A railway employee named William Kisby went to the District Locomotive Superintendent at Ipswich and made this statement. On the day of the accident a friend of his, a shunter named William Hume, had been dealing with a special coal train in the up yard at Witham. After the accident he had immediately run to the station and helped in the rescue work until he injured himself. That afternoon Hume was suspended for being drunk on duty although he stoutly maintained that he had only had one glass of beer and a few biscuits for his lunch. When he got home he took to his bed and it was not until six days later that Kisby visited him to see how he was getting on and was told the following story.

Hume said he was standing immediately opposite the point

of derailment when the accident happened. He had finished his shunting operations and was waiting for the express to pass before crossing the line to report to the signal box which was on the down side. As the engine of the express approached the crossing he noticed that a key was out of the rail and as soon as the train passed on to the crossing he saw a rail jump up and the leading coach plough into the ballast. He called to Foreman Pryke, 'That looks well,' to which Pryke replied, 'Oh, my God.' Asked why they had allowed six weeks to pass without divulging this information, Kisby made the illogical and unconvincing reply that both he and Hume thought it might injure the Company.

Needless to say, nothing could be more damaging to a railway company's reputation than an unexplained derailment, and the Locomotive Superintendent at Ipswich at once informed the Board of Trade. It was one man's word against three, for the permanent way gang categorically denied Hume's story and stuck to their original statement. But when they were recalled, the evidence of Driver Hills and Fireman Ward of the express was very significant. They said that as they approached Witham they saw the three men working very busily on the track ahead, so busily, in fact, that Hills became alarmed, fearing that they were not going to move in time. When, at the last minute, they stepped aside, all three had their eyes riveted on a particular point on the track, one of them, whom he now recognized as Foreman Pryke, from a kneeling position. John Smith, the guard of the express who was riding in the front van, said that the leading wheels of his van seemed to strike something hard as it ran over the crossing.

In view of these statements, Colonel Von Donop came to the conclusion that, despite their denials, the permanent way gang had rashly loosened the rail fastening at the 'V' of the crossing and had been unable to make good their mistake in time. As a result, he thought that the wing rail of the crossing had jumped up under the weight of the locomotive, striking the wheel of the leading van and so causing the derailment of the entire train. Although the inspector made no comment upon it, one can scarcely avoid the suspicion that the odd circumstances of William Hume's injury and suspension after the accident may have been part of a conspiracy designed to cover up Foreman Pryke's disastrous mistake.

Quite the oddest of the many accidents associated with permanent way work happened in the early days – on the line between Brighton and Lewes on June 6th, 1851. No 82, one of a class of twelve engines built for the Brighton line in 1847–8 by Sharp, Roberts and Co., was running down the incline between Falmer and Lewes with a passenger train. At a point where a high brick bridge known as the Newmarket Arch carries the line over a bridle road, No 82 struck a sleeper which was lying across the outside rail and became derailed. The engine and two coaches fell into the road below killing three passengers and the fireman. The driver was terribly injured and died later. How did the sleeper come to be there? There were a number of sleepers on the line side because relaying was in progress although the permanent way men were several hundred yards away from the spot where the accident occurred. They stoutly denied that they had left a sleeper in such a position, and it was alleged that it was a wilful prank on the part of Jimmy Boakes, a ten-year-old boy who lived with his parents in a cottage beside the line. Although it is highly improbable that he could have had the strength to lift a 9-foot sleeper across the rail, the wretched child was subjected to a third degree cross-examination by William Acton, the Railway Superintendent of Police. But Acton failed to trap the boy into making any admission and the mystery remained unsolved. Now comes the curious sequel. Exactly a year later, on the same day of the same month that the accident happened and on the same spot, little Jimmy Boakes was struck by lightning and killed instantly. Such an extraordinary coincidence proves nothing, but no doubt it was quoted with relish from local pulpits as an awful example of the visitation of divine retribution.

It was another of the Sharp, Roberts engines, No 79, which made a very unorthodox excursion from Petworth shed one dark October morning in 1859. She was raising steam in the shed and had only 15 lb pressure on the gauge when the cleaner who was working on her went out of the shed to find a fireman to help him to move her. Unfortunately he left her in forward gear and failed to close the regulator. When he returned with the fireman, No 79 had gone. They saw her moving majestically through the darkness of the yard and gave chase, but with the pull on her fire from the exhaust she was now making steam fast and gathering speed. The cleaner could only manage to get his hand on her rear buffer beam before he collapsed in breathless exhaustion while the fireman was an 'also ran'. Moving at a smart pace, No 79 disappeared down the line in the direction of Pulborough. It was a cleaner, walking to work along the line at Horsham who finally stopped the runaway. As she approached he noticed the splintered remnants of the three sets of crossing gates, which she had demolished en route, festooning her front buffer beam and suspected that something was wrong. So he managed to scramble on to the footplate and close the regulator. She had run for seventeen and a half miles.

So far as level crossings are concerned the journey made by the Great Western tank engine No 1032 in 1871 was much more destructive. She was standing in the yard at Pontypool Road when a Taff Vale engine, shunting four wagons, inadvertently gave her a forceful bump in the rear. Her driver, who was off the engine oiling the motion, saw what was coming and shouted 'Look out!' to his young fireman. The youth leaped from the footplate in a panic and in doing so he must have knocked the regulator open. Pushing a van before her, No 1032 set off on a wild career of over nine miles through Newport in the course of which she demolished no less than seventeen sets of level crossing gates. Fortunately, all this took place in the early hours of a Sunday morning or the consequences might have been more serious.

Much more alarming than this was the episode at Miles Platting on the Lancashire & Yorkshire Railway in 1868. A fireman named Philip Jones was moving engine No 275 in the yard when he suddenly fell in a fit. A pointsman at the yard entrance saw what had happened but he had no facing points under his control to enable him to divert the runaway. It went off in the direction of Ashton Junction where the lines to Rochdale and Ashton diverge while all the pointsman could do was to work his distant signal up and down to attract attention and shout to a driver on another engine to go in pursuit. The pointsman at the Junction saw Jones lying on the footplate with his head in the coals and the rapidly moving engine instantly confronted him with a hideous dilemma. Which way should he send it? As a Rochdale train was approaching he chose the Ashton branch, but unfortunately the 4.40 pm train from Ashton to Manchester was standing in the station platform just out of his range of vision. The driver and fireman of the train had just started away when they beheld No 275 bearing down upon them. The two engines met in head-on collision and after the rebound 275 advanced again and began vigorously to propel the train backwards out of the platform until the astonished driver collected his wits, made a dive for the footplate and shut the regulator. History does not relate what happened to the unfortunate Philip Jones.

It should not be supposed that tales of runaway locomotives belong exclusively to the giddy youth of railways. Even the staid adult has occasional lapses, and Colonel Woodhouse's report on an accident on the Somerset & Dorset Joint Railway on August 4th, 1936, tells a story which, for sheer knockabout comedy, stands unsurpassed in the sober and generally sombre annals of the Railways Inspection Department. The comic element in railway accidents is too often overlaid by tragedy, but in this case there was happily no personal injury whatever.

The six-coupled side tank engine No 7620 had been carrying out some shunting operations at Braysdown colliery sidings between Radstock and Wellow and was standing on the up main line, facing south, at the head of eight empty wagons. Her driver became somewhat concerned when he saw bearing down upon him the 9.50 am up freight train from Evercreech Junction to Bath. It was a heavy train consisting of thirty-seven wagons drawn by one of the massive eight-coupled goods engines built specially by the Midland Company at Derby for work over this steeply graded line. The goods was obviously overrunning signals and the concern of the driver of the shunting tank not unnaturally quickened to alarm when he saw the crew of the big engine leap off the footplate. He immediately flung his engine into back gear, and opened his regulator wide with the object of beating a hasty retreat. By the time he had done this the two engines were practically buffer to buffer and he realized that the goods was now moving very slowly. Quick as thought he jumped out of his cab, clambered on to the footplate of the 2–8–0 and brought her to a stand. Here indeed was cause for self-congratulation! What presence of mind and resource in emergency! How chagrined her craven crew who had so prematurely abandoned ship! But, alas, never had pride so speedy a fall. For as our hero had leaped from one side of his footplate, his fireman, a nervous youth, misunderstanding his motive for so doing, had jumped off the other side, and neither had closed the regulator. Triumph instantly turned to dismay when the intrepid driver looked up just in time to see his own engine rapidly disappearing backwards in the direction of Bath propelling the eight wagons before it.

Fortunately, it was possible to keep the line clear for the runaways. A few minutes later they roared through Wellow station at high speed – 50 miles an hour according to the signalman there. It must have been an alarming sight for him but one not to be compared with the experience of his colleague at Midford, the next station. For here the double line becomes single and the eight wagons proceeded to run well and truly amok on the points and to play havoc with the station and its surroundings. Signals and telegraph poles fell like ninepins; signalman Larcombe's cabin collapsed under his feet as one wagon demolished its masonry base; six wagons shot one after another over an embankment, and for a distance of 300 yards the line was littered with debris. Yet although the track was damaged, No 7620 held the rails and her powers were by no means exhausted. Having so successfully shaken off most of her load she continued at unabated speed, pushing before her like a handcart the remnant of one wagon running on two wheels only. Miraculously she succeeded in propelling this peculiar vehicle through Combe Down and Devonshire single line tunnels, but at Claude Avenue overbridge it brought about her undoing. The remaining end door of the wagon fell off, got under her rear wheels and derailed her. At about the same time the fusible plug in the crown of her firebox melted owing to shortage of water and her last breath was spent. The escapade was over.

In his narrative poem *Mazeppa*, published in 1819, Lord Byron tells how his hero, Ivan Stepanovich Mazeppa, was punished for an indiscreet amour with the wife of a local magnate by being bound naked to the back of a wild horse. The horse galloped away with him, never stopping until it fell dead after covering many miles on the plains of the Ukraine. It would almost seem as if something of the same impetuous spirit entered into the locomotive 'Mazeppa' of the London & North Western Railway, for no engine has ever stolen away more cunningly upon so wild a journey. 'Mazeppa' was a 2-2-2 of Trevithick–Allan design built at Crewe in 1849 and numbered 234. On the occasion in question she was working between Stafford and Shrewsbury over the line then owned by the Shropshire Union Railway & Canal Company but operated by the North Western.

When 'Mazeppa' arrived at Shrewsbury with the 9.5 am train from Stafford her driver reported to the shed foreman that the regulator gland was blowing and needed packing. The foreman told Joseph Thompson, the night cleaner, to deal with it and the engine was handed over to him outside the shed at 11 pm. Thompson drew the fire, blew down steam and then pushed 'Mazeppa' into the shed with another engine. He and his assistant William Clarke packed the gland, cleaned and oiled round and then lit up the fire at 4 am. At 5 o'clock Clarke left the shed to knock up some workmen, leaving Thompson alone. He made up 'Mazeppa's' fire at 5.45 and five minutes later, ten minutes before he should have done, he went home to bed. Daniel Tinsley, the day cleaner, was due on duty at six, but he was ten minutes late which meant that for twenty minutes there was nobody in the shed. Tinsley was accompanied by a fireman named Philips who had come to prepare his engine which was standing outside and was looking for his shovel. He said he thought Thompson might have used it on 'Mazeppa' but the engine was not to be seen. He asked Tinsley what had become of her, and the latter replied that she must have gone out early. Indeed she had. It was at this moment that a breathless platelayer arrived in a state of high agitation to say that as he was walking to work he had seen an engine go by on the line to Stafford with no one on the footplate. Thompson had left 'Mazeppa' in forward gear with the regulator open and she had taken advantage of that twenty minutes when no one was about to make her getaway.

In Shrewsbury shed there was now an immediate hue and cry. An engine with steam up in the yard was hurriedly manned and sent off in hot pursuit. Three miles out from Shrewsbury her driver caught a fleeting glimpse of flying steam in the distance, but that was all he saw of 'Mazeppa' until he reached Donnington, fourteen miles out. Meanwhile the 6 am train from Shrewsbury had reached Donnington and was standing at the station platform when her driver happened to look back down the line and saw to his horror a light engine bearing rapidly down upon his train. He did not know that there was no one on her footplate, but as she was only sixty yards away with steam on it was obvious that she was not going to stop. He jumped for his regulator in a desperate effort to draw his train away from the danger but he was far too late. In a matter of seconds he was knocked flat by the force of the collision as 'Mazeppa' leapt upon the rear brake van and smashed it to pieces. Fortunately there were few people in the little train of three coaches and they were in the third-class carriage next to the engine. For the fourteen mile run from Shrewsbury had in no way exhausted 'Mazeppa's' energy and steam was roaring from her safety valves as she proceeded to savage the train. She had demolished the first-class carriage next to the van, broken the next, a second-class, in two, and crushed the leading third against the engine tender before the driver of the train had time to collect his scattered wits, jump on her footplate and close the regulator. Before the injured passengers in the third coach could be released the coach end had to be prised out. One of them was found to be dead.

All this while Joseph Thompson, the unwitting author of this tragedy at Donnington, lay snoring peacefully in his bed at Shrewsbury. He woke up to find himself facing a charge of manslaughter, while the Board of Trade inspector had some pungent remarks to make in his report about the importance of staff punctuality and of observing shed regulations with regard to stationary locomotives. Indeed this chapter ends with the same cautionary moral with which it all began: that safety on the railway is the responsibility of all and that there is no item of railway equipment from a wagon sheet or a porter's barrow to a stationary locomotive that carelessness cannot convert into a potent instrument of disaster.

6

SINGLE LINE COLLISIONS

Menheniot – Norwich (Thorpe) – Radstock – Abermule

THE EARLIEST passenger carrying railways were laid out
as double lines, each of which was reserved exclusively, in
theory, at least, for up or down traffic, as the case might be. It
will be obvious that unless the strictest precautions are observed, the working of trains in both directions over a single
line of metals involves most appalling risks. Mistakes in block
working on double lines do not necessarily lead to disaster, but
on single lines there is no such margin for error. Once two
trains have been dispatched in opposite directions over a single
line section a head-on collision, that most invariably destructive of all types of railway accident, becomes almost inevitable. The Board of Trade recognized this danger from the
outset. They insisted on regarding a single line of railway as
incomplete even though Parliament might have sanctioned its
construction in that form. Before they would agree to the opening of such a railway the company concerned must sign a
solemn declaration under their seal to the effect that only one
engine in steam should ever be permitted to enter any single
line section at one time. This ruling holds good to this day and
the only permissible exception to it is that more than one
engine may enter if they are coupled together for purposes of
double-heading or banking so that they form one train.

The earliest single lines were short country branches where a
single locomotive carrying a distinguishing target was alone
sufficient to handle all the traffic. There are still a few lines
which are worked upon this principle today. On a long single
line divided into a number of sections by passing loops some
other method of working was obviously necessary. So the
single target became a series of suitably inscribed and coloured
staffs each of which gave the bearer the exclusive right to enter

a particular section. Though simple, this system was extremely effective from a safety point of view but it possessed the disadvantage that it could not be adjusted to meet traffic requirements. Two trains could never follow one another through a single line section. It was necessary for a train in the opposite direction to bring the staff back before the second could proceed. To overcome this difficulty the staff was made divisible. Successive trains could then be given a portion of the staff, while no train could start in the opposite direction until the complete staff had travelled through the section in this way. A variant of this was the 'staff and ticket' system. Under this arrangement the stationmaster was authorized to issue successive drivers with tickets permitting them to enter a single line section provided he could show the train staff as proof of his authority. Here again, no train could move in the opposite direction until the staff itself had travelled through the section. A typical train staff ticket would be inscribed as follows:

GRAND CENTRAL RAILWAY
Train Staff Ticket
Train No.........(Up)
To the Engine Driver
You are authorized, after seeing the Train Staff coloured
RED for the section to proceed from
SUMMERSEND to WINTERSTOKE
And the Train Staff will follow

Date............   Signed..................

The divisible staff and the staff and ticket systems were worked in conjunction with telegraph or latterly with block instruments to ensure that, in the case of following trains, the second did not enter a section until the first had cleared it.

In the early days of railways, however, it became accepted practice to work certain long and busy single lines solely by the method known as 'telegraph and crossing order' without any other precautions. It was argued that additional precautions would cause too much delay. Stations were in communication with each other by telegraph and the telegraph clerks, or alternatively a central control office, regulated the movement of trains in this way. Sometimes instructions were merely given verbally, but more often the driver was given a written authority to proceed. As we shall see, however, no matter what safeguards the working rules imposed, this system was very far from foolproof because it lacked the positive and tangible safeguard of the train staff. Its dangers were revealed very clearly by an accident which occurred on the Cornwall Railway in 1873. Inadequate signalling was in this case a contributory cause.

On the occasion in question, two goods trains were standing on the passing loop at Menheniot awaiting the instructions to proceed from the porter-signalman. The latter had gone into the telegraph office while the guard on the down goods, whose name was Dick, waited on the platform outside. The guard of the up goods was not in sight. In due course the porter-signalman received 'Line Clear' for the down train and, putting his head round the door shouted, 'Right away, Dick.' To his horror the up goods, a heavy train drawn by two engines, immediately pulled away in the direction of St Germans. Unknown to him, the other guard's name happened to be Dick also. He knew from his telegraph that a second down goods had already left St Germans but he was unable to attract the erring guard's attention. Both trains were travelling at about twenty miles an hour when they met on a sharp curve in a cutting halfway through the section. Such was the force of the collision that one locomotive, the 'Lance', was completely destroyed while the other two were very seriously damaged. All three engine crews were badly injured and one driver was killed. Had the wayside crossing stations on the Cornwall line been adequately signalled at this time, the accident would not have occurred. There was only one signal in each direction at Menheniot and these were 'homes' which admitted trains to the station. Consequently the departure of trains depended solely on verbal order. The accident led to the immediate introduction of starting signals throughout the line.

Despite its fatal outcome there is an element of comedy about the misunderstanding at Menheniot. But in the events at Thorpe station, Norwich, on September 10th, 1874, which culminated in the worst head-on collision in the history of British railways there is no such light relief. A mundane railway platform became, for sixteen critical minutes, a stage for high tragedy in which no dramatic ingredient was lacking. Unknown to the actors, we, their audience, can watch error upon trivial error leading in remorseless sequence to their terrible conclusion. And only when it is too late, when disaster becomes inevitable, does there come the sudden overwhelming realization of guilt and error.

Before beginning the action the stage must be set. The single line of the Great Eastern Railway between Norwich and Yarmouth was one of the first in the country to be controlled by electric telegraph. The installation of five-needle Cooke and Wheatstone instruments on the Norfolk Railway (as it then was) in 1848 was considered at the time to be a model of its kind. For twenty-six years it had controlled the traffic over the line without a single mishap. Now, the Great Eastern Company proposed to double the line and by the irony of fate a second set of metals had already been laid between Thorpe and the East Norfolk Junction at Whitlingham, the very section upon which the collision occurred, and was only awaiting inspection and approval by the Board of Trade. The movement of trains through this section was controlled by the telegraph instruments at Thorpe and at Brundall, the next station east of Norwich. At Brundall the stationmaster worked the telegraph himself. At Thorpe the instruments were worked by a telegraph clerk acting under the instruction of the station inspector. If late running made it necessary to alter the normal crossing arrangements, the procedure at Thorpe was as follows. The telegraph office had a window with a sliding wicket, like a booking office, which faced the platform. At this window was kept a message pad for the use of the station inspector. The inspector would write his instruction on the pad, sign it, and hand it to the telegraph clerk who would then transmit it to Brundall exactly as written with the signature as proof of its authority. Brundall would then acknowledge it in the same form and both the message sent and the reply received would be entered by the clerk in a record book. At the same time the station inspector would hand a signed instruction to the driver of the train concerned.

The 5 pm express from Liverpool Street to Yarmouth was normally booked to cross the 8.40 pm up Mail train at Brundall but on this occasion the express was running late. The drama began at 9.16 when Cooper, the night inspector, who had just come on duty, went to the stationmaster's office as usual to receive his orders for the night.

'What about having the Mail up, sir?' Cooper asked. Sproule, the stationmaster, consulted his watch and inquired what time the Mail was due to arrive at Brundall. 'Nine-twenty-five,' Cooper told him. 'We will not have the Mail up,' Sproule replied, 'certainly not.' 'You know, sir,' Cooper reminded him, 'there is an order allowing us to detain the 9.10 down as late as 9.35.' To this the stationmaster made an ambiguous reply. 'All right,' he said, 'we will soon get her off.' Now it seems clear that Sproule's 'All right' was delivered in a tone of impatient dismissal and that by 'her' he was referring to the express and not to the Mail. But evidently Cooper thought that Sproule had conceded his point. He left the office, walked straight to the telegraph office, tapped on the wicket and said to the young clerk, Robson, 'Tell Brundall to send the Mail on to Norwich.' Robson wrote the message down on the pad but Cooper had hurried away without stopping to sign it. The time was then 9.22.

One minute later the express drew in to the down platform drawn by the four-coupled mixed traffic engine No 218. She was met by the day inspector, Parker, who, thinking the train might arrive punctually, had already made out an order authorizing her driver to proceed. He was standing by the engine when Cooper came up and he asked him whether he had arranged for the Mail to come on. Inexplicably, Cooper answered, 'No, certainly not; let us get the train away as soon as possible.' Parker then handed the order to the driver and told him to proceed to Brundall. Events now moved swiftly. Parker gave the express the 'right away' at 9.30 and from his office window the stationmaster watched it pull away. It had scarcely cleared the platform when Edward Trew, an inspector of railway police, wishing to speak to the telegraph clerk upon some other business, knocked on the office wicket. Robson immediately opened it and asked where the express was.

'She has just left,' Trew replied. 'What, left the yard?' asked Robson. He seemed about to make some exclamation when Cooper hurried up. 'You haven't ordered the Mail up, have you?' he asked. 'You told me to order her up,' Robson retorted. The clerk at once went to his instrument and signalled 'Stop Mail' to Brundall. Immediately the deadly reply came back: 'Mail left'. He returned to the wicket, put the pad with its fatal message in front of Cooper and asked him to sign it. 'No,' cried the wretched man, 'no. I never gave you that message. I did not, I did not.' Robson's reply was unanswerable. 'Why, if you did not, have you now come back to cancel it?' At this moment Hayden, the ticket collector came up. 'What's the matter?' he asked, and Cooper answered, 'The Mail is coming up.' 'Good God,' said Hayden, 'this is a frightful thing.' The stationmaster, overhearing the raised voices and the word 'Mail', guessed that something was wrong and rushed out of his office. He described the scene at the inquiry. 'What about the Mail?' he asked. Cooper was standing against the window with his back to him as he said this. When he turned towards him his face was as white as chalk; 'he had the appearance,' said the stationmaster, 'of a man paralysed.' 'I have ordered the Mail up,' he answered. Both men knew very well what these words meant. They meant that on this dark and rainy autumn night with visibility down to 300 yards

Cooper had sent two trains to certain destruction. No power on earth could save them now. Sproule was so unstrung that he said he scarcely knew what happened after this. He felt so deeply for Cooper that he could hardly speak, but he remembered suspending him and telling Hayden to take his place.

While this little stricken group of men stood helplessly upon the platform at Norwich in the overwhelming knowledge of what they had done, the tragedy was being played out in the blackness beyond the station lights where the express and the Mail were speeding towards each other. They met between the Yare Bridge and the East Norfolk Junction, and the noise of their collision, said those who heard it, was like a great clap of thunder. Of the last few terrible moments of that drama there was no witness for both engine crews perished. But on the engine of the up Mail, the 7-foot single No 54, they found the regulator shut and the tender brake screwed hard down. In all, twenty-five lives were lost in the Thorpe disaster and seventy-three were injured.

The unfortunate inspector, Cooper, was not alone to blame. The telegraph clerk Robson was even more culpable and the Board of Trade inspector, Captain Tyler, commented adversely upon the fact that this youth of eighteen had no less than four young men in the telegraph office with him to distract his attention from his work. He knew perfectly well that the working rules stated clearly that no message should be transmitted unless it bore the station inspector's signature. Yet when he had taken down Cooper's verbal instruction he had almost immediately transmitted it to Brundall as 'signed A. Cooper', whereas in fact, Cooper had never signed it. Asked why he did this he replied: 'I see my error. I did it to oblige Cooper; I never did such a thing before in my life.' He added that Cooper had promised that he would return immediately to sign his order but that he had failed to do so. At this Captain Tyler pointed out that he was provided with a bell with which to summon the inspector if required and that he should have rung it when Cooper failed to return. Robson replied that he did not use the bell because it made the inspectors angry. Cooper, on the other hand, declared that he had no sooner given his order than he heard the express approaching and cancelled it, Robson replying: 'All right, Captain.' Robson denied this.

The precise proportion of blame attaching to Cooper and to Robson can never be certainly determined, but, as Captain Tyler pointed out, the moral to be drawn from the tragedy was obvious. It was that a system which allowed such mistakes to occur was gravely defective. The railway companies' arguments about the delays occasioned by other methods of working should not be allowed to outweigh consideration for the public safety. There could be no doubt whatever that the staff system, in conjunction with the telegraph, was the safest combination for single line working. In laconic phrases, a page in the telegraph book at Norwich sums up the circumstances of this tragic collision. It reads as shown in the table on page 148.

Within two years of the Thorpe disaster another terrible single line collision occurred, this time on the Somerset & Dorset Railway, where a similar telegraph and crossing order system was in operation. Shortly before midnight on August 7th, 1876, a down excursion train from Bath ran head on into an up relief train from Wimborne near Foxcote signal box at Braysdown colliery siding on the section over the Mendips between Radstock and Wellow. Fifteen passengers were killed.

Granted the defects of the system, the Norwich line had been efficiently worked for many years without mishap and the eleventh hour catastrophe was a cruel misfortune. The case of Radstock was quite otherwise. The Somerset & Dorset's extension to Bath on which the accident took place had only been opened for traffic two years before and the operational methods were such that disaster was inevitable from the beginning. Indeed it is remarkable that the railway should have worked even for two years without serious accident. The

SINGLE LINE TRAIN MESSAGES

TIME RE-CEIVED	SUBJECT OF MESSAGE	STATIONS TELE-GRAPHED	TIME SENT	CLERK'S SIGNA-TURE	SUBJECT OF ANSWER	TIME RE-CEIVED	CLERK'S INITIALS	RAILWAY OFFICER'S SIGNA-TURE
9.24 pm	Send up Mail train on to Norwich before the 9.10 pm down passenger train leaves Norwich.	Brundall	9.25 pm	R.	I will send the up Mail train on to Norwich before the 9.10 pm down passenger train leaves Norwich. W. Platford.	9.25 pm	R.	
	When the up Mail train has arrived at Norwich will line be clear for 9.10 pm down passenger train to Brundall?	Brundall						

9.32 pm Norwich to Brundall 'Stop Mail'.
9.32 pm Brundall to Norwich 'Mail Left'.
NORWICH, Thorpe Station,
Sept. 10th, 1874.

public inquiry conducted by Captain Tyler disclosed a most shocking state of affairs. In the first place, Foxcote signal box had no right to exist at all. Its presence was a direct breach of the Company's customary undertaking, delivered under seal, that only one engine in steam should occupy any single line section at one time. For Foxcote was not a crossing station; it was merely a block post set in the middle of the three mile section between Radstock and Wellow which enabled two trains to follow one another through that section in flagrant breach of Board of Trade regulations. The Company's lame excuse was that they thought that Foxcote constituted a station between sections in the meaning of the regulation. The line was equipped with block instruments, but the telegraphic arrangements left much to be desired. Radstock and Wellow were not in direct touch with each other but could only communicate through the signalman at Foxcote. A telegraph control office at Glastonbury issued instructions to all crossing stations, but it had no communication with Foxcote at all so that the signalman there was left in blissful ignorance of any special arrangements which might have been made.

Even in the best of hands the working of such a system to pass an extremely heavy traffic (on the day of the accident alone there had been seventeen extra trains) would have been fraught with peril, but when we read the roster of the Company's staff who were on duty on this fatal night the hair rises upon the scalp. The fact was that the construction of the extension to Bath had exhausted the Company's finances and they were attempting to run the railway with an inexperienced staff deficient both in quality and quantity. It is true that the Midland and the London & South Western Railways had very recently come to the rescue of their ailing neighbour and had formed a joint managing committee, but their reforms had not yet taken effect, and there existed meanwhile a state of affairs that must surely have been without parallel on any English railway.

In charge at Radstock was the telegraph clerk, Herbert

John, a youth of eighteen who worked from 6.30 am to 9.30 pm for a wage of 17s. 6d. a week. The signalman at Foxcote was another youth named Alfred Dando who had been with the Company four months and was unable to read the telegraph instruments. He admitted at the inquiry that he 'could not write well nor read excellent', nor was he very strong. His only training as a signalman consisted of one week in the box at Radstock where he was unable to pull over the levers, yet John Jarrett, the Radstock stationmaster, said he thought he could manage the few levers at Foxcote and forthwith posted him there. On the night of the disaster, John Hamlin, the driver of the up relief train, said he found the Foxcote distant signal lamp out and the arm 'nearly at caution'. There was nothing unusual about this, he added. The signals never were lit for the simple reason that Dando was not supplied with enough paraffin for the lamps, while the drivers knew that he was not strong enough to work the signals. Dando stopped him with a handlamp and then told him to proceed. The collision occurred a few moments afterwards.

James Sleep, the Wellow stationmaster, had come on duty at 5.30 that morning. At 6.30 in the evening he went off to Midford 'chiefly for pleasure', as he put it, leaving in sole charge of the station Arthur Hillard, a boy of fifteen. Hillard's working hours, officially, were from 8 am to 10 pm but were often, as on this occasion, much longer. He not only worked the telegraph but issued tickets and kept the station accounts. His wages were 7s. 6d. a week. These three, John, Dando and Hillard were the 'men' responsible for working the traffic on this August night while Stationmaster Sleep was making up for a long and thirsty day at Midford.

The evidence of Caleb Percy, the superintendent at Glastonbury control, gives a revealing glimpse of the chaos which prevailed on the Somerset & Dorset metals that night. Percy himself was grossly overworked. He had come on duty at nine o'clock that morning and in the normal course of events he would not have gone off until 11.30 pm. As it was, owing to the accident, he was on duty until 8.30 the next morning. It was the height of the holiday season and throughout that long day it had been his exacting task to find paths and arrange crossings for the seventeen extra trains which passed over that congested single line. Neither of the trains involved in the collision appeared in the working timetable. The down train was the return working of an excursion to Bath regatta which was due to leave Bath at 9.15 pm. The other train, the up special, had to be arranged on the spur of the moment to relieve the 6.10 pm regular train from Bournemouth which was overcrowded. The first the station staffs knew of this train was when Percy sent out the following message at 7.18:

'Percy Glastonbury to all stations. A special train will leave Wimborne at 7.10 for Bath. I will arrange crossings.' This message, of course, did not go to Foxcote and as neither Radstock nor Wellow advised him, the unfortunate Dando remained in ignorance of the existence of the train. The down excursion was extremely late for it was not until 10.23 pm that Bath advised Glastonbury that it had left. From this time forward until the moment of collision both trains disappeared so far as the Glastonbury control was concerned. The harassed Percy and his telegraph clerk, Locke, made frantic efforts to trace them, but the replies they received were either conflicting and vague or sheer gibberish. To begin with they could get no reply at all from Wellow until 11.13. Then, in answer to their question, 'Where is down special?' the boy Hillard returned the enigmatic reply 'Over T'. Percy said he concluded from this that the Bath excursion must have been taken on the Foxcote block; in other words, that it had passed through Wellow and was on its way to Radstock. But Hillard then added, 'Up is on from T.' From this Percy assumed that the excursion must have reached Radstock and there crossed the up relief train which was now on the Foxcote–Wellow block. Percy therefore told his clerk to get in touch with Herbert John at Radstock and the following fantastic exchange took place:

Glastonbury: 'Where is down special?'
Radstock: 'Don't know.'
Glastonbury: 'Where is special?'
Radstock: 'Good.'
Glastonbury: 'Where is special?'
Radstock: 'Good.'
Glastonbury: 'Do you refuse to answer my question?'
Radstock: 'Don't know.'

Asked afterwards why he had given a repeated 'OA' (good) signal in reply to Glastonbury's questions, John replied that they had often done the same to him. 'It is not pleasant to be treated so,' he said. And while those responsible were suffering from fits of pique and talking double Dutch to each other over their instruments, the farce ended in tragedy like a bad practical joke that has gone too far. Percy was informed of the collision at 11.37 pm.

Not only had no timetable been drawn up for the working of the up relief train, but although the driver had crossed no less than six trains en route he had received only one verbal instruction and no written crossing orders. It transpired that the boy Hillard at Wellow had allowed the Bath excursion to leave without advising Dando at Foxcote and without putting on the block instruments which, it transpired, were frequently neglected in this way. Six minutes later, and before the excursion had reached Foxcote, Hillard had accepted the up relief train from Dando with the inevitable consequence.

The Radstock disaster revealed a state of affairs so chaotic, so irresponsible and so lacking even the most elementary precautions that it was impossible to lay blame upon any particular individual. The whole staff were culpable and all were grossly over-worked, shouldering responsibilities which they were quite unfitted by training to bear. This particularly applied to the wretched boy Hillard whose actions were the immediate cause of the accident. So Captain Tyler contented himself with this terse conclusion: 'Railway working,' he said, 'under such conditions cannot, whatever the system employed, be expected to be carried on without serious accidents.'

Happily for west country travellers the Radstock accident roused the new joint managing committee of the S & DR to immediate and drastic action. So effectually was this ne'er-do-well among railways reformed that it soon became one of the most efficient and smartly worked cross-country lines in England. Much of the line has been doubled, while on such single line sections that remain passenger trains can run to express schedules by means of automatic tablet exchange apparatus of which more anon. Hauling 'The Pines Express', streamlined 'West Country' Pacifics now thunder past the site of that illicit cabin at Foxcote where once the hapless Alfred Dando minded, or failed to mind, his unlit signals.

The two accidents of Thorpe and Radstock made a deep impression on the public mind. There was considerable alarm and concern. It was clear from the Board of Trade reports that on single lines such as these which passed a considerable volume of traffic the safeguards were inadequate. There was an urgent need for some new device which would combine the advantages of the telegraph with the positive security of the staff and ticket system.

Where a demand of this kind exists an ingenious inventor invariably appears to supply it, and it was the great signal engineer Edward Tyer who provided the answer. Tyer devoted the whole of his long life (1830–1912) to the improvement of railway telegraph instruments and it would be difficult to find a signal cabin of traditional type today which did not contain some instrument bearing his name. No other man made a greater practical contribution to railway safety than Tyer. As early as 1851, when he was only twenty, he was responsible for considerable improvements in the first crude telegraph instruments and he took out his first patent in the following year. His electric block instruments were already revolutionizing railway working on double lines and after the Thorpe disaster he set himself to perfect machines which would provide similar protection on single lines. The result of his efforts, patented in March, 1878, was the Tyer electric tablet instrument.

This invention of Tyer's contained, like some automatic slot machine, a number of appropriately inscribed tablets or tokens each of which authorized the driver of a train to occupy the section to which they referred. But this machine was electrically interlocked with another at the other end of the section in such a way that once one tablet had been withdrawn from either, both became locked and it was not possible to release a second tablet until the first had been replaced in one or the other machine. It will be seen that with this apparatus, the direction of running through the section could alternate, or trains could follow one another successively with perfect safety. The so-called 'electric staff' system is a variant of this 'electric tablet' and operates in the same fashion.

These Tyer instruments not only brought a far higher standard of safety to single lines; they also made possible far more efficient and expeditious working. Alfred Whitaker on the Somerset & Dorset, and James Manson and William Duncan on the Great North of Scotland Railway each evolved locomotive and lineside apparatus for the exchange of tablets at high speed. Accompanied by the suitable re-alignment of the passing loops, the installation of this apparatus enabled express schedules to be maintained with perfect safety on single line routes.

Now signalling and train protection devices make a fascinating subject for study by anyone deeply interested in railways, but their detail is proper matter for a textbook and would be out of place in a work of general interest such as this. But the description just given of Tyer's single line apparatus is essential in the light of what was to follow. If the reader has been able to grasp the principle of the invention he may very well conclude that it was absolutely foolproof; that where such instruments were installed there could be no possibility of a recurrence of the tragedies of Menheniot, Thorpe or Radstock.

Their inventor himself probably thought so too, and when he died in 1912 nothing had occurred to disillusion him. But on January 26th, 1921, on a single line protected by Tyer's instruments, two passenger trains met in violent head-on collision. The railway was the Cambrian and the place was Abermule.

The story of the events which resulted in the Abermule disaster is a classic example of the truth that no electrical or mechanical safety devices can altogether eliminate the human element: that the safety of the travelling public must always depend, in the 1st analysis, upon the efficiency and vigilance of the railway staff. The 10.5 am stopping train from Whitchurch was scheduled to cross the Aberystwyth to Manchester express shortly before noon at Abermule, a small country station in the valley of the upper Severn and the junction for the short Kerry branch. But this arrangement was not rigidly enforced. If either train happened to be behind time then they might pass each other at the next station to the north or south of Abermule. If the stopping train was late it might be held for the express at Montgomery but if it was running to time and the express was delayed, then Abermule might send it on to Newtown. On this January day the staff at Abermule station was as follows: relief Stationmaster Lewis, deputizing for the regular stationmaster who was on leave; Signalman Jones; a youthful porter named Rodgers and a boy named Francis Thompson who collected tickets and helped in the booking office. It is important to remember these four for although they remained remote from the actual scene of the accident they were the chief actors in the drama. For the tragedy was entirely due to their combined carelessness added to the fact that there was no proper co-ordination at the station in the carrying out of their respective duties. In the light of this lack of proper organization, the fact that the Tyer electric tablet instruments were installed in the station building and not in the signal cabin was most unfortunate. Only the stationmaster and the signalman, Jones, were supposed to work the tablet instruments, but it had become the practice for anyone to work them who happened to be handy.

When Montgomery advised Abermule at 11.50 am that the stopping train had arrived there and was waiting to proceed it was Signalman Jones who replied. He was in the instrument room with Rodgers and Thompson. Stationmaster Lewis had gone for his dinner. Jones accepted the train and pressed the release on the Montgomery–Abermule instrument which enabled his mate at Montgomery to withdraw the necessary tablet. Having done so he rang up Moat Lane Junction, the next station south of Newtown, to ask the whereabouts of the express. Moat Lane replied that it had left there and was on its way to Newtown. Having received this information, the signalman left the instrument room and went along to his cabin at the end of the platform to set the road and open the level crossing gates for the stopping train. On his way out he met the returning stationmaster but he did not say anything to him about the position of the two approaching trains. Lewis did not stay in the instrument room but went off to the goods yard to superintend the movement of some wagons, leaving the young porter, Rodgers, and the boy Thompson in charge. At this juncture Newtown rang up saying that the express had arrived there and asking permission to send it forward. This time it was Rodgers who accepted the train and pressed the release on the Abermule–Newtown instrument which enabled Newtown to withdraw a tablet. So far, everything was in order; the two trains were approaching Abermule from opposite directions, each bearing the correct tablet for the section it occupied while both the tablet instruments at Abermule were now automatically locked so that no other tablet could be withdrawn. Rodgers now left the instrument room and went to the ground frame at the opposite end of the platform from the signal cabin with the object of setting the road for the express to enter the passing loop. Lewis the stationmaster was still in the goods yard so the youth did not tell him that he had accepted the express. The ground frame levers were locked from the cabin. Had Rodgers called on Signalman Jones to release the lock, the latter would have realized that the express was approaching, but at this moment Rodgers was diverted from his intention by the arrival of the stopping train from Montgomery. Jones knew from his telephone inquiry to Moat Lane that the express was running to time, but only Rodgers knew positively that the express was actually occupying the Newtown–Abermule section and even having regard to his youth his subsequent inaction is hard to explain. The boy Thompson was beside him when he accepted the express but evidently he did not realize what Rodgers had done. Thompson was alone on the up platform when the stopping train ran in on the down side. He immediately crossed the line and collected the Montgomery–Abermule tablet from the driver. He climbed back on to the up platform with the intention of returning the tablet to the instrument when he met the stationmaster hurrying up from the goods yard. Lewis asked Thompson where the express was and the boy inexplicably replied that it had just passed Moat Lane, thus giving Lewis the false impression that it was running late. As he gave this misleading information the boy made another terrible mistake; without any explanation he handed the Montgomery–Abermule tablet he had just collected to the stationmaster with the remark that he must go to the station exit to take the tickets. Now it was Lewis's turn to make confusion worse confounded. He had not been on the platform to observe the boy's actions and he assumed that Thompson had already replaced the Montgomery–Abermule tablet and, since he understood that the express was behind time, that the tablet he now held in his hand authorized the train in the station to proceed towards Newtown. In fact it would have been impossible to obtain such a tablet for the Abermule–Newtown instrument was locked. Had Lewis looked at the inscription on the tablet he would have seen that it was the wrong one, but he took it for granted that the boy had changed it, crossed the line and handed it back to the driver. Under working rules it was the driver's duty to examine the tablet and so ensure that it was correct, but he failed to do so. Like the stationmaster he took it for granted. For years the Tyer electric block system had protected the line infallibly and he conceived no possibility of error. Without troubling to remove it from its pouch, the driver placed it in his cab. It was his death warrant. Both the boy Thompson, who had returned from his ticket collecting, and Signalman Jones saw Lewis hand over the deadly tablet, but neither saw any reason to intervene. Thompson assumed that the stationmaster had changed the tablet in his absence. Jones, knowing the express was running to time, was surprised, but he too took for granted the infallibility of the system and assumed that for some reason unknown to him the express had been held at Newtown. Presumably Rodgers thought likewise and imagined that Newtown's request for acceptance had been cancelled and that the tablet whose release he had authorized had been replaced in the Newtown instrument. The road was accordingly set for the train to proceed towards Newtown, the signals were pulled off and the train went on its way. Only when it was too late did the Abermule staff discover that the Montgomery–Abermule instrument had not been cleared by the return of the tablet and so realized their terrible mistake.

The crew on the express locomotive miraculously escaped death and were afterwards able to give an account of the collision. They were travelling fast on a falling gradient about a mile from Abermule when, to their horror, they sighted the engine of the stopping train coming towards them at close range through a shallow cutting and labouring hard on the upgrade. Driver Pritchard Jones at once made a full emergency brake application, but to pull up his heavy train in time was quite impossible. Moreover, the crew of the oncoming train did not appear to see them for the locomotive continued to belch steam and smoke until the moment of impact. In that terrific collision the engine of the stopping train was overwhelmed and irreparably damaged by the heavier locomotive of the express, both enginemen being killed instantly. The framing of the express engine reared itself on end while the boiler was torn clean out of the frame and twisted through 180 degrees. The coaches of the slow moving 'local' and the rear coaches of the express remained on the rails and were little damaged, but the leading express coaches were telescoped and wrecked. In them, fifteen passengers were killed including Lord Herbert Vane-Tempest, a Director of the Cambrian Railway Company. The wreckage was so inextricably locked together that it took the breakdown gang over fifty hours of continuous work to clear the line.

Although he was lying seriously injured under a pile of wreckage, Driver Pritchard Jones's first thought was to discover the cause of the accident. He had examined his tablet before leaving Newtown and found it was correct. Could he possibly have been mistaken? In desperate anxiety he called to his fireman, Owen, and although the latter had also been injured he began frantically to search among the twisted wreckage of the two locomotives for the tablet. He eventually managed to recover two tablets: one was their own and correct, but the other was for the Montgomery–Abermule section and at once the presence of the stopping train was explained. Mr George, the Cambrian's Chief Traffic Inspector, who had been a passenger on the express, took both tablets from Owen and ran with them to Abermule station. The fatal tablet now became an instrument of mercy. In the presence of witnesses, George placed it in the Abermule–Montgomery machine, an action which cleared that section and allowed the breakdown train from Oswestry to proceed.

After commenting upon the mistakes and breaches of working rules at Abermule which had led up to the disaster, the inspecting officer, Colonel Pringle, went on to make certain recommendations which, he said, would prevent any recurrence. The fact that the tablet instruments were installed in the station building was a practice inherited, no doubt, from the old telegraph offices which the new system had replaced. The Colonel condemned it. The instruments should be in the signal cabin under the control of the signalman. No such misunderstanding could then occur. He also suggested that the tablet instruments should be interlocked with starting signals so that a starter could not be pulled off unless the relevant instrument had been cleared. Finally he criticized the layout at Abermule. Although it was locked from the box, the use of a separate and remote ground frame for controlling movements on running lines was objectionable.

In the forty-five years that have gone by since Abermule there has been no serious single line collision on any British railway and there is good reason to hope that there never will be another. But for anyone connected with railways the name of this quiet little country station in the Welsh border country will always carry sinister and tragic overtones. The story of the apparently trivial events which defeated the most ingenious mechanical devices and so led to this appalling disaster has not staled with the passing of the years. On the contrary it still teaches so salutary a lesson that it should be compulsory reading for every newcomer to the railway service in any capacity. For at Abermule the locomotive crew of the stopping train and each member of the station staff from stationmaster to ticket boy contributed to the tragedy by their slackness and irresponsibility, by breaches of rule and by relying too much upon the infallibility of a mechanical system. We may take it as certain that the errors committed on this occasion were by no means unique. Not only at Abermule but at many another single line crossing station unauthorized staff had worked the tablet instruments or had passed tablets from hand to hand. Many another stationmaster had, for one reason or another, failed to be present on the arrival of a train and then authorized the 'right away' without proper assurance that all was as it should be. Many another driver had received a tablet without examining it. Time and again one or other of these mistakes had been made with impunity, but at Abermule on that disastrous day, like the scattered pieces of a jig-saw puzzle, these trifling faults fitted one into another until the sombre picture was complete.

7

HIGH SPEED DERAILMENTS

Wigan – Wennington – Welshampton – Salisbury – Grantham – Shrewsbury – Ditton Junction

QUEEN VICTORIA'S love of Balmoral made fashionable among her more affluent subjects an annual summer pilgrimage north of the Border. In reserved first-class compartments or family saloons, with their numerous progeny, with their companions, nurses and servants, their horses, carriages and coachmen and their mountains of luggage, the gentry headed north from Euston and King's Cross, their annual exodus giving traffic superintendents on the West and East Coast Routes many grey hairs. Such was the complement of the 'Tourist Special' which left Euston for Scotland at 8 pm on the night of August 2nd, 1873. It was drawn by two locomotives, and by the time it left Crewe it consisted of no less than twenty-five vehicles of mixed North Western and Caledonian stock, many of them family coaches. As one of the distinguished travellers, Sir John Anson, boarded his reserved carriage, a Caledonian Composite, he pointed to the red lion of Scotland rampant in its golden field on the maroon lower panel and jocularly observed to his party that they were halfway to Scotland already. They were fated never to arrive.

As the long train was running through Wigan station in the small hours of the morning, Driver Will Stawpert on the train engine happened to glance back and saw to his dismay that sparks were flying from the rear of the train. He promptly whistled for guard's brakes but, fearing that part of the train might have become detached, he applied his own cautiously and came to a stand over a quarter of a mile beyond Wigan North signal box. He then walked back to find out what was amiss but, to use his own words, he was so overpowered by the sight that met his eyes at the south end of Wigan down platform that he hurried back to the north box.

Wigan down platform was an island, a loop road passing round the back of it. The first fifteen vehicles of the fast moving train passed safely over the loop line facing points but two wheels of the sixteenth coach, a family saloon occupied by Lady Florence Leveson Gower and her companion Miss Braggs were derailed. Next to it came a luggage van in which Conductor Alexander Harper was riding. This was derailed completely. It demolished a lineside shunters' cabin, carrying away its side in the process, but the couplings held and both vehicles travelled the length of the platform and were miraculously re-railed by a crossing at the north end. Harper was dazed and half stunned by the avalanche of luggage which overwhelmed him while the two ladies in the saloon were naturally terror struck. The Wigan station staff were so appalled by the spectacle of the two derailed vehicles reeling through the station and so deafened by the noise they made as they cannoned against the platform face that they knew nothing of the happenings at the south end of the station until a dishevelled figure staggered into view crying 'What station is this?' They then hurried down the platform to be greeted by the spectacle which so unmanned Driver Stawpert. The coaches behind Harper's van had all been completely derailed on the facing points, had broken away from the train and lay shattered in hideous confusion. Some had run up the ramp on to the platform carrying away part of the awning; others were heaped upon the loop line. The eighteenth vehicle, Sir John Anson's Caledonian Composite, stood upon its roof on the platform and five of its occupants lay dead beside it. Another composite carriage had burst through a retaining wall and landed on the roof of a foundry, one of its occupants, a Mrs Roberts, falling through the roof on to the moulding floor below. Only the last coach and the rear brake van in which the head guard, May, was travelling, were undamaged. They came to rest beside the loop platform with their wheels in the ballast. Thirteen passengers lost their lives and thirty were injured. It was 1.20 am when the disaster occurred, and at 2.53 the front portion of the train continued on its way to Scotland, its passengers unaware of the fate which had overtaken their fellows in the rear until they reached their destination.

The public inquiry into the Wigan disaster, which was conducted by Captain Tyler, lasted five weeks and in the course of these protracted proceedings no less than 104 witnesses were examined. Subsequent accounts of the accident frequently state that it was caused by the facing points moving under the train, yet in fact this was never established. The facing points were locked and the most minute examination failed to reveal the smallest defect either in the locking gear or in the points themselves. Indeed they sustained so little consequential damage from the derailment that traffic was passed over them with perfect safety an hour or so after the disaster. The interlocking gear in the south signal box which controlled them was found to be worn so that certain levers could be partially freed, but this defect had no bearing upon the accident. On the other hand, all but one of the passengers who gave evidence said that many times on the journey up from Euston they had been alarmed by the speed of the train and the rocking and swaying of the carriages. The exception, significantly enough, was the Reverend C. W. Dod. He was a keen student of railways, he said, who frequently amused himself by timing the speeds of the trains. He noticed nothing unusual about either the speed of the train or its motion. In fact he thought the quality of the riding was particularly good. Obviously that love of railways which so many pillars of the established church display is no recent phenomenon.

Despite this clerical championship, Captain Tyler accepted the majority view. In the circumstances he considered that the speed of the train had been too high for safety and he referred to the keen competition between the East and West Coast Routes for Scottish traffic which tempted the Companies concerned to take unwarrantable risks. The speed of the train at the time of the accident had been estimated at forty miles an hour but it was probably higher. He did not think that trains should run through a major station such as Wigan so fast as this. Bearing in mind the motley collection of six- and four-wheeled vehicles which made up an express train in those days, there can be little doubt that the Captain was right. As to the precise cause of the derailment he could only conjecture. He thought that the flange of a wheel of the sixteenth coach may have struck the 'joggle' in the offside running rail which was made to receive the blade of the facing points when set over for the loop. This might have caused the flange of the nearside wheel to slip over the tongue of the points. Yet this can hardly explain why all the following vehicles should have run amok. All the circumstances seem to suggest that they 'split' the points, yet if this were so how could those points have remained perfect and revealed no clue? Alexander Harper, in his evidence, said he felt the front wheels of his van 'wrenched' as though they had hit some obstruction. Did something undiscovered fall from the train to lodge between running rail and check rail? We can only speculate; the mystery of the Wigan disaster remains.

Wennington Junction, where the Midland and Furness joint line leaves the Leeds to Lancaster section of the Midland Railway, was the scene of the next serious high speed derailment in 1880. Eight lives were lost when the 12.15 pm train from Leeds to Lancaster became completely derailed on the junction points, ploughed its way forward for 166 yards and then struck the abutment of a bridge. The immediate cause of the accident was too high a speed over a junction where there was no super-elevation owing to the use of continuous crossing timbers. But, as the inspector, Colonel Yolland, pointed out, the train would not have hit the bridge and there might have been no loss of life had the braking power been adequate. The engine alone was fitted with the Westinghouse brake, while there was only one brake van on the train. The Colonel spoke his mind in no uncertain terms.

It is all very well [he said] for the Midland Railway Company now to plead that they are busily employed in fitting up their passenger trains with continuous brakes, but the necessity for providing their passenger trains with a larger proportion of brake power was pointed out by the Board of Trade twenty years since; and with the exception of a very few railway companies that recognized the necessity and acted upon it, it may be truly stated that the principal railway companies throughout the kingdom have resisted the efforts of the Board of Trade to cause them to do what was right, which the latter had no legal power to enforce, and even now it will be seen by the latest returns laid before Parliament that some of those companies are still doing nothing to supply this now generally acknowledged necessity.

That there were so few serious defaulters among British railway companies when automatic continuous brakes on passenger trains became compulsory nine years later was in a great measure due to the salutary effect of such hard-hitting pronouncements as this.

Welshampton, a sleepy little Welsh border station on the Cambrian Railway between Whitchurch and Ellesmere was the scene of the next serious derailment on June 11th, 1897. Eleven lives were lost when a long day excursion train of mixed Cambrian and Lancashire & Yorkshire rolling stock, double-headed, ran off the road on its return journey from Mid-Wales to Lancashire. Earlier in the day a Cambrian guard had complained of the rough riding of a small four-wheeled L & YR brake van which, on the return working, was attached to the front of the train. Cambrian officials maintained at the inquiry that this vehicle caused the derailment, and Company loyalty has perpetuated this version of the accident to this day as I know from conversation with old Cambrian men. But the inspecting officer came to a different conclusion. This was that the speed of the train was too great having regard to the con-

dition of the permanent way in the neighbourhood of Welshampton. The rails were too light in weight for high speed
running and many of the sleepers were in need of renewal. In
fairness to the Cambrian, they were at that time in process of
relaying with a heavier rail.

We might suppose that with the general improvement in
permanent way which accompanied the introduction of steel
rails, and the use of bogie rolling stock fitted with continuous
brakes on all express passenger trains, derailments due solely
to excessive speed would become a thing of the past. But we
should be quite wrong. Strangely enough the early years of the
twentieth century were marred by a most extraordinary and
terrible sequence of accidents of this kind. They were terrible
in their destructiveness; they were extraordinary because the
aberrations which caused the first three of them were inexplicable. They must for ever remain subjects for conjecture. Dead
men can tell no tales.

On the night of June 30th, 1906, the weekly London &
South Western Railway boat express left Plymouth for Waterloo with forty-eight passengers from the American liner *New
York*. It was a light train consisting of only five eight-wheeled
vehicles: a brake van, three first-class corridor coaches, and a
kitchen/brake composite at the rear. Although the load was
small the schedule was smart over this difficult west of England main line and the 4-4-0 No 288 did well to bring her
train into Templecombe one minute ahead of time. Here the
boat express made its only scheduled stop between Plymouth
and London – for engine purposes only. No 288 came off and
No 421, a four-coupled bogie express engine with Driver
Robins and Fireman Gadd in charge backed on to the train.
Driver Robins was a man of long experience and good record
who knew the road thoroughly. Richard Furze, the night inspector, and a shunter named Walter Mullet both talked to the
engine crew while they were waiting for their train to arrive
and said afterwards that they were sober and in good health
and spirits. Mullet said: 'The boat train's running well to

time,' and Robins replied: 'Yes, but I shan't get into Waterloo before time else I shall have to go up and see the governor.'

Robins made a poor start from Templecombe and when he passed Dinton box, twenty miles out, he was running four minutes late. But at this point No 421 was given her head, averaging seventy miles an hour over the six miles to Wilton. The express had a clear road through Salisbury but there was a permanent speed restriction of 30 mph over the curves at the west and east ends of the station. Although Robins must have been perfectly well aware of this restriction he appears to have made no attempt to slacken speed. It was a clear summer night so that it is scarcely conceivable that a driver so familiar with the road should have mistaken his whereabouts. At Salisbury up distant signal Robins opened his whistle and kept it open for several hundred yards. Screaming, and still steaming hard the express tore past Salisbury West box to the consternation of the signalman, Herbert Mundy. Miraculously, the train held the curve on the western approach and roared through the station, but on the 10 chain reverse curve between the east end of the platform and the Fisherton Street overbridge it became completely derailed and dashed into the rear vans of a milk train which, by ill fortune, was at that moment passing through on the down line. According to Signalman Haines in Salisbury East box the derailment occurred at 1.57 am which meant, if it was correct, that the train had covered the eight and a half miles from Dinton to the point of disaster at an average of 72 miles an hour.

In his report, the Board of Trade inspector, Major Pringle, said he had no doubt whatever that when the disaster occurred the train was running at least double its permitted speed. All the evidence and the terrible destruction caused proved this. The locomotive overturned across the down line. The three first-class coaches and five vans of the milk train were completely destroyed. A light engine which was standing on the down bay platform line was also damaged, the driver being badly scalded by escaping steam. Forty yards of the down line were demolished and where the northern rail had been there was a trench three and a half feet deep. The disaster claimed no less than twenty-eight victims: twenty-four passengers – precisely half the complement of the express – Driver Robins and Fireman Gadd, the guard of the milk train and the fireman of the light engine. In addition, seven of the surviving passengers were seriously injured. One remarkable feature of the accident was that the engine of the boat train was so little damaged that it was run upon its own wheels to Nine Elms for repairs. The regulator was found to be closed but the vacuum brake, which was in perfect order, had not been applied.

Competition between the South Western and Great Western Companies for the West of England traffic was very keen at this time but inquiries found no truth in rumours that boat train passengers made a practice of tipping drivers to put up fast runs or that the Company encouraged record breaking. Indeed Driver Robins' remark to Mullet at Templecombe showed that he was well aware that he would be reprimanded if he arrived before time at Waterloo. Beyond suggesting that the thirty miles an hour speed restriction should be reduced to fifteen over the eastern curves at Salisbury, Major Pringle had few comments to make. The recklessness of Driver Robins, he concluded, was inexplicable.

It is possible to dismiss the Salisbury accident as a gross error of judgement on the part of the unfortunate driver, but no such simple solution can suffice to explain the cause of the disaster which occurred at Grantham on September 19th of the same year. Of all the major accidents that have occurred in our railway history it remains the most mysterious. The train involved was the 8.45 pm semi-fast mail from King's Cross to Edinburgh which was booked to stop at Peterborough and Grantham. On this occasion it consisted of twelve vehicles, five of them, including two sleeping cars, being twelve-wheeled East Coast Joint Stock. It was usual on this run for engines to be changed at Peterborough, and when the train arrived there No 276, one of the famous Ivatt 'Atlantics', then only two years old, was waiting to work it forward. On the footplate were Driver Fleetwood of Doncaster and Fireman Talbot. Several of the station staff at Peterborough spoke with them before the train arrived and declared afterwards that both men were perfectly sober and in normal health. Fleetwood knew the road intimately. He had had eighteen years driving experience and had been in sole charge of No 276 since she first came out of the shops. His fireman was a highly competent and intelligent young man who was perfectly capable of taking over the controls from the driver should the need arise. He had served a premium apprenticeship at Doncaster works and was now working under the district locomotive superintendent, firing on various types of locomotive for the purpose of taking notes on their behaviour under working conditions. Both men had booked on duty at Doncaster that afternoon. They had worked the 2.55 pm train to York and the 6.50 pm express from York to Peterborough. Now they were returning to Doncaster where they would book off. They had worked precisely the same rota the previous day.

The train was due to stop at Grantham at 11 pm and Henry Pile, the night station inspector, was standing on the down platform ready to receive it together with three postmen who were waiting to load mails. Alfred Day, who was on duty in Grantham south signal box had his own distant signal at 'caution'. Richard Scoffin in the north box had all his down main line signals at 'danger' to protect the Nottingham line junction where he was crossing the 10.57 pm up Leicester goods train from the up Nottingham line to the up main. This meant that the goods had to cross over the down main, so the down line facing points at the junction were, very properly, set for the Nottingham line also. It was a dark night with occasional scuds of rain which made the rail greasy but it was perfectly clear and the red eyes of the Junction signals glowed brightly. Suddenly, Cecil Cox, one of the postmen, stepped to the platform edge and looked up the line. 'It's coming in,' he called. His mate joined him, took one look at the swiftly approaching headlights and shook his head. 'It's a run through,' he said. A moment later the train was thundering through the platform and Cox was shouting above the din, 'It isn't, it has our mail carriage on it.' Inspector Pile estimated the speed of the train as forty miles an hour, others thought more, but all agreed that the brakes were not applied. None of them noticed the driver and fireman. The only man at Grantham that night who did so was Alfred Day in the south signal box. He said he saw them both standing motionless, one on either side of the footplate, each staring ahead through his cab spectacle glass. The bewildered little group on the platform turned to watch the train disappear into the darkness under the red danger lights. A moment later they heard a great noise like an explosion and then the night sky over the north yard was lit with flames. They ran then, stumbling over the network of rails and point rods, to give what help they could.

The 'Atlantic' rode the points on to the Nottingham line and the reverse curve which followed it, but on this second curve the tender, with its long fixed wheelbase, was derailed and swept away the parapet wall of an underbridge for a length of 65 yards. It then broke away and fell over the side of the bridge. In doing so it derailed the locomotive which slewed broadside across the tracks with the leading three vehicles piled against it. The following six vehicles plunged down the embankment just beyond the bridge and only the last three remained upright and unharmed. Fire broke out almost immediately in the wreckage both above and below, the one being started by coals from the engine firebox and the other by escaping gas. Driver Fleetwood and Fireman Talbot were killed instantly and their locomotive was so badly damaged that it was impossible to determine the position of the regulator and brake lever at the time of the accident. Fortunately three brake vans and the mail coach were at the front of the train otherwise casualties might have been much heavier, but even so eleven passengers and a postal sorter lost their lives.

The Grantham disaster produced an unprecedented crop of

rumours and fantastic theories. The driver was drunk. The driver had gone mad. As the train approached Grantham the driver and fireman had been seen struggling desperately with one another on the footplate. The driver was accustomed to join the train at Grantham, had thought he had done so on this occasion and believed that he faced a clear run to Doncaster. All these stories were either disproved at the inquiry or else the facts made them quite preposterous. The theory most favoured and most credible was that Fleetwood was suddenly taken ill and that Talbot was so concerned in aiding him that he did not realize the position of the train until it was too late. Certainly Fleetwood had complained of illness which he had said was sciatica. He had been taken ill on the footplate in the previous June and was off duty for a week. He was not given a medical examination when he returned to work and the inspector, Colonel Von Donop, gave his opinion that all drivers should in future be so examined before being allowed to resume footplate duty. Yet, convincing though this theory is, it cannot be reconciled with the evidence of Signalman Alfred Day. His claim to have seen Fleetwood and Talbot standing on the footplate, and the fact that the train did not whistle in accordance with invariable custom on approaching Grantham both seem to suggest that the men mistook their whereabouts. But here again, such an extraordinary aberration on the part of two intelligent men, both of whom knew the road intimately and had worked over it with the same train on the previous night, seems incredible. Not only was it a clear night, but a number of Great Northern footplate men testified at the inquiry that the approach to Grantham was quite unmistakable under any conditions. What precisely took place on the footplate of Ivatt 'Atlantic' No 276 on this September night sixty years ago is a question that Sherlock Holmes himself could not answer. It remains the railway equivalent of the mystery of the *Marie Celeste*.

On October 15th, 1907, little over a year after the Grantham disaster, there occurred the third in this extraordinary series of inexplicable tragedies. Once again the accident happened in the small hours; once again the train involved was a night mail consisting of modern stock and drawn by a newly built locomotive. In this case it was the 1.20 am London & North Western mail train from Crewe to Shrewsbury, Hereford, Bristol and the West of England. It was a heavy train, assembled at Crewe from three through portions arriving from Glasgow, York and Liverpool. On this particular night it consisted of fifteen vehicles, some Great Western, some North Western, some West Coast Joint Stock, and one Caledonian covered truck. It was hauled by the six-coupled North Western locomotive *Stephenson* of the 'Experiment' class which had been built at Crewe the previous year. The train left Crewe eight minutes late, but on the eighteen and three-quarter mile run between Whitchurch and Shrewsbury, the first booked stop, the driver maintained an average of sixty miles an hour and regained five minutes. Now in order to enter Shrewsbury platform the train had to traverse a curve of only 610 feet radius over which speed was restricted to ten miles an hour. Two signal boxes controlled the approach to the station : Crewe Bank and Crewe Junction. When Crewe Bank offered the train to the Junction it was accepted under the 'section clear but station blocked' signal which meant that the Crewe Bank signalman must stop and caution the train. He therefore kept his signals at danger but, to his horror, he saw the train run past his box, only 600 yards from the junction curve, at full speed and realized that disaster was inevitable. He immediately sent the 'train running away on right line' signal to Junction, but by the time the signalman there received it the train was, in his own words, 'all across the junction'. The engine travelled for 75 yards over the sleepers and ballast before it was flung over on its side whereupon the coaches piled themselves upon and beside it, tearing up two sets of metals for a distance of 140 yards. Eighteen lives were lost : eleven passengers, the driver and fireman, two guards and three Post Office sorters.

Once again there was no certain explanation. The driver was an experienced man who knew the road well and the night was fine and clear. It was conjectured that the driver must have dozed off, but if that was so what of the fireman? Surely he would have noticed at least one of the danger signals and realized that his train was heading for certain destruction? To suppose that he too had nodded off would be incredible. Perhaps he was too preoccupied with his firing to notice his whereabouts.

With the Shrewsbury disaster this tragic sequence of accidents comes to an end, but there was to be another high speed derailment in 1912 which was more easily explicable and was destined to be the precursor of similar accidents which have occurred in more recent times.

The multiplication of running lines which took place in the latter part of the nineteenth century certainly relieved the congestion of traffic on many busy main lines and made possible more expeditious working, but it also created new dangers. The increased complexity, the great gantries of signals, all added to the possibilities of error and called for additional safeguards. At Ditton Junction on the London & North Western Railway near Widnes there were no less than eight running lines: down goods, up goods, up St Helens local, down slow, up slow, down fast, up fast, Runcorn local. The 5.30 pm express from Chester to Liverpool was signalled to cross from the fast to the slow line at Ditton but the driver, who had little experience of the road and had never been switched at Ditton before, misread his signals and obviously thought he had a clear run through on the fast line. He approached a crossover with a fifteen miles an hour speed restriction at a speed of at least a mile a minute. The result was horrible in the extreme. Needless to say the entire train left the rails. The locomotive, a 2–4–0 of the 'Precedent' class, turned over on its side and travelled in this fashion for some distance, ploughing up both the up and the down slow lines, until it struck the pier of an overbridge, bringing down a large part of the brickwork. As it struck the pier, the locomotive broke its back, the boiler barrel shearing clean away from the firebox throat plate. The six following coaches leapt right over the engine and tender and formed a compact heap of wreckage beyond the bridge, between the station platforms and against the wall of the booking office. Before any move could be made to rescue passengers from the dreadful heap of shattered woodwork and twisted steel, gas from punctured gaslighting cylinders ignited and in a matter of minutes the scene became an inferno of flame. Chemical extinguishers were brought into play and hoses run out from hydrants on the station platform but all to no avail. The driver and fireman and thirteen passengers perished in this fearful holocaust.

'It is not for me,' said the inspector, Colonel Yorke, 'to describe the horrors of the scene. There is, I believe, no record of any previous accident in which the engine has broken its back, as in this case, and rarely has there been such wholesale destruction of rolling stock.' The lesson to be learnt, Colonel Yorke went on, was the urgent necessity of ensuring that drivers shall be properly acquainted with the road. It was clear from the evidence that the driver, Robert Hughes, had insufficient knowledge and that he should have applied for a pilot at Chester. The inspector also criticized the signal installation at Ditton. It was inconsistent and confusing to provide a separate distant signal for this crossover route when none existed for the similar goods line crossover which was subject to exactly the same speed restriction. As in the latter case, a single distant signal which should stand at danger when a train was to be crossed was all that was required. Alternatively, if the fast to slow line distant was retained, then it should carry on its post a speed restriction warning sign.

There have been repetitions of the Ditton Junction accident at Leighton Buzzard in 1931 and at Great Bridgeford in 1932 but fortunately, though there was loss of life in both cases, they were not attended by such catastrophic results. In the former case the locomotive involved was one of the original

'Royal Scots' and the driver's view of his signals was obscured by steam and smoke hanging round the boiler. This was a chronic fault of these engines which was only partially cured by fitting deflector plates beside the smoke box.

With the exceptions of Wigan, Wennington and Welshampton, all these serious accidents might have been averted or at least mitigated. For the automatic vacuum brake can be applied by the guard in his van as well as by the engine driver, and the former, no less than the latter, is responsible for the safety of the train. Yet it would be a mistake to criticize too harshly the men concerned. A guard on a fast passenger train is often preoccupied with other duties, he has not the driver's view of the road ahead and on a dark night he may not always be precisely aware of the position of his train. Inevitably he puts his trust in the good judgement of the driver. There is another point which must also be remembered. When these disasters occurred the automatic vacuum brake was still only twenty years old and the older railwaymen did not readily alter the habits of a lifetime. In this connection the statement of William Harrison, the guard of the Plymouth boat train, after the Salisbury disaster is of some interest. He knew that the train was running into Salisbury much too fast. Asked by Major Pringle why he did not apply the vacuum brake, he replied that he did make 'a gentle application' with the object of warning the driver, but that he then released it. He was afraid, he said, that a coupling might break or that he would otherwise damage the train. The inference is that Harrison was instinctively thinking in terms of the old non-continuous brakes, for no damage could possibly have resulted from his applying the automatic vacuum even in the highly unlikely event of a coupling parting. It would seem therefore that in the case of the vacuum brake familiarity has spelt, not contempt, but greater safety. For the mysterious tragedies of Salisbury, Grantham and Shrewsbury remain without parallel in railway annals and it is happily improbable that we shall ever see their like again.

8

STRAY WAGONS AND BREAK-AWAYS

Shrivenham – Round Oak – Abergele – Stairfoot – Chelford – Armagh

A T T H E end of the first chapter I referred to the introduction in 1845 of the famous Great Western broad gauge expresses from Paddington to Exeter. The 'Cornishman', the 'Flying Dutchman' and the 'Zulu', as they were later called, were for many years the fastest trains in the world and it speaks volumes for the 7-foot gauge and for the Great Western Company that over all the years they were running only one really serious accident befell them. The victim was the twelve o'clock up express from Exeter on May 10th, 1848, and Shrivenham station was the scene of the mishap. Unseen by the policeman stationed at the level crossing at the opposite end of the station, two porters pushed a horse-box and a cattle van out on to the up main line in order to clear a wagon turntable. They were struck and flung on to the station platform by the engine of the express, the 'Sultan', one of Daniel Gooch's classic 8-foot single drivers. There was no derailment and the locomotive swept past practically undamaged but unfortunately the wreckage of the vans fell back upon the following train, tearing the side out of the leading coach, killing six passengers and injuring thirteen.

Two years later a somewhat similar accident, fortunately not of serious consequence, occurred at Wootton Bassett where an excursion train collided with a straying horse-box. In this case the stray had not been properly braked or scotched and had been blown out of its siding on to the main line by the wind created by the passing of a previous train.

These two accidents are typical of many which occurred in the early days and which emphasized the necessity of pro-

tecting fast running lines from erroneous or accidental movements on adjacent tracks. After the Wootton Bassett accident
the Great Western directors issued an edict. Wherever there
was sufficient room all sidings must be fitted with safety or
'trap' points leading to stop blocks. Otherwise permanent
chock blocks must be installed which could be swung over the
rail and locked there. Later, these trap points would be interlocked so as to make impossible any conflicting movement
when the main running line was set for the passage of a train.
Coincident with this safety provision, siding layouts were
gradually altered so that all shunting operations would be
carried out clear of main running lines.

Another closely analogous danger was that of vehicles running back down a gradient either as a result of injudicious
shunting operations or owing to a breakaway caused by a coupling failure. It is the great virtue of the automatic brake that if
vehicles so fitted break away from their train, the brakes
immediately come on and no accident should occur. But if a
considerable portion of a loose coupled goods train breaks
away when ascending a steep gradient its weight may be more
than the single brake van at the rear can hold and an accident
is almost inevitable although under present working conditions
it can seldom or never be attended by serious consequences. In
the first place it is the duty of the signalman to note from its
rear lamps that each train that passes his box is complete. If it
is not, he sends out the 'train divided' signal in both directions.
The leading portion will be stopped at the next block post in
advance and following traffic halted in the rear. Similarly if a
signalman sees a detached portion of a train run past his box
out of control he will send out the 'train running away on right
line or wrong line' signals as the case may be. But the danger
of runaways colliding with following trains by running back
down inclines is minimized by the provision of 'catch points'
on steep gradients on double lines which will automatically
derail runaways and deflect them harmlessly into the bank of a
cutting. Such a catch point derailment may cause a major pile-

up of wagons and block both running lines, but this is in-
finitely preferable to the terrible head-on collision which might
otherwise ensue.

All these safety precautions: siding trap points, shunting
spurs and catch points and the interlocking and block systems
which accompanied them were not installed in a day and before their provision became universal some terrible disasters
were caused by straying wagons and divided trains.

The construction of the Oxford, Worcester & Wolverhampton Railway was accompanied by many vicissitudes financial
and otherwise. While the half completed line languished for
lack of money it was bitterly fought for by the rival gauge
factions. The spoils ultimately went to the Great Western, but
it was a hollow victory which signalled the decline of Swindon's broad gauge empire. For it was a narrow gauge line that
the Western acquired and the 7-foot gauge outer rail which it
had compelled the Worcester Company to lay was seldom or
never used and was soon removed. During its brief independent career the OW & WR was a shocking railway, so much so
that it acquired the local nickname of 'the Old Worse &
Worse'. Its trains never kept time; its locomotives were continually breaking down. Finally, on August 23rd, 1858, it distinguished itself by staging what the Board of Trade inspector,
Captain Tyler, then described as: 'Decidedly the worst railway accident that has ever occurred in this country.'

The Company had decided to run a special day excursion
train from Wolverhampton to Worcester and back. It was
advertised as being for school children only, but in the event it
appears to have become a glorious free-for-all. It was a vast
train of packed four-wheelers that pulled out of Wolverhampton at 9.12 am on August 23rd. Everyone became infected
with the holiday spirit including Guard Cook in the rear van.
He had half a dozen passengers smoking and drinking with
him and invited them to try their hand at his screw brake.
This they proceeded to do to such effect that train couplings
and side chains broke three times before Worcester was

reached, and Cook had to make temporary repairs. At Brettell Lane he found some goods coupling links, at Hagley a spare screw coupling, while at Droitwich he made do with two links on one side and a single link and hook on the other. No doubt these minor contretemps only contributed to the general hilarity. While the train was standing at Worcester the broken side chains were repaired but nothing was done to the centre couplings.

On the return journey the train had to face a gradient of 1 in 75 between Brettell Lane and Round Oak so it was decided to divide it into two parts. The first consisted of twenty-eight coaches plus a brake van at each end and a second locomotive was added at Stourbridge to assist it up the long gradient. Guard Cook and his convivial friends occupied the rear van of this train. The second train of fourteen carriages and two vans was drawn by one locomotive throughout. The first train reached Round Oak at 8.10 pm, one minute before the second ran into Brettell Lane. By this time the night had fallen very dark, scuds of rain had made the rail greasy and a gusty wind was beating down the smoke of the locomotives making visibility difficult. Just as the first train drew to a standstill at Round Oak, a foreman platelayer who was standing on the platform heard a snap and immediately Cook's van and seventeen coaches packed with 450 passengers began to move back down the incline. According to Cook's evidence, this was what happened: he applied his brake about twenty yards before the train stopped and then eased it off again. The train stopped with a jerk and the coupling snapped on the recoil. When he realized that the train was running back he braked again, locking the wheels of his van. At first the runaways seemed to be slowing, but then they gathered speed again. As his van passed under the Moor Lane bridge Cook saw the second part of the excursion approaching only a short distance away and leaped out on to the lineside shouting to the passengers 'Jump! Jump! or we'll all be killed.' The enginemen of the second train sighted the runaways when they were 300 yards away;

they were naturally travelling slowly up the steep gradient and had practically drawn to a standstill when the violent collision occurred. Cook's van and the two coaches next to it were, in the words of Captain Tyler, 'broken all to pieces with the most dreadful consequences'. Fourteen passengers died, fifty were badly injured and a further 170 claimed compensation. Curiously enough, the locomotive of the second train was neither derailed nor seriously damaged and was later able to proceed on its way minus its funnel and front buffers.

Two men who said they were in the van with Cook and jumped with him corroborated his evidence and so did a woman living by the lineside who said she saw Cook jump and heard him shout. Moreover, the engine crew said they saw sparks flying from the wheels of the brake van. The sequence of events leading up to the disaster therefore seemed conclusive, yet Captain Tyler was not convinced and by investigations worthy of the great Sherlock himself he was able to show that Cook's evidence was completely false. In the first place he staged an elaborate experiment. The runaway vehicles were reassembled at Round Oak on his instructions with the addition of two coaches and a van similar to Cook's to replace the casualties. Weights were placed in the compartments to represent the passengers and with the inspector in the van the train was set rolling down the bank. It was certainly not an experiment to be lightly undertaken, this deliberate release of a train of seventeen loaded vehicles on a gradient of 1 in 75. But the gallant Captain had the courage of his convictions. He screwed the van brake hard down as Cook claimed he had done – and the runaways stopped. This was not all. Tyler recovered from the debris the brakescrew of Cook's van. The nut was in the fully 'off' position and he pointed out that the screw had been bent in such a way by the force of the collision that the nut could not have been moved subsequently.

In his summing up, Tyler said he was quite satisfied that the brake in the van had not been applied and that, in fact, Cook was never in the van at all but had stepped out on to the platform at Round Oak at the moment the train came to rest. He considered that Cook's evidence was a complete fabrication and that he was a thoroughly unreliable employee who should never had been entrusted with such a responsible post. It was true that certain of the train couplings had been found to be defective, but they would not have parted had it not been for Cook's mishandling of the van brake and his folly in permitting others to work it. The inspector also severely criticized the Company for allowing an excursion, advertised for school children only, to become a general free-for-all with such appalling results.

Next in this sequence of accidents we have to consider the fate of the Irish Mail at Abergele on August 20th, 1868. Other accidents have claimed a heavier toll in human life but never in railway history has disaster struck more swiftly or in so hideous a form. Readers may be surprised by the frequency with which the name of the Irish Mail crops up in these pages. This does not cast any adverse reflection upon the operational methods of the London & North Western Railway Company which were no better and no worse than those of other lines; nor does it imply that the Mail was ill omened. The truth is that this famous express has been operating continuously over a far longer period of time than any other 'named' train in the world and against its misfortunes must be set the thousands of journeys it has made, the millions of miles run, in perfect safety.

On the morning of August 20th, while the Mail was speeding north from Euston, a 'pick up' goods left Crewe for Holyhead. At the Flintshire Oil Works siding at Saltney, three miles west of Chester, this goods picked up two wagons loaded with $7\frac{3}{4}$ tons of paraffin oil in fifty casks. These wagons were marshalled at the rear of the train next to the brake van. The goods then proceeded on its way and arrived at Abergele at 12.5 pm. When it left at 12.15 it consisted of twenty-six empty and seventeen loaded wagons. When this long train jerked to a standstill with a clash of buffers at Llandulas, the next station west, the time was 12.24 pm and the Mail was due to pass at 12.39. The Llysfaen Lime sidings at Llandulas were partially occupied by wagons, but by dividing the goods there was room for it to shunt clear. Before doing so, however, the stationmaster ordered some shunting movements to be carried out on the main line. This was a flagrant breach of the Company's rule which stated: 'Goods trains when likely to be overtaken by a passenger train must be shunted at stations where there are fixed signals at least ten minutes before such a passenger train is due.'

While the rest of the train drew a rake of three timber wagons out of the Llysfaen sidings, the brake van and six wagons were left standing on the main line on a gradient of 1 in 147 and 1 in 100 falling towards Abergele. The wagon brakes were not pinned down, but the senior brakesman screwed the van brake hard on while the junior brakesman was working the points and controlling the shunting operations. The timber wagons were drawn out and then fly-shunted back on to the standing vehicles. Running beside them, the brakesman attempted to put down a brake but failed with the result that they cannoned into the six standing wagons and the van with some force. At once the whole lot began to move away down the incline followed, after the initial recoil, by the timber wagons. The brakesman ran in pursuit, but they gathered speed so rapidly that he was easily outdistanced. He signalled frantically to the driver of the goods to come back with the futile idea that he could pursue and retrieve them. Meanwhile the runaways had disappeared out of sight round a curve in a cutting and a few moments later the brakesman held up his arms as a signal to the driver to stop. He had heard the distant sound of a collision.

The Irish Mail had left Chester at 11.47 am, four minutes late, after attaching to the front of the train the Chester portion which consisted of a brake van, two first-class coaches, one composite and one second-class. The rest of the train was composed of a Post Office van and tender, a van, one first-class

carriage, three composites and a guard's van. At 12.39 the
Mail ran through Abergele, five minutes late, at a speed of
about forty miles an hour. It was at a point one and three-
quarter miles west of Abergele that Driver Arthur Thompson
saw the runaway wagons approaching. Owing to the cutting
and the reverse curves at this point they were only 200 yards
away when he first sighted them and for a moment he thought
they were running on the up line. When he realized they were
on the down line they were almost upon him. He shouted to his
fireman: 'For God's sake, Joe, jump for it, we can do no
more,' and as he shouted he leaped from his footplate. But Joe
did not follow him. Above the thunder of the collision Thompson recognized his fireman's voice in one despairing cry but he
heard no other human sound.

Thompson landed safely. He was struck by flying splinters
but otherwise unhurt and in a moment he had scrambled to his
feet. Yet in that moment the front van and the following three
coaches of the Mail had become enveloped in a roaring inferno
of flame. The contents of the bursting paraffin casks had de-
luged them and had been instantly ignited by spilt coals from
the locomotive firebox. The runaway wagons had been flung to
the north side of the up line where they were also blazing
furiously, likewise the engine tender which lay across the up
metals ahead of the locomotive which had come to rest on its
left side. The rear portion of the express was quite undamaged
and its occupants unharmed. Willing helpers uncoupled it and
pushed it back out of reach of the flames. But of the thirty-two
passengers in the leading coaches no soul survived. 'They can
only be described,' wrote Colonel Rich, the Board of Trade
inspector, 'as charred pieces of flesh and bone.'

One of the problems which Colonel Rich had to solve was
precisely how the wagons had run away from Llandulas in the
way they did. He did not doubt the senior brakesman's statement that he had screwed down the brake on the van, for if he
had not done so the vehicles would not have remained standing
on the gradient at all. On the other hand, all the eye-witnesses

agreed that after the recoil the fly-shunted timber wagons never overtook the leading runaways but followed them down the incline at a little distance. This proved that the brake van must have been running perfectly freely. In a careful search of the charred debris, the inspector recovered the cast iron cogs which worked the brake gear on the van. They were broken. He concluded that they had not been broken by the collision but by the rough shunting which preceded it.

The fact that the compartment doors of the burnt coaches were locked caused considerable outcry in the Press. While the inspector condemned a practice the dangers of which had already been demonstrated in the train fire at Versailles, he did not think that the passengers could have saved themselves in this case even if the doors had not been locked. The fire overwhelmed them too rapidly.

Colonel Rich strongly criticized the stationmaster at Llandulas for ordering the train to shunt in breach of the Company's rule, but he also criticized the North Western's working timetable for permitting the goods to precede the Mail within so short a time interval. When goods vehicles were left standing on main running lines their brakes should be pinned down or their wheels spragged whether or not they were attached to a brake van. Finally, Colonel Rich condemned the layout of the Llysfaen Lime sidings which, contrary to regulation, had never been inspected and approved by the Board of Trade, and which were, he said, 'quite unfit in extent and means of safety'. Here as elsewhere provision must be made for goods trains to carry out shunting operations clear of the running lines.

A little over three years after the Abergele calamity we find Colonel Rich conducting the inquiry into the disastrous accident at Stairfoot station near Barnsley on the Manchester, Sheffield & Lincolnshire Railway. In many respects it was a repetition of Abergele except that there was no fire and the passenger train involved was stationary at the moment of collision.

A goods train bound for Mexboro' was shunting in Barnsley top yard and in the course of this operation a rake of ten wagons was left standing on a gradient of 1 in 119. A single sprag was thrust through the spokes of a wheel to hold them. When two gas tank wagons were fly-shunted against them this sprag broke and the guard, who was acting as shunter, failed to couple up. The ten wagons, plus the two tankers, began to move. The pointsman controlling the crossover at the outlet from the top yard heard the guard's warning shout and managed to pin down one brake but slipped and fell as he was trying to secure another. The pointsman at the south end of Barnsley station also made an heroic attempt to stop the runaways which were by this time moving at about seven miles an hour. He took a running jump at them as they passed but was knocked off by the centre girder of an underbridge which obstructed the 6-foot way. At this point the descending gradient steepened to 1 in 72 and the wagons rapidly gathered speed. The signalmen at Pinder Oaks, Quarry and Old Oaks Colliery junctions had no facing points under their control by which they could safely deflect the runaways and looked on helplessly as they dashed past. Meanwhile a passenger train which had left Barnsley at 6.15 pm was standing in Stairfoot station one and a half miles away. The attention of those upon the platform was first drawn to the approaching runaways by the roar that they made as they crossed over an iron bridge, but by then it was far too late to do anything to avert or even to mitigate disaster. The bridge was only 200 yards away and the wagons were by this time moving at a speed of at least forty miles an hour. They struck the rear of the standing train with such violence that the driver was knocked flat on his footplate and when he got up and released his brake his engine shot forward forty yards as a result of the buffer compression. It was as though a tornado had struck the station. Debris flew everywhere. The guard of the train and the stationmaster who were standing together on the platform had miraculous escapes from death. Both were knocked senseless and must have been hurled through the air for when they recovered consciousness they found themselves lying on a line of metals at the back of the station and beyond the platform railings. In the rear coaches of the train, which were splintered to pieces, fifteen passengers died and fifty-nine were injured.

Colonel Rich's comments on the Stairfoot accident were very similar to those he had made after Abergele. The goods guard was gravely at fault for not ensuring that the standing wagons were better secured. True, the wagons were not standing upon the main line in this case, but the layout of Barnsley top yard was open to grave criticism because there were no trap points to protect the running lines in the event of a mishap of such a kind.

After 1870 the gradual introduction of the full interlocking of points and signals was accompanied by a progressive improvement in the layout and protection of sidings and marshalling yards. Yet an extraordinarily unlucky accident on the London & North Western Railway at Chelford in December, 1894, showed that circumstances might still conspire to confound the ingenuity of man. John Hyde, the Chelford station-master was superintending some shunting operations in the station yard. It was rapidly falling dark and a strong wind was blowing. A high-sided North Western wagon was fly-shunted into a siding, the goods train drew forward and then proceeded to set back once more to fly-shunt another six wagons into the adjoining road. As these wagons were running back, Hyde noticed that the high-sided wagon was moving out of its siding to meet them. It was being blown forward by the force of the wind. The wagons met in sidelong collision on the siding points at such a precise moment and angle that the runaway was derailed and deflected on to the 6-foot way where it came to rest foul of the up main line. No sooner had this happened than Hyde heard the roar of an approaching train on the up line. It was the 4.15 pm Manchester to Crewe express, a heavy train drawn by two locomotives, No 418 'Zygia' as pilot and No 520 'Express' as train engine. Hyde ran along the 6-foot towards them waving a red lamp, but the drivers thought he was signalling to the shunting goods and made no attempt to slacken speed. 'Zygia' struck the wagon, became immediately derailed, and fell over on her side while her tender dashed up the platform ramp. 'Express' was also derailed but remained upright. The third vehicle of the train, a Great Western bogie composite, struck the signal cabin. Signalman Frank Feam said afterwards that he heard a rumbling noise and the next instant the whole of the front of his box was carried away. Uninjured and undaunted by this petrifying experience, Feam stuck to his post amid the ruins of his box. He first tried to send out the 'obstruction danger' signal on the block instruments and, on finding that they were dead, managed to send out his warning on his speaking telegraph which was still working.

On this most unlucky disaster in which fourteen lives were lost the inspector, Captain Marindin, had little comment to make. But he stressed that although it had never been found necessary to do so at Chelford in the past, in future the brakes of all shunted wagons should be immediately pinned down.

So far in these pages there have been few references to Irish railways. After the rear collision at Straffan in 1853 no major disaster occurred in Ireland until June 12th, 1889, when the Armagh collision took place. This was not only Ireland's worst accident but it caused greater loss of life than any accident that had occurred on any British railway up to that time, the Tay Bridge disaster not excepted. The circumstances were somewhat similar to the Round Oak breakaway but the results were far more terrible. Once again, as at Round Oak, the train concerned was a special excursion for school children. It had been arranged by the Great Northern Railway of Ireland and was to be run over that Company's Newry & Armagh branch from Armagh to Warren Point.

The Newry & Armagh line began life as an independent concern which had only been absorbed by the Great Northern in 1879 and it possessed its own station at Armagh. From this terminus the railway climbed almost continuously on gradients of 1 in 75 and 1 in 82 for three miles to Dobbins Bridge Summit. The single line was worked by staff and ticket but not on the absolute block system, trains being dispatched at a ten minute time interval, or twenty minutes for a passenger train following a goods. Thomas McGrath, a driver with very little experience of the Newry road, was sent from Dundalk to Armagh with a four-coupled engine to work the excursion. Knowing the gradients he had to face he was somewhat disconcerted to find himself called upon to haul a train of fifteen vehicles packed with no less than 940 passengers. He sought out John Foster, the Armagh stationmaster, and said that according to his instructions, given to him at Dundalk, his maximum load would be thirteen vehicles. If he was to take more he must have pilot assistance over the bank. 'I did not write those instructions for you,' Foster replied. 'No,' said McGrath, 'Mr Cowan [the Superintendent] did.' To this Foster retorted: 'Any driver who comes here doesn't grumble about taking an excursion train with him.' 'Why didn't you send proper word to Dundalk?' the driver retorted, 'then I should have had a proper six-coupled engine with me.' With this McGrath turned on his heel and returned in high dudgeon to his footplate. A few moments later Superintendent Cowan's chief clerk, James Elliot, who was in charge of the running of the excursion and proposed to travel on the engine, joined McGrath on the footplate. He had heard about the brush between the driver and the stationmaster and suggested that, in default of a pilot, Patrick Murphy, who was in charge of the regular train which was due to follow the excursion at 10.35 am, should provide banking assistance in the rear. But McGrath was still nettled by the stationmaster's remarks. He refused the offer and a few moments later, with steam roaring from the safety valves and his reversing lever in full forward gear, he opened his regulator and put his engine at the bank.

Although the rail was dry and his engine was steaming well, McGrath gradually lost speed on the long gradient. They were within sight of the summit at Dobbins Bridge when the labouring locomotive finally stalled. It was a case of so near and yet so far, for there was 125 lb of steam on the gauge, only five pounds below the full working pressure, and McGrath knew that it was hopeless to attempt to restart. McGrath and Elliot then debated the question of what was to be done. There were two alternatives. Either they could protect the train in the rear and then wait for Murphy to arrive with the lightly-loaded regular train to push them over the summit, or they could divide the train. Although it would have been somewhat irregular practice, the first course would not only have been the simpler and safer but would also have involved less delay to both trains. Yet Elliot decided to divide and McGrath agreed. It was a fatal decision. Elliot called to a porter named William Moorhead who was acting as guard in the front van and asked him how many carriages he thought the siding at Hamilton's Bawn (the first station over the summit) would hold. Moorhead replied that it was already partly filled with wagons but that he thought it should take five. After the leading five had been shunted there the engine could return for the rest of the train. Elliot therefore instructed Moorhead to uncouple between the fifth and sixth carriages.

Now the excursion train was fitted with a vacuum brake of the old 'simple' or non-automatic type which worked in the opposite fashion to the automatic brake, the vacuum applying the brake and the admission of air to the train pipe releasing it. This meant that as soon as a flexible brake pipe was disconnected the brakes would cease to function. All the men in charge of the train knew this. Thomas Henry, the rear guard, was wedged in his brake compartment with no less than fifteen passengers when Elliot ran back down the train to tell him what they were about to do. He ordered Henry to screw his handbrake down hard and then to come down and scotch some of the wheels with stones. By giving such an order, Elliot completely disregarded the Company's rule which stated: 'With a heavy train the guard must not leave his van until perfectly satisfied that his brake will hold the train securely. . . .' But Henry did as he was bid. Meanwhile Moorhead had placed stones under the wheels of the sixth carriage and now proceeded to uncouple, undoing the screw coupling to its full extent so that he could do so without calling upon McGrath to ease back. No sooner had he lifted the link of the hook, than McGrath did ease back. It was not much, but it was enough. With a lurch and a crunch the coach wheels rode over the stones and the long, crowded train began slowly to move back down the gradient. Panic ensued. Henry leapt back into his crowded van and, urged on by Elliot who was standing on the step, attempted with the assistance of two passengers to get another turn on the handbrake. It was useless. The brake would not hold. The van wheels continued to revolve. Elliot leaped off the step crying, 'Oh, my God, we will all be killed,' and rushed forward. 'My God,' he shouted to McGrath, 'what did you come back against the carriages for?' McGrath was now setting back on Moorhead's instructions and the latter was vainly trying to re-couple the two portions of the train. Twice he managed to get the link raised ready to drop over the drawhook of the sixth coach; twice at the crucial moment he tripped and fell over some old rails which were lying by the lineside. No one thought of lifting one of these rails and thrusting it through a wheel as a sprag. Instead they stumbled along making futile efforts to stop the runaways by putting more stones from the ballast under the wheels. They slipped aside or were crushed to powder. The runaways rapidly gathered speed and soon outpaced their pursuers. 'We went so fast,' said Henry, 'that we could not see the hedges as we passed.' To prevent unauthorized entry, as the Company phrased it, all the compartment doors had been locked before the train left Armagh. Except for those in the van with Henry, not a soul could escape from the train.

While these events were taking place at the top of the bank, Patrick Murphy had left Armagh with the regular train and, with only a horse-box, two vans and three coaches on his drawbar, he was forging up the gradient at a steady thirty miles an hour. They were approaching a point one and a half miles from Dobbins Bridge when Murphy's fireman suddenly yelled, 'Hold! Hold! Hold!' Rocking down the track towards them at frightful speed came the ten carriages of the excursion. The leading van was empty. Its occupants had already jumped for their lives. As soon as his fireman shouted, Murphy shut off steam and applied the vacuum brake so that at the moment of impact his speed was reduced to five miles an hour. In the terrific collision which ensued the first three vehicles of the excursion were completely destroyed, their shattered, twisted fragments being scattered down the 40-foot embankment, while those behind them piled in crazy confusion, some on the metals and some on the steep embankment sides. The locomotive fell over on to its side but its following train broke away and began to run back towards Armagh in two portions, first the three coaches and two vans and then, some distance behind it, the horse-box and the engine tender. The guard managed to pull up the first portion on his screw brake a quarter of a mile farther down the bank and a second violent collision might then have followed but for a lucky chance. As the tender broke away from his engine, Patrick Murphy contrived to cling to the coal plate. Dazed and shocked after his terrible experience, Murphy none the less managed to scramble to his feet and screw down the tender brake. By doing so he stopped the tender and horse-box three carriage lengths short of his train. Eighty lives were lost in this appalling catastrophe, many of the casualties being young children, while the roll of those seriously injured was equally high.

Like his predecessor Captain Tyler after Round Oak, the Board of Trade inspector, Major-General Hutchinson, carried out experiments on the Armagh incline with a train of precisely similar composition and weight drawn by the same engine. He found that the engine was able to lift the train over the summit without any undue difficulty and that a van of the same type as Henry's was quite capable of holding a train of nine loaded vehicles on the gradient. He therefore found McGrath's failure to get the train over the summit and Henry's inability to stop the runaways quite inexplicable. He could only assume that in the former case the failure was due to inexperience and that, despite the evidence to the contrary, the screw brake in Henry's van was either not in proper working order or it had been tampered with by passengers. Nevertheless, in fairness to McGrath, the inspector pointed out that such a load on such a gradient was approximately equal to the maximum drawbar pull which a locomotive of this class could exert and he criticized the Company for assigning to their locomotives duties so near the limit of their capacity. General Hutchinson also criticized the shed foreman at Dundalk who had allotted such a difficult duty to a driver with so little experience of the Armagh & Newry line. But the heaviest share of responsibility, he went on, must rest with James Elliot who was in charge of the excursion train and who authorized such rash procedure in flagrant disregard for the Company's working rules.

So much for the immediate causes of the disaster. But there were other and wider considerations. The concluding paragraph of Major-General Hutchinson's report on Armagh is of historic significance. He said:

As the President of the Board of Trade has stated in Parliament his intention to introduce a Bill to make compulsory the adoption of continuous automatic brakes, should the report on this collision point out that it would have been avoided had the excursion train been fitted with them, it is unnecessary for me to say more upon the subject.

Under whatever aspect the circumstances are viewed, it seems manifest that if the block telegraph system had been in force between Armagh and Hamilton's Bawn the results of this collision would have been considerably mitigated, and it becomes consequently a grave question whether legis-

9. Harrow & Wealdstone, 8 October 1952: the scene at the station immediately after the disaster

10(a). Welwyn Garden City, 7 January 1957: the Aberdeen–King's Cross express wrecked after collision with a local train

10(b). St. John's, Lewisham, 4 December 1957: the wreckage beneath the fallen bridge

lative power should not be sought to make the block system compulsory on old lines as it has been for many years on new lines.

The public had been profoundly shocked by the Armagh disaster and the General's words took speedy effect. Before the year was out a Bill making both continuous automatic brakes and absolute block working compulsory on all British railways passed into law. It is true that very considerable progress in the installation of both these safeguards had already been made and that what the Act of 1889 did was to give the Board of Trade power to compel the defaulters to conform within a specified period of time. Nevertheless the Armagh disaster represents a most significant milestone in railway history, possibly, indeed, the most significant of all. For in those shattered coaches of the ill-fated excursion train the old happy-go-lucky days of railway working came to their ultimate end and the modern phase of railway working as we know it began.

9

SIGNALMEN'S ERRORS, 1890-1937

Norton Fitzwarren (1) – Thirsk – Hawes Junction – Quintinshill – St Bedes – Hull – Winwick Junction – Welwyn – Castlecary

A L T H O U G H   A S we have seen in previous chapters, the responsibility for railway safety is borne in some degree by all railwaymen, by far the heaviest burden rests upon the signalman and the engine driver. Electrical and mechanical safety devices may ease that burden but they can never remove it. In the last analysis the safety of the railway traveller lies in the keeping of the signalman in his lonely cabin and of the man whose hand holds the regulator. For, as this chapter and the next are designed to show, the most modern equipment and the most painstaking precautions cannot be altogether proof against their mistakes or errors of judgement.

The mistake which has probably caused more serious accidents in the last sixty years than any other is that of a signalman forgetting, especially at night, that he has a train standing near his box. It may be a train that has halted in obedience to his danger signals, or it may be one that he has 'wrong roaded', that is to say transferred to the wrong running line to wait there until a fast following train has passed. A terrible example of the consequences of the latter mistake occurred at Norton Fitzwarren on the main West of England line of the Great Western Railway on the night of November 11th, 1890.

About half an hour after midnight a down goods train of thirty-eight wagons arrived at Norton Fitzwarren and proceeded to shunt. It was a narrow gauge train but it was assisted by a broad gauge pilot engine.[1] This pilot was detached and

[1] E. T. MacDermot (*History of the Great Western Railway*) and other authorities maintain that mixed gauge working was never permitted under any circumstances. Apart from its obvious dangers,

sent up the Devon & Somerset branch to wait until the goods was ready to proceed. When the shunting operations were completed the goods was crossed to the up line to allow a fast down goods to run through, and Charles Noble, the driver of the goods, duly changed his headlight from green to red. As soon as the goods had passed, however, he assumed that George Rice, the signalman, would give him the road at once and he therefore replaced his green headlight. But the 'right away' did not come. Seven minutes later his fireman called out: 'Here's a train a-comin' on our line and he's never going to stop.'

George Rice had forgotten about the goods or, as he said afterwards, he thought it was on a siding. The fast goods had run past his box at 1.17 am. Two minutes later he gave 'Line Clear' to Victory (the next block post to the west) for a special conveying passengers from a South African Cape liner from Plymouth to Paddington. At 1.23 he received the 'Train on Line' signal for the express. The featherweight broad gauge special – it consisted of only two eight-wheeled composite coaches and a van drawn by a four-coupled saddle tank engine – came flying down Wellington Bank into the trap prepared for it at a mile a minute. Misled by the green headlight on the goods engine, her driver received no warning of disaster until the moment of impact. Once again the extraordinary stability of the broad gauge was convincingly demonstrated. Despite the extreme violence of a head-on collision at sixty miles an hour the locomotive and its train remained upright and in line, and the engine crew, though badly injured, survived. But it was too much to hope that the fifty passengers could escape the consequences. Ten were killed and nine others seriously injured.

---

misalignment of buffing and drawgear would seem to make such working impracticable. Yet the Board of Trade report on Norton Fitzwarren specifically refers to the use of the broad gauge pilot engine, while the absence of adverse comment suggests that the circumstance was not unique.

Colonel Rich, the inspector, criticized the driver of the goods for changing his headlight to green before he had received permission to proceed. It was a clear night and the sighting on the up line was good so that if the light had been red the collision might have been much less serious. He also pointed out that the guard of the goods should have gone to the signal box to remind Rice that the train was standing on the up line. But it was obvious that Rice must carry the blame for the accident and indeed the wretched man frankly admitted his responsibility. He explained that he had been knocked down by a light engine the previous January and had never felt well since. He had been 'bad in the head' the whole evening, 'worse than usual', he said

I am informed [wrote Colonel Rich in his report on Norton Fitzwarren] that many signalmen put one of their flag sticks in the spring catch of the signal levers of the line that is blocked to prevent their forgetting that a train is waiting to proceed and pulling off the signals of the line that is occupied. I would suggest that a slide-bar, a loop, a wedge or some other mechanical contrivance marked 'Train Waiting' should be fixed to the levers in the cabin to do this, and prevent these levers from being pulled by mistake.

Colonel Rich's suggestion was widely adopted and lever 'collars' or 'clips' are still used today for this purpose in situations where no more modern safeguards exist. Another vital precaution against this danger is Rule 55 which was adopted by all British railway companies. This decreed that when a train was brought to a stand at a stop signal the driver must whistle and if that signal was not lowered after three minutes in clear weather, or immediately in fog or falling snow, then he must at once dispatch his fireman, the guard or a shunter to the signal cabin to inform the signalman of the presence of the train. Having arrived at the box, this individual must sign the signalman's train register book and not leave the box until the signalman had given him the 'all clear' or until he was satisfied that all proper precautions, such as the use of lever collars, had been taken to protect the standing train. Additional safety devices which will be mentioned later have led to certain modifications and exceptions being made to this rule, but it remains one of the most important of all rules of railway working and we shall see in the following pages the dire consequences which could follow failure to carry it out.

It is obviously of the utmost importance that a man in so responsible a post as a signalman should be alert and in good health, so that the condition of the unfortunate George Rice at Norton Fitzwarren caused some public concern. But this was nothing to the outcry which followed the collision at Thirsk in 1892 when the tragic figure of James Holmes the signalman responsible, was finely calculated to rouse popular sympathy.

James Holmes was signalman at Manor House cabin on the North Eastern main line between Northallerton and Thirsk. The two block posts immediately north and south of Manor House were Otterington and Avenue Junction. The night before the accident, Holmes's child had been taken seriously ill and he had had no sleep. Next morning he tramped the countryside trying to find the local doctor who had gone out on his rounds. He returned to find the child dead and his wife so distressed that he did not like to leave her alone. He had a telegraph message sent to York to ask his mother to come down by train to join her. Holmes then went to Thomas Kirby, the stationmaster at Otterington, told him what had happened and said that he felt quite unfit to go on duty at Manor House that night. Kirby then sent the following telegraph message to Signals Inspector Pick: 'Can you send relief to Manor House tonight? Holmes child dead.' The reply came back that a relief could not be found. Holmes later spoke to the Otterington signalman and asked him to let him know by telegraph if his mother arrived on the York train. 'Harry,' he added, 'I am just about done to start duty. I haven't been off my legs since 12 o'clock.' Holmes then set off to walk to Manor House.

The first part of the up night Scotch express left Edinburgh at 10.30 pm that evening but the second part was delayed by the late arrival of connections from the north and did not leave until 11.2. After the first part had passed Northallerton North Junction at 3.33 am and cleared the block, the signalman there let an up goods from Middlesbrough to Starbeck out on to the main line. His action was subsequently criticized in the Press but, as the accident inspector, Major Marindin, pointed out, he was perfectly justified in so doing. The line was worked on the absolute block system, there was an ample margin of time between the two portions of the express, and the goods had only to run six miles on the main line to Avenue Junction where it would pass on to a running goods line.

James Holmes passed the first part of the express through normally. He then accepted the following goods train. When he received the 'Train on Line' signal for the goods from Otterington he acknowledged it but did not send the 'Be Ready' signal for it forward to Avenue Junction. For at this juncture he was overcome by sleep and, as he had not cleared his signals, the goods train came to a standstill only a few yards from his box. When he awoke thirteen minutes later his mind was confused and he had forgotten about the goods train. So, when Signalman Eden at Otterington gave him the 'Be Ready' signal for the second part of the express and he saw that his instrument still showed 'Train on Line', he concluded that he had never cleared after the first part of the express had run through. He therefore unpegged his block instrument giving 'Line Clear' to Otterington, accepted the train and offered it forward to Avenue Junction. But having done so, Holmes had a sudden misgiving. He called Eden on the speaking telegraph and asked: 'Is this the EP (Express Passenger)?' So soon as Eden received this message he realized too late that something must be wrong at Manor House. The express roared past his box at that moment, into a section only a mile and a half long and in a matter of seconds he heard the distant thunder of a collision.

Driver Roland Ewart of the Scotch express had no chance. He was running at a mile a minute, the night was slightly foggy, and he only sighted the red tail lights of the goods at a distance of 40 yards. The engine and tender fell on their sides across a siding on the up side with their wheels together. The first three vehicles of the train were a brake van, an East Coast Joint Stock third-class carriage, and the Pullman Sleeping car 'India'. The body of the Pullman came off its bogies and demolished the third-class coach, killing eight passengers and injuring thirty-nine. But it was a tribute to the strength of Pullman construction that no passenger in the sleeping car was even slightly injured.

Forty minutes after the collision, a fire, started by live coals from the firebox, spread rapidly through the wreckage. Roland Ewart, who had been thrown clear on to the lineside, watched the blaze start from a flicker no larger than a candle flame but was too badly injured to prevent it spreading. His fireman had wandered off down the line towards Otterington. He, too, was injured and suffering from shock but his one idea was to protect the up line. He eventually made his way to a neighbouring farmhouse from which he was taken to hospital.

The unhappy James Holmes was subsequently charged with the manslaughter of George Petch, the guard of the goods train, and committed for trial at York Assizes before Mr Justice Charles. Holmes, weeping bitterly, was found guilty, but the Judge ruled that he be discharged and it is a measure of the popular feeling which the case had aroused that this decision was greeted with prolonged cheering from the body of the court. Reinforced by the recommendations made in the inspecting officer's report on Thirsk, the case of James Holmes led to a reduction in the working hours of signalmen and to a better system of relief. In this connection Major Marindin criticized Stationmaster Kirby for the wording he used in his telegraphic request for relief. He should have stated positively that Holmes had declared himself unfit for duty.

Major Marindin also pointed out that responsibility did not

rest wholly with Holmes. There was contributory negligence. Joseph Baines, the driver of the goods train, stood for seven minutes at the Manor House signals without sounding his whistle or making any attempt to inform Holmes of his presence there. Moreover, after the collision occurred his engine was quite undamaged so that there was nothing to prevent him going forward to Thirsk to summon assistance in which event the fire might have been prevented. He had not done so. Henry Eden, the Otterington signalman, had said that he took Holmes's fatal 'Line Clear' signal as referring to the goods train, yet he ought surely to have wondered why, over so short a section, thirteen minutes had elapsed before he received it. That he had accepted the express and given Holmes the 'Be Ready' before he had received the latter's 'Line Clear' was quite in accordance with the Company's rules, but the inspector considered that this was wrong. He thought that a train should not be accepted into a block section until 'Line Clear' had been received from the block post in advance.

To reach the scene of the next drama in this series involves no long journey from Thirsk yet it is one which takes us into a country very different from the levels of the North Riding. A branch line from Northallerton leads directly to that storm-swept junction on the high Pennines with which we are already familiar. Yes, it is Hawes Junction near the summit of the Settle & Carlisle line with its unique stockaded turntable. Like that desert heath near Forres there could be no more appropriate setting for scenes of terror and tragedy than these wild and desolate moorlands. And strangely enough the Settle & Carlisle has had more than its fair share of disasters. We have visited the line before and we shall visit it yet again. It is as though the solitude resented the steel rail's arrogant invasion.

It was Christmas Eve, 1910, and Signalman Sutton was having a busy night in Hawes Junction box. Through traffic was heavy, while he had no less than five light engines on his hands, two waiting to return north to Carlisle and three south to Leeds. This was nothing unusual. Owing to the small engine policy of the Midland Company the majority of the trains had to have pilot assistance up either side of the 'big hump'. It was a wild night and pitch dark. A strong wind, sweeping down from the fells, beat the rain against Sutton's cabin windows like grape-shot. There was nothing unusual about this either – not at Hawes Junction.

Driver George Tempest was standing on his footplate in the station yard waiting his turn to move on to the turntable. The two four-coupled bogie tender engines from Carlisle had already been turned and were standing coupled together in the back platform road waiting to leave. A down special express swept past in a momentary blur of lights which was rapidly lost in the curtains of rain to the north. The other two Leeds engines ran back from the turntable and Driver Tempest moved up. As he did so he saw the Carlisle engines swing out over the crossovers on to the down main line and halt at the advanced starting signal.

Tempest was ten minutes or more turning his engine and by the time he returned the Leeds engines had gone but the two Carlisle engines were still standing on the down main line where he had last seen them. Two 'Class A' fast goods trains now ran through in quick succession on the up line and hardly had the sound of the second died away towards Dent than Tempest saw all the down main line signals come off. As soon as the advanced starting signal dropped the drivers of the light engines sounded their whistles and moved away in the direction of Ais Gill. The time was 5.44 am. To Tempest's surprise the signals did not return to danger and he heard above the wind the sound of a train approaching at speed from the south. A moment later the midnight sleeping car express, St Pancras to Glasgow, thundered through the station. She was running late but making time, the two engines working hard and fast, taking advantage of the short favouring grade before tackling the final ascent to Ais Gill summit. Tempest turned to his mate. 'How far do you think them engines have got?' he asked. 'I reckon it would take them all their time to clear Moorcock

Tunnel,' his fireman answered. The words were scarcely out of his mouth before they both heard, borne down the wind from the north, the long piercing scream of an engine whistle. Then there was silence except for the buffeting of the gale in the rainswept yard. 'He's catched 'em,' said Tempest. He moved his engine down to the signal box as the ground signal came off, jumped from the footplate and ran up the steps into the cabin. 'Hello,' said Sutton, 'I'd intended coupling you on to those two engines going south, but you've been longer on the table than I reckoned for and I've let them go.' Tempest ignored this remark. 'What have you done with those two engines for Carlisle?' he asked. 'They've gone to Carlisle,' Sutton replied. 'They've not,' Tempest retorted. 'When you pulled off for the down express them two engines was standing on the down road behind the advanced starter waiting for it to come off, and when it came off they went.' The signalman laughed incredulously. He crossed to his desk and consulted his train register book; then he looked at his instruments for a moment before taking a second glance at his book. He next picked up the Ais Gill telephone and asked: 'Where's them two light engines I sent on, Ben?' Came the reply: 'You haven't given me any; they haven't come.' 'Has the down express arrived yet?' 'There's been nothing passed.' Sutton hung up the receiver and turned to Tempest. 'I've done it,' he said simply. He walked to the north window of his box and looked out. An angry glare of light was staining the sky crimson over Ais Gill. Signalman Simpson, who was due to relieve Sutton at 6 am, had just come up into the box. Sutton turned to him. 'Go to Bence' (the stationmaster), he ordered, 'and tell him I am afraid I have wrecked the Scotch Express.'

Drivers Scott and Bath on the two light engines ran at an easy twenty-five miles an hour after they left the junction. They had passed through Moorcock Tunnel and were crossing the Lunds viaduct when Bath, who was on the second engine, happened to look back and saw in the dark of the tunnel the two yellow eyes of express headlights. For a moment, but only for a moment, he could not believe what he saw. Then the locomotives of the Scotch Express burst out of the northern portal of Moorcock at sixty-five miles an hour and the sparks that shot skywards from the two funnels left Driver Bath in no doubt as to what was behind him. He at once opened his regulator and his whistle, while on hearing his signal Driver Scott in front did likewise. But by this time the express was close upon them and there was no escape. Near Grisedale Crossing between Lunds viaduct and Shotlock Hill tunnel the pilot engine of the express, 2–4–0 No 48, crashed into the tender of Bath's engine. The two light engines were carried forward for a considerable distance and finished up nearly 200 yards ahead of the express. Scott's engine held the rails and only its tender was derailed, but Bath's ploughed up the down line for over 350 yards before it finally came to rest minus its front bogie. The leading engine of the express, though derailed, stayed upright, but the train engine fell over on its side against the slope of the cutting and the coaches piled themselves against it. The two twelve-wheeled sleeping cars were electrically lit, but the rest of the train was fitted with Pintsch oil gas-lighting, the gas being stored in cylinders between the sole-bars at a pressure of 85 lb per square inch. The high pressure main gas pipe on the cylinder of the leading coach was broken off and this allowed the entire contents of the cylinder to escape in two minutes. From his cottage at Quarry Lunds a shepherd saw it ignite instantaneously in a single brilliant flash of flame and in a matter of minutes the whole wreck was ablaze.

Although he was badly injured in the leg, Driver Bath managed to struggle for one and a half miles down the line to Ais Gill to give warning and to summon assistance. Benjamin Bellas in Ais Gill box heard him shouting 'Signalman! Signalman!' as he approached and he immediately ordered Driver Judd on a light engine to take Bath with him and go forward on the up line. Judd drew up as near as he could to the blazing train where he made heroic efforts to free the trapped passengers and to extinguish the flames by bucketing water from his tender tank. Meanwhile another light engine had come from Hawes Junction on the down line and her crew were struggling to draw back the rear coaches of the express before the flames reached them. They managed to move the brake van, which was still on the rails, out of danger, but the rest of the train was immovable and was completely gutted. Nine passengers perished.

As Colonel Pringle stated in his report, the man chiefly responsible for this disaster was the signalman at Hawes Junction. Sutton frankly admitted that while he was preoccupied in passing the two fast goods trains on the up line he had forgotten that he had left the light engines standing on the down. But the Colonel pointed out that Drivers Scott and Bath were also gravely at fault. Their engines had remained stationary on the down line for at least thirteen minutes, yet in all that time they had made no attempt to carry out Rule 55 or to remind the signalman of their presence there in any way. The Midland Railway Company had stated that they did not hold with the use of lever collars, but had Sutton been provided with these reminders and placed them on his down signal levers as soon as he let the engines out on the main line, the accident would have been avoided.

The Hawes Junction accident was the first to reveal unmistakably that along with the new safeguards had come also a new and terrible menace – the danger of fire from gas-lit coaching stock. 'This is actually the first occasion when it can be proved beyond question of doubt that fire was occasioned by burning gas,' wrote Colonel Pringle. He went on to advocate stronger gas cylinders and automatic cut-off valves which would act in the event of the main pipe breaking. 'But,' he concluded, 'I still hold that electricity is the more desirable and should be adopted wherever possible.' In the next few years this recommendation would be repeated many times.

The widespread introduction of electricity which distinguished the first quarter of the twentieth century not only reduced the danger of fire in passenger trains; it also started a revolution in railway signalling and safety measures. Thus we find Colonel Pringle advocating in his report the installation at Hawes Junction of a device which has not so far been mentioned in these pages – the track circuit. This was the invention of an American, William Robinson, who patented it in 1872. During the last two decades of the nineteenth century it was introduced widely on American railways, but in this country, apart from a few isolated installations such as at St Paul's and King's Cross stations, track circuiting made little progress until 1901. The principle of the track circuit is simple. A section of track is insulated at the rail joints from adjoining sections. An electrically operated switch or relay is maintained in the closed position by a low voltage current which is passed continually through the rails. The effect of the entry of a train on to the insulated section is to short circuit this current through its wheels and axles with the result that the electric switch opens. It will be appreciated from this that should the current fail or should an accidental short circuit take place the device will behave as if a train was on the section. The track circuit thus gives the equivalent of a danger signal in the event of failure, an essential feature of every railway safety device. If a line of railway is divided into a number of these track circuited sections it will be realized that this simple principle can be applied in a number of ways. In its simplest application it can merely work an indicator in the signal cabin which will reveal the progress of a train or show whether or not a certain line, or section of line, is occupied. In its most complex form – continuous track circuiting – the trains can be made to operate their own signals as they do on London's underground system. Such a combination of continuous track circuiting and multi-aspect light signals can make the signalman obsolete but, as was shown by the serious accident on the District Line at Charing Cross in 1938 due to a circuit breaker being wrongly wired, his responsibilities do not dissolve, they pass to the linesman and electrician. Electrified lines are outside the terms of reference of this book. Moreover, what is quite practicable on London's underground is not either financially or practically feasible to install over all the thousands of miles of our main railway system. It is therefore unlikely that the track circuit will ever put the British railway signalman out of a job, but its more limited application helps him very considerably. Had track circuits been installed at Hawes junction as recommended by Colonel Pringle, the presence of the light engines on the down line would have been revealed by the indicator in Sutton's box. In that case a lozenge-shaped indicator on the post of the advanced starting signal would have told Drivers Scott and Bath that their engines were standing on a track circuit which exempted them from carrying out Rule 55 by going to the box. But the track circuit can, as we shall see, do more than this. It can be interconnected with the electrical locking gear in the signal box in such a way that, when a train is standing on a track circuit, conflicting movements cannot be made or the block instrument cannot be cleared.

In the early years of the twentieth century electricity was already making a great contribution to safety on some of the more congested main lines in other directions besides the track circuit. It made possible electrical interlocking between the block instruments and the lever frame with the effect that it became impossible for a signalman to lower his signals for the passage of a train unless that train had been duly accepted by the box in advance. Thus the starting signal would remain locked electrically until it was released, for one pull only, by the 'Line Clear' indication from the signal box in advance. Again, what was called 'Rotation Locking' was introduced between successive signals in one box whereby once a signal had been lowered and replaced it could not be lowered again until the signal next following had been similarly lowered and raised again after the passage of a train.

The block instruments themselves also underwent a change. Many old instruments, whether of needle or disc type, had only two positions: 'Line Clear' and 'Train on Line', the former being the normal indication. All the new instruments had three positions: 'Line Blocked', 'Line Clear', 'Train on Line'. 'Line Blocked' was their normal indication so that they were only pegged to the 'Line Clear' position for the actual acceptance of a train, a virtue which needs no explanation. It was a change similar to that which had taken place after the Abbots Ripton disaster when 'danger' or 'caution' instead of 'all clear' became the normal indication of railway signals.

All these developments and new devices increased the complexity of railway signalling systems, but they spelt greater simplicity and safety in operation. They were elaborations of those two cardinal principles of safe railway working – the interlocking of points and signals and the absolute block system, and like them they could not be installed overnight. Apart from the immense cost and labour involved, the years of the first world war seriously retarded progress. It was natural that in the installation of these new safety devices congested lines and important junctions should receive priority so that the Caledonian Railway Company could scarcely be blamed for the fact that Quintinshill, the scene of the worst disaster in British railway history, was not so equipped. For it was an unimportant country block post near Gretna Junction, just over the Scottish border, ten miles north of Carlisle.

On the morning of May 22nd, 1915, the two Scotch expresses which had left Euston at 11.45 pm and midnight were approaching Carlisle half an hour late. Because they were behind time, a northbound local train which normally followed them was dispatched from Carlisle before they arrived. This was the usual practice when the trains from the south were running late because the local had to provide a connection for Edinburgh and Glasgow at Beattock for passengers from Moffat. On this occasion it was decided to send the local forward as far as Quintinshill and to shunt it there to allow the expresses to pass. Quintinshill was a block post provided with 'lay by' loops on the up and down sides. Signalman Meakin

had been taking the night turn there and although he was due
to book off at 6 am he was still on duty when the local train
arrived at 6.30. This was a result of a private arrangement
made between Meakin and James Tinsley who was working
the day turn and who lived at Gretna Junction. Whenever the
local was going to stop at Quintinshill, as on this occasion, the
Gretna signalman gave Tinsley the tip and he then travelled
down on it. Meanwhile Meakin would write down all the train
movements occurring after 6 am on a piece of paper so that
Tinsley could afterwards copy them into the Train Register,
thus making it appear that he had come on duty at the proper
time.

The down loop at Quintinshill was already occupied by the
4.50 am goods train from Carlisle which Meakin had received
at 6.14. He therefore switched the local across on to the up
main line where it came to a stand in broad daylight only 65
yards from his box. Meakin was provided with lever collars for
use on such occasions but he failed to place them on his up
signal levers. Kirkpatrick, the next block post to the north, had
previously offered him an empty coal train on the up line. On
offering it forward to Gretna he was told that Carlisle Kings-
moor could not take it so Meakin decided to turn it into his
up loop. The empty wagon train arrived and ran into the loop
at 6.34, just as his mate, Tinsley, came up into the box. There
were thus three trains standing at Quintinshill, a goods on each
loop and the local on the up main. Just prior to this, Meakin
had accepted the first part of the Scotch express from Gretna
Junction. It was the last signal he made before handing over
the box to Tinsley. The two men talked for a few moments
and while they were doing so a message came through from the
north to the effect that a special troop train conveying a regi-
ment of the 7th Royal Scots from Larbert to Liverpool had
passed through Lockerbie at 6.32. Meakin then settled down
in a chair at the back of the box to read the morning paper
which Tinsley had brought with him and to chat to the brakesmen of the two goods trains who had come up into the cabin.

11(a). After the Shipton disaster, GWR, 24 December 1874

11(b). Charfield, 13 October 1928: the frames of the burned-out coaches piled against the bridge

12. Sutton Coldfield, 23 January 1955: the wreckage of the York–Bristol express

Meanwhile Tinsley busied himself at the desk copying Meakin's entries into the Train Register. Presently, Hutchinson, the fireman of the local train, joined them for the purpose of carrying out Rule 55. Without diverting his attention from what he was doing, Tinsley handed him a pen over his shoulder so that he could sign the book. Hutchinson then left the box and went back to his engine without satisfying himself that the collars were on the up signal levers.

Now although both men denied having done so, it is clear from subsequent events and from the evidence of the signalman there, that after the empty coal train had run into the up loop either Meakin or Tinsley sent the 'Train out of Section' signal to Kirkpatrick and cleared the Kirkpatrick–Quintinshill block section indicator. They certainly did not, as they should have done, send any 'Blocking Back' signal to Kirkpatrick showing that the local train was occupying the up line.

Tinsley now began methodically to set the stage for this most shocking catastrophe. At 6.38 he pulled off his down signals for the Scotch express and gave 'Train entering Section' to Kirkpatrick. At 6.42 he accepted the up troop train. At 6.46 he acknowledged Kirkpatrick's 'Train entering Section' signal for the troop train and offered it forward to Gretna Junction where it was accepted at once. He then pulled off all his up main line signals. Two minutes later the troop train, drawn by a four-coupled bogie express engine No 121, came into sight travelling very fast on the falling gradient of 1 in 200. The engine of the standing local was No 907, a heavy 4–6–0, and a head-on collision of great violence took place. The tender coupling on the local train broke and the coaches ran back for 136 yards. The engine itself was driven back 40 yards and came to rest lying in the '6-foot' with its tender across the down line. The engine of the troop train finished up lying on its right side across both running lines, its tender on the down line and its smokebox against the empty wagons on the up loop. The troop train consisted of fifteen old Great Central coaches with wooden under frames, eleven of them six-wheeled. They were smashed to pieces, the foremost shooting clean over the top of their engine and landing some distance in front of it. That a crowded train of fifteen coaches of a combined length of 213 yards was reduced in an instant to a length of only 67 yards will convey some conception of the force of the collision and its terrible results. But worse was to follow.

When Meakin, still sitting at the back of the box reading the paper, heard the thunder of the collision he cried out, 'Whatever have you done, Jimmy?' 'Good heavens!' Tinsley exclaimed, 'whatever can be wrong? The frame's all right and the signals are all right.' 'You've got the Parly[1] standing there,' said Meakin, and as he spoke a sudden fearful thought struck him. 'Where's the 6.5?' he shouted and rushed to the down signal levers. But he was too late. The same thought had already occurred to the engine crew of the empty coal train and to Guard Graham of the local. They all started to run up the down line, Graham in the lead, but they were also too late.

The Scotch express consisted of thirteen bogie vehicles, some L & NW and some, including three twelve-wheeled sleeping cars, West Coast Joint Stock. It was drawn by two four-coupled bogie express engines. Altogether the train weighed over 600 tons and it was travelling at high speed under clear signals. As soon as the driver on the leading engine saw Guard Graham's frantic waving he shut off steam and made a full emergency application of the automatic vacuum brake. But no brake on earth could stop a train of that weight from full speed in the 270 yards which was all the distance that Graham had managed to cover. The two engines ploughed into the wreckage running down many of the survivors of the first collision who were trying to rescue their injured comrades. Then the leading locomotive came into violent collision with the prostrate tender of the troop train engine and drove it for 30 yards clean through the wagons of the goods

[1] I.e., the 'Parliamentary' – see Chapter 1.

train on the down loop. Its own tender mounted the framing of the train engine behind it which was also derailed, while the three following coaches of the express telescoped into one another. This second collision occurred one minute after the first. There were now five trains at Quintinshill, all of them damaged, and around and on top of the engine of the local, the troop train engine and the pilot of the express there was piled a mountain of wreckage. The troop train had suffered the worst; indeed, as a train it had ceased to exist at all except, by the irony of fate, for the Caledonian baggage and equipment wagons which had been attached at the rear. The recoil of the first collision had caused them to break away and to run, in spite of the adverse gradient, for some distance down the up line where the brakesman of the empty coal train had the presence of mind to bring them to a stand and prevent them from running forward again.

All the Great Central stock of the troop train was gas lit and just before leaving Larbert the gas cylinders had been fully charged to a pressure of from five to six atmospheres. Coals from the overturned engine of the troop train immediately ignited this gas as it escaped at high pressure and the flames spread with fearful speed. Extinguishers were brought into play. Water was taken from the tanks of the two goods engines. A pump and hose was connected to a stream at a neighbouring farm. The Carlisle fire brigade arrived at 10 am. But all these efforts were of no avail. All that day and throughout the following night the fierce holocaust of Quintinshill blazed on. When the Carlisle brigade left the still smouldering remains at 9 am the next morning after twenty-three hours continuous duty the fifteen coaches of the troop train, four coaches of the express, five goods wagons and all the coal in the engine tenders had been completely consumed.

In the express eight lives were lost and fifty-four were injured. In the local train two passengers were killed, the driver and fireman having jumped from the footplate and taken refuge under a wagon when they saw the troop train bearing down upon them. The precise number of men who lost their lives in the troop train was never established, for the roll of the Royal Scots was lost in the accident. But it was estimated that 215 officers and men were killed in addition to two railway servants while 191 men were seriously injured. Because the Quintinshill disaster involved a troop train in wartime it did not receive the publicity which has attended many lesser accidents. Consequently, although it was by far the worst catastrophe ever to occur on a British railway, the recent disaster at Harrow and Wealdstone not excepted, Quintinshill has not left so deep an impression on public memory as the fall of the Tay Bridge or the Armagh collision.

As the accident inspector, Colonel Druitt, pointed out, the calamity was caused entirely by the inexcusable carelessness and inattention to duty of Signalmen Meakin and Tinsley. That they had overlooked the presence of a train standing within a few yards of the box in broad daylight could only be explained by the fact that they had been preoccupied in discussing the news of the day with the two brakesmen who should never have been permitted to remain in the box and, where Tinsley was concerned, in copying out the false train entries from Meakin's paper. The only other railwayman in any way culpable was Fireman Hutchinson who, had he carried out Rule 55 correctly, should not have left the box until he was satisfied that the proper precautions had been taken to protect his train. It had been said, the inspector went on, that if the Caledonian Railway Company had track circuited Quintinshill the accident would not have occurred. This might be true, but he considered it unreasonable to expect the Company to install such apparatus in such a situation where the layout was extremely simple and where the view of both running lines from the signal box was quite clear and unobstructed. Once again the terrible danger of fire caused by escaping gas had been demonstrated and Colonel Druitt strongly urged the abolition of gas lighting. He also recommended the introduction of all steel rolling stock and the pro-

vision of more wrecking tools and fire extinguishers on all passenger trains.

Imagination can scarcely conceive what the feelings of those
two unhappy men Meakin and Tinsley must have been when
they watched, as from some grand stand, the frightful consequences of their carelessness taking place below. No punish-
ment that any law could inflict could be more terrible, for the
memory of the scene must have haunted them for the rest of
their lives. Surely they are to be pitied rather than blamed, for
have we not all been equally careless and forgetful on occasion
but with no such fearful result? Unfortunately, however, the
delicate mechanism of railway operation, though designed to
eliminate human errors, does not lightly tolerate them when
they occur.

Seven months after Quintinshill another disastrous triple
collision occurred at St Bedes Junction near Jarrow on the
North Eastern Railway. St Bedes is situated on the line between Newcastle and South Shields, and from it a mineral line
descends on a gradient of 1 in 100 to Tyne Dock Bottom.
Early one dark December morning a goods train came up this
mineral line and ran out on to the main line past St Bedes
signal box. It had been banked in the rear up the incline by a
six-coupled tank engine which, as was usual on this line,
carried red headlights and a green light at the rear to avoid
changing the lamps round at St Bedes. As the train ran past
his box Hodgson, the St Bedes signalman, failed to see the
banking engine. He said afterwards that he thought the red
lights were on the brake van and that he must have missed the
green tail light. After passing his box, the banker, which was
not coupled, dropped away from the train and came to a stand
on the up main line just south of a trailing crossover which
would enable it to return to Tyne Dock on the down line. A
few minutes later Hodgson accepted the 7.5 am passenger
train from South Shields to Newcastle on the up line and the
6.58 empty stock train from Hebburn to South Shields in the
opposite direction with fearful results. The 7.5 train which

consisted of seven eight-wheelers drawn by an 0–4–4 tank engine ran into the rear of the stationary banking engine at thirty miles an hour. Both engines toppled down an embankment and the two leading coaches were telescoped. Almost immediately the down stock train collided with the wreckage and this engine also plunged down the embankment, killing the fireman and seriously injuring the driver. The passenger train was gas lit and there was the all too familiar and terrible sequel. Fire instantly broke out in the two telescoped coaches. The coaches behind them had fortunately escaped derailment so it was possible to uncouple them and pull them out of reach of the flames. But the two leading coaches together with the bodies of eighteen passengers were totally consumed. In addition eighty-one passengers were injured.

The accident was primarily due to the failure of Signalman Hodgson to observe that the goods train was banked. The weather was clear and there was no excuse for his failure to see the green light. But Driver Hunter on the banking engine was also greatly to blame, for he stood for thirteen minutes before obeying Rule 55 by sending his fireman back to the box. As soon as the latter entered the box, Hodgson had thrown his signals to danger but by then it was too late. Because the branch from Tyne Dock was used by mineral traffic only, the special bell code signal 'Banking engine in rear' had never been used, but the inspector, Colonel Von Donop, urged that the Company should alter their rules in this respect. He also strongly recommended the installation of track circuiting at St Bedes. There was absolutely no doubt that the resulting fire was caused by escaping gas, and the sequence of disastrous train fires had by now so alarmed the inspecting officers that a circular was sent to every railway company impressing upon them the vital importance of substituting electric for gas lighting as quickly as possible. Unfortunately war conditions inevitably delayed both the building of new steel coaching stock and the conversion of existing stock to electric light.

How error and unlucky chance can conspire to seek out the

smallest chink in the armour of the most elaborate and carefully planned assembly of safety devices was never better
illustrated than by the circumstances which caused two passenger trains to meet in head-on collision on the approaches to
Hull, Paragon station, on February 14th, 1927. Scarcely any
safety device existing at that time was lacking on the network
of lines outside Paragon station and all movement over them
was controlled and protected by an electro-pneumatic signalling system.

Driver Robert Dixon was running into Hull behind time
with the morning train from Withernsea. As he passed under
the Argyle Street bridge he was looking for the West Park
starting signals and as soon as he dropped his eyes from them
he saw to his horror that a train was rapidly approaching him
on his own line and was already close upon him. This was a
train from Hull to Scarborough with Driver Sam Atkinson in
charge. He had pulled out of Paragon station as usual under
clear signals and it was not until he ran under a signal gantry
at Park Street that he thought his train appeared to be out of
position. Such a thing seemed to him to be so incredible that
he crossed from one side of his footplate to the other and back
again to make sure. As soon as he realized that he was undoubtedly running on the wrong road he made a full application of the vacuum brake. He had not then sighted the other
train. The next thing he knew was that there was a violent
collision and he found himself half buried in coals from his
tender. Although, with the exception of three coaches, both
trains were equipped with gas lighting, there was happily no
fire on this occasion. But there was serious telescoping as a
result of which twelve passengers lost their lives and twice that
number were seriously injured.

Driver Atkinson extricated himself from the coal, climbed
down from his engine and sat on the ballast for a few moments
to recover himself. He then walked across the tracks to Park
Street signal box. This large and busy box was staffed by three
signalmen, Alfred Campling, the chargeman, Edwin Gibson

and John Clark. Atkinson clambered into the cabin and said to Campling: 'What are you playing at this morning?' For answer, Campling turned to Clark and asked, 'Did you put that lever over?' Clark did not reply.

Because the Withernsea train was running late, the three signalmen had been anxious that she should not be checked by the outgoing Scarborough train. Campling had called to his two assistants, 'Right away Scarborough,' and 'B to D for the Withernsea as soon as the Scarborough is out.' Signalman Gibson returned the signals behind the approaching Scarborough train while Clark set the road for the Withernsea to run in. They heard a curious clicking noise in the lever frame and then, as the Scarborough train was running out of sight Gibson said, 'Where has that chap gone?' 'What chap?' asked Clark, to which Gibson replied: 'Well, I thought the Scarborough looked a bit too far over.'

'I can recollect no case of an accident having occurred in similar circumstances,' said the inspector, Colonel Pringle, and he set out to discover how, despite all the elaborate safety equipment, a train could have been switched to the wrong running line. By careful investigation, experiment and timing Colonel Pringle found the following answer. It is inevitably a little technical but it is of much interest. The numbers mentioned are those of the relevant levers in the Park Street signal box which were arranged in numerical order and they are of great importance. The vital lever was No 95. This operated a pair of facing slip points by means of which, without a doubt, the Scarborough train had passed from its proper line, via the trailing points No 83, to the line on which the Withernsea train was travelling. This crucial set of slip points was protected in two ways. They were locked by bolts in such a way that the locking lever controlling the bolts was not freed unless No 171 signal controlling movement over the points was cleared. There were also facing point locking bars between the rails at the approach to the points. The action of the locking lever moving to the 'locks on' position was to raise these bars

with the effect that the presence of wheel flanges on the locking bars made it impossible to withdraw the point locking
bolts. This made it impossible for the points to be moved
under a train. Signal No 171 had to be cleared to permit the
Scarborough train to approach the points and so long as it was
cleared the points would remain locked, yet somehow or other
these points had been reversed in front of the oncoming train.
How was it done?

It will be remembered that Signalman Gibson was returning
the signals to danger behind the Scarborough train at the same
time that Clark was setting the road for the Withernsea train.
Gibson admitted at the inquiry that he returned No 171 signal
to danger as soon as the engine and the first three coaches of
the Scarborough train had run past it. Colonel Pringle calculated that at this moment the leading wheels of the locomotive
would be 37 feet $9\frac{3}{4}$ inches away from the slip point locking
bars. This meant that for the fleeting instant which it would
take the locomotive to cover this distance No 95 point lever
was free. Now in order to set the road for the Withernsea
train, Signalman Clark had to pull levers 96 and 97 and the
only possible explanation of the accident was that he had mistakenly pulled 95 instead of 96 in that second when it was
freed by Gibson's premature return of lever 171, and before it
became automatically locked again by the train itself. The
clicking noise which the men heard in the frame was simply
explained. It was made by lever 83 and its connections as the
Scarborough train ran through the trailing points which it controlled.

Both Clark and Gibson were to blame for the disaster, Clark
for mistakenly pulling the wrong lever as he must surely have
done, and Gibson for returning No 171 signal prematurely to
danger. By doing so the latter had acted contrary to the Company's Rule 61 which stated:

When a signal other than a distant signal has been lowered for the passage of a train, it must not (except in the case

of accident or obstruction) be again placed at danger until the last vehicle of the train has passed it, or the train has been brought to a stand. . . .

Had Gibson obeyed this rule the engine would have reached the locking bars before the signal was returned and no accident could have occurred. Colonel Pringle recommended that a track circuit be installed between No 171 signal and No 95 points to hold the latter automatically for any train approaching them.

> The root cause of this accident [the Colonel concluded] is psychological. Gibson and Clark acted more rapidly than they should have done so as to avoid recording a stoppage of the Withernsea train which was already running late. Clark should not have commenced setting the road for the Withernsea train until the Scarborough train was clear.

Thus in a split second and by the most extraordinary ill chance was a major disaster brought about.

It is noteworthy that the recommendations of successive generations of accident inspectors down the years at once foreshadow and reflect the changes whch have taken place on our railways. Thus the nineteenth-century inspectors were almost wholly concerned to eliminate the *causes* of accidents by urging the installation of improved protection devices, notably interlocking and absolute block working. As a result, in the twentieth century every improvement which they had so tirelessly advocated, often against considerable opposition and inertia, had become accepted practice. The result was a great improvement in the safety record of British railways. Yet the twentieth century brought new dangers as locomotives and trains became progressively heavier and scheduled speeds higher. Consequently we find the inspecting officers' recommendations becoming more and more concerned to mitigate the *effects* of accidents. For every increase in the speed and weight of a train makes a disaster the more destructive. Hence although prevention was naturally as important as ever, the emphasis shifted and the twentieth-century campaign was chiefly concerned to make the express train safer in the event of accident by combating the two greatest consequential dangers: fire and the telescoping of rolling stock. The answer to the first was the elimination of gas lighting. The answer to the second was stronger rolling stock, steel framed and steel bodied, and also two other things: shock absorbing buffers and buck-eye in place of screw couplings to prevent overriding and to hold coaches upright and in line in the event of derailment. In the 1930s these recommendations took effect on an increasingly wide scale on main line passenger trains. The fact that disasters involving heavy loss of life have occurred to trains of modern rolling stock does not mean that these improvements were made in vain. The true answer is that casualties would have been very much higher than in similar accidents in the past had these recommendations not been acted upon. For example, the collision on the LMS at Winwick Junction in 1934 cost twelve lives, but it might have been a second Quintinshill had not the express involved consisted of all steel rolling stock fitted with shock-absorbing buffers and electric light.

The disaster at Winwick Junction, near Warrington, was another sorry case of a signalman forgetting a local passenger train which was standing at his signals. The junction box was a busy one and the signalman there had a booking lad to keep his Train Register for him. The local train was being closely followed by the 5.20 pm express from Euston to Blackpool, but the former was due to be turned off on to a branch line at Winwick. After accepting the local from Winwick Quay, the signalman intended to offer it forward immediately to Vulcan Bank, the first block post along the branch. But he then became preoccupied in dealing with traffic on the up side and forgot that the local was standing at his signals. Signalman Wheeler at Winwick Quay then rang 'Call attention' for the express and, seeing that his block instrument still showed 'Train on

Line', he intended to follow this with the signal 'Shunt train for following train to pass', but the Junction signalman thought he must have failed to clear after a previous train had passed. 'Goodness!' he exclaimed to his booking lad, 'I haven't given the two-one here yet.' He forthwith gave Wheeler the 'two-one' out of section signal, cleared the instrument, accepted the express and pulled off his signals. The boy failed to remind the signalman that his entries for the local were incomplete and filled them in by guess work. Meanwhile Driver Hope of the local had dispatched his fireman to the box to carry out Rule 55, but so short was the section from Winwick Quay that he had not reached the box when the collision occurred. The express pitched in as Driver Hope was moving slowly forward to pick up his fireman, the signal, as he thought, having cleared for him. It was a dark night, but visibility was good. A curious feature of the accident was that in spite of a collision so violent that three steel coaches were badly telescoped, the locomotive of the express, a 4–6–0 of the 'Prince of Wales' class, was so little damaged that when the wreckage had been moved from her she was able to steam away; in fact she assisted the wrecking operations by dragging the damaged vehicles clear.

Colonel Trench dealt leniently in his report with the signalman who was directly responsible and more severely with his booking lad. He should have made no entries in his book without the confirmation of the signalman; otherwise the whole point of the Train Register, which was to remind a busy signalman of the position of trains at any moment, was completely lost. As for the fact that the fireman of the local had not reached the box when the collision occurred although he left promptly, it was clear that either a track circuit must be installed or that a fireman's telephone must be placed at this home signal.

Another accident which showed how the human element could defeat the most elaborate safety precautions occurred at Welwyn Garden City on the London & North Eastern main line on the night of June 15th, 1935. Three expresses left King's Cross that night for the North in quick succession. The first left at 10.45 pm and passed through Welwyn at speed at 11.20. The second was the Newcastle express consisting of eleven bogies drawn by 'Atlantic' locomotive No 4441 which pulled out at 10.53. Finally, at 10.58, No 4009, a 'K3' class 2–6–0 drew away with the express passenger and mail train to Leeds. The 'K3' was a more powerful engine than the 'Atlantic' and, although it comprised the same number of vehicles, its load was lighter and it began to overhaul the Newcastle train. Approaching Welwyn at seventy miles an hour, Driver Morris on the 'Atlantic' saw the distant at 'Caution', shut off steam and applied his brakes. He had slowed to twenty miles an hour when he saw in the distance the home signal come off. Imagining that he must be overrunning the train ahead, Morris let his train roll gently forward. There was a 'berth' track circuit 200 yards in rear of this home signal which, when occupied, sounded a buzzer in Welwyn signal box until the block instrument for the section ahead had been placed in the 'Train on Line' position. But Driver Morris had not reached this track circuit, and in that brief interval Welwyn accepted the Leeds express from Hatfield. Driver Morris was still moving slowly when he approached the starting signal, saw that it was clear, 'popped' his whistle and then put on steam. Almost immediately he felt the impact of a violent collision in the rear. Running at nearly 70 mph the 'K3' had crashed into the rear of Morris's train.

No rolling stock on earth could have withstood the fury of that onslaught. The rear coach of the Newcastle express was completely demolished and no passenger in it survived. Their bodies were found scattered among the debris along the lineside. The crushed frame of the coach wrapped itself round the front of the locomotive while the bogies, together with those of the coach in front of it, were pushed forward by the 'K3' for a distance of 140 yards. The behaviour of this next coach was a most remarkable tribute to the wisdom of the recommendations to which I have previously referred. It was an all steel vehicle with buck-eye couplings and shock absorbing buffers. There was no telescoping and, although it had lost both its bogies, the buck-eye coupling at its leading end held fast, not only supporting that end, but holding the coach upright and in line until it came to rest. Not one of the thirty passengers in it was seriously injured. The rolling stock of the Leeds train was of older pattern, but here again there was no telescoping, while it was to some extent protected by the locomotive which, despite the terrific force of the collision, never left the rails. In all, thirteen passengers were killed and eighty-one injured in this Welwyn collision.

How had it happened? Clearly the fault must lie with the signalman at Welwyn South, an inexperienced man only recently promoted to that box. In the first place it became clear that the second express was not overrunning the first but had been slowed quite unnecessarily. After its acceptance, a porter at Welwyn station had rung the south box to ask the signalman to inquire about a missing parcel and the latter had answered the call before pulling off his signals. But what happened after this was never perfectly clear. Signalman Crowe at Hatfield said that when he received the 'out of section' from Welwyn at 11.23 pm he promptly offered the third, Leeds, train which was immediately accepted. He thought this was 'rather smart' so he called Welwyn South and asked: 'Is that out, Fred?' 'Yes,' came the simple reply. A few minutes later he received the 'obstruction danger' signal. The Welwyn signalman, on the other hand, maintained that his 'out of section' signal referred to the first, the 10.45 express, and that he thought Crowe was referring to that train when he rang and asked, 'Is that out?'

It would be tedious to detail the complicated evidence of the Welwyn South signalman and his colleagues at Hatfield and Welwyn North. Suffice it to say that it was conflicting. The inspector, Colonel Mount, stated that he could not accept the evidence of the Welwyn South signalman and that he had formed the opinion that he had become thoroughly confused.

He had been passing a train on the up line at the time and the Colonel believed that he had been giving and receiving signals and pegging trains on the wrong set of block instruments. He suggested that block instruments might be painted in different colours and the tones of block bells more widely differentiated to guard against such confusion. He also criticized the porter's telephone call. A busy signal box should not be treated as a general inquiry office. But the Colonel also made another suggestion which was to have far reaching results. He proposed that track circuit control over block instruments and signals should be such that acceptance of a second train would be impossible until the first had occupied and cleared the 'berth' track circuit approaching the home signal. In some cases, to provide an additional margin of safety, this control could be extended to a second track circuit ahead of the home signal. Had such an arrangement been in operation that night it would have meant that the Welwyn signalman could not possibly have cleared his instrument and accepted the Leeds express until Driver Morris had passed the advanced starting signal and was well clear of the section. This arrangement, which has since been widely adopted, has become known as the 'Welwyn Control'.

For the last accident in this series we move northwards once more, over the Border to the little station of Castlecary on the old Edinburgh to Glasgow main line of the North British Railway which we last visited many years and many pages ago at Bo'ness Junction, only a few miles away. It was as darkness fell on a snowy December evening in 1937 that disaster struck at Castlecary. The trouble began three sections away to the west at Gartshore where a set of down main line facing points became blocked by snow. The inexperienced lengthmen who attempted to clear them did not do so sufficiently to enable the facing point locking bolt to engage and there was a delay of half an hour before the linesman arrived to set things right. As a result a succession of trains were brought to a standstill between Gartshore and Castlecary, the last being a goods train which was halted at Dullatur East box, the next block post west of Castlecary. The signalman at Castlecary, whom I will call Jones, was informed of this and set his signals against the next down train. This was an express from Dundee to Glasgow. It consisted of seven eight-wheeled coaches with a six-wheeled fish van at the rear and it was drawn by the four-coupled locomotive 'Dandy Dinmont' of Class D29. In spite of the snow it was running only two minutes late. Much to Jones's alarm he saw in the rapidly failing light that the express was approaching at speed. He waved a red hand lamp out of the box window and blew a whistle as the train ran past, but it disappeared through the station out of his range of vision. Jones feared that the express would certainly collide with the standing goods train and became almost panic stricken. He immediately sent the 'Train running away on right line' signal to Signalman Smith at Dullatur East and then called him on the telephone. 'That was the Dundee that's gone through my "sticks",' he called. 'Oh God!' said Smith and at once shouted to the fireman of the goods to run back and protect his train. His anxiety was needless for if, before jumping to conclusions, Jones had paused to look at his down line station track circuit indicator he might have seen that it showed 'occupied'. For the crew of 'Dandy Dinmont' had in fact seen his hand signal and pulled up within station limits.

Jones knew that the Edinburgh to Glasgow express was nearly due and he straightaway rang up Signalman Beattie at Greenhill Junction, the next box east, to ascertain where the express was and was told it was running to time. Jones then told Beattie what he thought had happened and that he was not sure whether he ought to accept the Edinburgh. What did he advise him to do? The following exchanges then took place:

Beattie: 'Have you sent the "Train running away on right line" signal?'

Jones: 'Yes.'

Beattie: 'Have you put down detonators?'

Jones: 'No.'

Beattie: 'You should.'

Jones: 'Why?'

Beattie: 'It's always a precaution.'

Jones: 'Am I justified in clearing back the Dundee and taking the 4.3?'

Beattie: 'There's nothing to stop you provided you saw the tail-lights and the regulations applied. Are you certain all your signals are at danger?'

Jones: 'Undoubtedly.'

Beattie: 'Have you got your quarter mile clear ahead of your home signal?'

Jones: 'Yes.'

Beattie: 'Then there's nothing to prevent you accepting the 4.3.'

Acting upon Beattie's advice, Jones thereupon accepted the Edinburgh express at 4.32 pm. Three minutes later Fireman Fleming of the Dundee express, closely followed by Stationmaster Scott, came up into the box to sign the Train Register in accordance with Rule 55. Jones seemed relieved to know that the Dundee train had stopped. 'I'll have to see about getting the 4 o'clock stopped,' he said. 'It's time there were detonators on the track,' Fleming remarked, and as he spoke a bell rang and Jones answered it. 'That's the "entering section" for the 4.3,' he said, turning to Scott. Scott immediately seized some detonators and rushed out of the box closely followed by Jones and Fleming. The trio had not got far, and Scott had only had time to fix one detonator satisfactorily when there thundered down upon them out of the dusk and the drift of snowflakes, terrible in speed and majesty, the Class A3 Pacific 'Grand Parade' with the Edinburgh express. She was running dead on her time at an effortless seventy miles an hour.

The moment Driver Anderson heard the crack of the detonator exploding under his wheels he snapped his regulator shut, threw open his steam sanders and made a full application of the vacuum brake. But, alas, the warning was far too be-lated. Apart from her following train of nine bogies, the weight of 'Grand Parade' alone was over 150 tons and she proceeded to give an even more awful demonstration than the 'K3' had done at Welwyn of the lethal power of the modern express train. When she struck the rear of the Dundee express she was still travelling at a mile a minute, and Colonel Mount calculated that her momentum must have been no less than 54,000 foot tons. In the second that elapsed before 'Grand Parade' came to rest embedded in the side of the cutting 100 yards beyond the point of collision the six-wheeled fish van quite literally disappeared while the two coaches next ahead of it were destroyed past all recognition. The steel frame of one of them was folded in two so that the headstocks were practic-ally touching one another. The bodies and frames of the first three Edinburgh coaches left their bogies and the latter, piling up against the engine tender, acted as runners. By this agency the first two bodies leapt clean over the locomotive and landed, upright, beyond it. The third came to rest on the top of the engine, twelve feet in the air. Thanks entirely to the fact that 'Grand Parade's' tender had a solid steel front, her engine crew had miraculous escapes. Driver Anderson was quite un-hurt and his fireman was only slightly injured. The leading bogie of the 'Pacific' was found under the trailing coupled wheels. One bogie wheel had been torn off its axle, indicating a shearing force of at least 80 tons. In this catastrophe thirty-five passengers were killed and 179 injured. Yet, even in this extreme test, steel construction, shock-absorbing buffers, buck-eye couplings and electric light proved their value. There was no fire and, apart from the vehicles immediately involved, there was no telescoping. The passengers in the rear coaches of the Edinburgh express, which did not leave the metals, were quite uninjured. They stepped out on to Castlecary platform to be conveyed by buses to their destination quite unaware that a major disaster had occurred.

The whole of the Dundee train had been pushed forward 50

yards by the force of the impact with the result that even
Driver Macaulay was badly injured. Nevertheless he managed
to drag himself along the line, past the fearful tangle of
twisted steel and up into the signal box. There was only one
burning question in the driver's mind, and it was indeed the
crucial point – the position of the Castlecary down distant
signal. 'Have you got a repeater on that distant?' he asked as
he staggered into the box. 'No,' said Jones. 'Well,' said the
other, 'it gave me the clear.' At this Jones lost his temper. 'Oh
don't come that stuff,' he retorted. 'All right, all right,' said
Macaulay, 'no use getting angry about it,' and he limped away.

What *was* the position of that distant signal? This was the
question to which Colonel Mount tried to find an answer at the
inquiry without any positive success. 'The distant was standing clear for me,' declared Macaulay in answer to the
Colonel's question. 'I have no doubt about that whatever.'
Driver Anderson was equally emphatic. There could be no
question of the arm drooping, 'it was distinctly and properly
clear,' he said. Both men frankly admitted that they had failed
to see the home signal at danger. When they saw that the
distant was 'off' they naturally assumed that they had a clear
road until Macaulay saw Jones's hand signal and Anderson
heard the detonator explode. Jones, on the other hand, told a
completely conflicting story. He said: 'I could see my signal
plainly go to danger at 4.9 after passing the Cadder goods
train, since when my levers were not moved. I could see the
distant signal back light at 4.22 and again at 4.32 when I
accepted the two expresses.' But Jones also declared that the
station track circuit indicator had failed. He maintained that
before he held his telephone conversation with Signalman
Beattie as to whether or not he should accept the Edinburgh
train he had looked at the indicator and that it was showing
clear. This track circuit, however, was tested after the accident
and was found to be working perfectly. By observing the distant signal for himself from the signal box at the same time of
day, Colonel Mount came to the conclusion that owing to fail-

ing light and falling snow Jones had not been able to see the signal return to danger after the goods had passed, nor would he have been able to see its backlight when he accepted the expresses. Although no fault could be found in the signal and its mechanism, it was a significant coincidence that both drivers had accepted it so positively as clear. It was plain, said Colonel Mount, that, fearing an imminent collision, Jones lost his head when the Dundee train ran through his signals; that he had not looked at the track circuit indicator or taken any proper steps to discover whether the Dundee train had come to a stand. For this reason he considered that Jones's evidence about the distant signal was equally untrustworthy. If he was unable to see the signal he should never have accepted the Dundee train unless he had received the 'out of section' for the goods. Moreover, when the Dundee train had run through his signals he should immediately have taken steps to ascertain why it had done so and to protect the line if necessary. Like his predecessor Captain Tyler in his report on the Abbots Ripton disaster, Colonel Mount also questioned the wisdom of permitting express trains to maintain such high speeds when visibility was so limited by falling snow.

In his recommendations, the Colonel said that even a repeater could be ignored by a signalman and was thus an inadequate safeguard. The repeater circuit could be used to prove the distant so that a train could not be accepted unless the distant arm was at 'caution', a device which had already been installed on 81 per cent of main lines and should be extended. He also recommended the installation of the Welwyn Control. Finally, he concluded, if the distant signal *was* passed at 'caution', then the disaster showed the need for some form of Automatic Train Control or 'ATC', a device which will be the theme of our next chapter.

10

DRIVERS' ERRORS, 1890–1940

Carlisle – Glasgow St Enoch – Ais Gill – Ilford – Darlington – Charfield – Ashchurch – Port Eglinton – Norton Fitzwarren

T H E B O A R D of Trade's long and hard fought campaign to secure the adoption of automatic continuous brakes which was brought to final victory after the Armagh collision had a curious and somewhat ironical sequel. Scarcely had the Act of 1889 passed on to the Statute Book than an accident occurred which appeared to make nonsense of the arguments of successive inspecting officers since the days of the Newark brake trials. On March 4th, 1890, the night Scotch express from Euston, consisting of fifteen vehicles drawn by the 6-foot Webb compound No 515, got out of control on the descent from Shap summit, ran through Carlisle and came into collision with a stationary Caledonian locomotive, causing the deaths of four passengers. It was a bitterly cold night and Driver Rumney declared that the automatic vacuum brake on his train had failed owing to icing in the train pipe between his engine tender and the leading coach. When the train was examined immediately after the collision the brakes were found to be off on all the coaches, but some of the wheel tyres were warm, suggesting that the brake had acted partially. A small quantity of ice was found in the train pipe behind the engine tender. At the subsequent inquest the jury exonerated Rumney from all blame and announced that: 'The London & North Western Railway are incurring a very grave responsibility in using a brake of such an uncertain and unreliable character.'

Now for years Francis Webb, the uncrowned king of Crewe, had stubbornly championed his chain brake against the claims of the vacuum system and it was only with reluctance that he had been forced to give way. This verdict must therefore have created a somewhat delicate situation, to say the least, and it would be interesting to know what passed between Crewe and the Railways Inspection Department of the Board of Trade. It was obviously of the utmost importance to the latter that this slur on the reliability of the vacuum brake should be removed. Colonel Rich went north on as difficult an assignment as ever an inspecting officer has had to face. Counsel for Driver Rumney was extremely well briefed in the technicalities of the vacuum brake and there took place a brilliant battle of wits between Counsel and Colonel Rich, with occasional questions fired at Driver Rumney by both combatants. For a long time the honours were even, first one and then the other scoring a point, but in order to appreciate the contest and its conclusion it is necessary first to give a brief explanation of the working of the vacuum brake.

It has already been explained that the old type of simple, non-automatic vacuum brake worked in precisely the opposite way to the automatic type. In the former the creation of vacuum in the train pipe applied the brake, whereas in the latter it held the brake off. Locomotive No 515 had two steam ejectors of different sizes. The smaller ejector was designed to work continuously when the train was in motion in order to maintain the vacuum in the train pipe by offsetting the leakage of air which inevitably occurs, particularly in the flexible connections between the coaches. For if the vacuum is lost it will mean that the brakes will 'leak on'. The large ejector was used to exhaust the air from the train pipe after a brake application had been made. The locomotive itself was fitted with a steam brake inter-connected with the vacuum brake which was quite a usual arrangement. But it also had another device which has long ago passed into limbo. Owing to the fact that the London & North Western Railway at this time still possessed a lot of rolling stock which was fitted with the old simple non-automatic vacuum brake, No 515 was arranged to work brakes of either type. When the brake lever was pushed *in* the working was automatic, but when a pin was removed and it was pulled right *out* it worked simple.

Now the first point which Colonel Rich made was this. If the train pipe had indeed become blocked by ice (and the ice which had been found was not, in fact, sufficient to block it) then the brakes on the coaches would have gradually leaked on the irrevocably remained on until the pipe was cleared and vacuum restored. Yet the brakes were found fully off when the train was examined immediately after the collision. This was the technical conundrum over which the argument raged and became at times quite heated. Again and again Counsel attempted to trip up and confuse his adversary, but the Colonel remained unshaken – icing *could* not have caused the brake to fail in this way. Yet Driver Rumney's story sounded straightforward enough. He had received pilot assistance up to Shap summit where he had stopped while the pilot was detached. This meant that the vacuum was lost so he had restored it with his large ejector. He had then run normally down the bank towards Carlisle and it was only when he reached his braking point that he saw from his gauge that he had lost vacuum. He had tried to restore it by using the large ejector but in vain; the brakes would not act. Again and again Colonel Rich questioned the driver as to the sequence of his handling of the brake controls and at last his patience and persistence were rewarded.

> There's one thing I wish to say [announced Rumney suddenly] when I was trying to create vacuum I pulled the pin out and pulled the (brake) lever right back so as to put the steam brake on the tender at the same time as I was creating vacuum; so I did not take the brake off the engine at all.

By saying this Rumney thought he was defending himself, yet in fact he had at last acknowledged his error as the Colonel instantly realized. The detective had discovered the vital clue. At once the whole sequence of events became clear to him and the reliability of the automatic vacuum brake was vindicated.

What had happened was this. After the pilot engine had been detached at Shap summit Rumney had, as he said, 'blown off' his brakes with the large ejector, but at the same time he had shut off the small ejector and had forgotten to put it on again. As a result, on the descent of Shap, the brakes on the train had gradually leaked on. This accounted both for the loss of vacuum and for the fact that some of the wheel tyres were warm when the train was examined. For the brake shoes had, of course, been rubbing. When Rumney was trying to restore the vacuum he admitted that he had taken the pin out of the brake lever and pulled it right back. This was a fatal mistake. By doing so he had moved it into the position for working simple vacuum which meant that on this train, the brakes were immediately fully released.

Colonel Rich's conclusion was brief and obvious. This arrangement of dual brake operation by means of a single lever was highly confusing to drivers and therefore dangerous. The remedy was for the London & North Western Railway Company to make it obsolete as quickly as possible by speedily equipping all their rolling stock with the automatic vacuum brake. It was a notable victory for the Railways Inspection Department.

Driver Rumney made an unfortunate mistake on this occasion, but even when a driver is in full command of an efficient continuous brake, to bring a heavy train smoothly to a standstill within platform limits is a feat which calls for very considerable skill. Practice makes perfect, but where so many variable factors are involved – the speed and weight of the train and the state of the rail – it is inevitable that errors of judgement sometimes occur which, if the train is running into a terminus, can have fatal consequences. The driver's task is made more difficult when the terminus lies at the foot of an incline, and it is an unfortunate fact that so many of our busier termini are so situated. Euston is a particularly bad example where from the earliest times there have been periodic mishaps due to drivers – to borrow a motor racing expression – 'running out of road'. Against this danger there can be no safe-guard except the driver's judgement, although the hydraulic buffer stops produced by the famous firm of Ransomes and Rapier do much to mitigate the effects of collision. Otherwise, a collision with a buffer stop backed by a solid masonry plat-form, even at relatively low speed, can have most disastrous results. This was revealed at the St Enoch terminus of the Glasgow & South Western Railway on July 27th, 1903, when the worst collision of this kind in British railway history occurred.

The accident was entirely due to an error of judgement on the part of the inexperienced driver of a special train from Ardrossan to Glasgow. St Enoch station had then been re-cently rebuilt and Platform No 8 into which the train was signalled was a new platform, not so long as the others and terminating short of the station's all-over roof. The driver was evidently misled by this. He ran in too fast, braked too late and was still travelling at ten miles an hour when his engine hit the stops. No less than sixteen passengers lost their lives and sixty-four were injured, the first and second coaches being completely telescoped.

For the next accident in this series we return for the last time to those familiar metals – the Settle & Carlisle line. Twenty-three years have gone by since Driver Rumney's train came sweeping down Shap out of control, but in imagination we are back in the yards at Carlisle, for it was there that the first scene in the drama of the Ais Gill disaster took place.

On the night of September 1st, 1913, two four-coupled Midland express locomotives were coaling up at Carlisle pre-paratory to working the night Scotch expresses on their way south to St Pancras. The first was No 993, Driver Nicholson and Fireman Metcalf, who were booked to work the Stranraer and Glasgow train which was due out of Carlisle at 1.35 am. No 446, Driver Caudle and Fireman Follows, would come after with the Inverness and Edinburgh portion, due out at

1.49 am. Their tenders were being filled up with South Tyne coal. It was a good quality steam coal, but it had not been screened and contained a very large proportion of small coal and slack. Driver Caudle stirred it critically with his boot and was heard to remark: 'If she'll steam on this she'll steam on anything.'

Driver Nicholson had the same misgivings which were by no means relieved when he found that his train consisted of ten coaches, three of them twelve-wheeled sleeping cars, weighing 243 tons. This was 13 tons over the maximum rated load for his engine on 'the long drag' up to Ais Gill summit. He therefore asked for pilot assistance, but was told that no pilot was available.

When No 993 pulled out alone with her train at 1.38 am – three minutes late – she had to lift her load from near sea level to a height of 1,167 feet in forty-seven miles, the last nine of which from Crosby Garret tunnel to Ais Gill summit were on an almost continuous gradient of 1 in 100. To make things more difficult, it was, needless to say, typical Pennine weather – a pitch dark night of rain with a strong wind blowing from the northeast. No 993 was soon in trouble. Fireman Metcalf did his best and Nicholson himself took a turn with the shovel but with such small coal they could not keep a lively fire and, despite all their efforts, when the gradient stiffened, so the needle of the steam pressure gauge remorselessly crept back. Over the eight and a quarter miles between Ormside and Kirby Stephen they were able to average only twenty-nine miles an hour as against the scheduled forty. At Mallerstang the speed of the labouring engine had dropped to twenty miles per hour and they were running ten minutes late. By this time steam pressure had fallen so low that Nicholson had to put on his large ejector to maintain the vacuum and so prevent the brakes on the train from rubbing. Three miles south of Maller-stang box, pressure had fallen to 85 lb and No 993 came to a stand. She was only half a mile short of Ais Gill summit and, incidentally, but two miles away from Grisedale Crossing where, less than three years before, disaster had befallen the down Scotch express.

As soon as the train stopped, Donelly, the front guard, jumped down and asked Nicholson what was the matter. 'We'll be a few minutes, we're short of steam,' shouted Nicholson above the dull roar of the blower. He stood in the glare from the open firedoor as Metcalf, wielding his long pricker, was cleaning the bars. The rear guard, Whitley, had also got out of his compartment, and now Donelly turned and called to him: 'Only a minute.' Whitley therefore took no steps to protect the train by placing detonators in the rear. Meanwhile Signalman Sutherland at Mallerstang was wondering why he had received no 'out of section' signal from Clemnet at Ais Gill box. Clemnet told him on the telephone that he had no information, so Sutherland kept his signals at danger when he was offered the Inverness and Edinburgh train.

Driver Caudle was making better progress with No 446 for he had only six bogies weighing 157 tons behind his tender. But his engine, too, was steaming badly owing to the small coal. As they were approaching the short Birkett tunnel near Mallerstang, Caudle left the footplate and went out on to the framing to oil the left-hand driving axle box. Owing to the force of the wind it took him longer to make his perilous way round the framing than he had expected and by the time he got back to the footplate the train had run past the Mallerstang distant signal which was just over 1,000 yards from the south end of the tunnel. Neither man saw it. There was a minor crisis on the footplate when Caudle returned. Water was short; it was out of sight in the bottom fitting of the gauge glass and Follows was trying in vain to get the right-hand injector to work. Caudle immediately went to his aid. 'Injectors need humouring sometimes,' said the driver. Delicately he manipulated the steam and water controls until at last the coughing and hissing of the obstinate injector ceased and it broke into its reassuring song. But by this time they had run past all the

Mallerstang signals without observing them. The next thing that happened was that Follows suddenly shouted: 'Look out, Sam, there's a red light in front of us.'

Signalman Sutherland at Mallerstang was watching Caudle's train approach. At first he thought it was slowing down and that Caudle had seen the distant signal at 'Caution'. He therefore lowered his 'home' with the idea of stopping the train at his starting signal. The next instant he realized that the locomotive was still steaming hard. Immediately he flung the home signal back to danger, grabbed his red handlamp and waved it from the box as the train went past. It did not stop and Sutherland sent the 'Train running away on right line' signal to Clemnet at Ais Gill. A minute or so later he heard the distant sound of an engine whistle followed by a sinister rumbling noise.

Signalman Clemnet, too, was wondering what was happening down the line and, just as Sutton at Hawes Junction had done two years before, he was staring northwards into the darkness through the rain bleared windows of his lonely cabin. It had just turned three o'clock when he saw what he afterwards described as a red mist rising and falling away in the night sky beyond his up distant signal. Five minutes afterwards he heard someone stumbling up the steps to his box. It was Fireman Metcalf in a state of collapse bringing the news of disaster. Clemnet at once stopped a down goods train which was just about to pass.

Driver Nicholson was the first to see the Edinburgh express approaching. Glancing back down the line he saw in the sky the moving glare from an open fire door. At once he sent Metcalf running back and opened both his whistle and his regulator. But No 993 still could not move her heavy train. Guard Whitley rushed down the line waving a red lamp and blowing a whistle but it was of no avail. Driver Caudle's engine crashed into the rear van of the stationary train, demolished it completely, and buried itself in the third-class coach next to it. The roof of the wrecked van slid over the top of No

446 and cut through three compartments of the first carriage
behind the tender. Fire caused by escaping gas broke out instantly in the rear of the leading train, completely consuming
the remains of the van, the partially demolished third, and the
sleeping car which was coupled next to it. It was a funeral
pyre for fourteen passengers who perished almost without
trace. In addition, thirty-eight passengers in the second train
were seriously injured. It was as though the ancient gods of
this high, wild country, still unappeased, had demanded a
second sacrifice.

The inquiry into the Ais Gill disaster, which was conducted
by Colonel Pringle, was opened in private at Kirby Stephen
station, but the accident had excited so much concern that
subsequent sessions were held in public in Leeds and London.
Once again the Colonel stressed the terrible danger of fire
from gas-lit coaching stock, but he also had a number of comments and criticisms to make on the events leading up to the
accident. He criticized the Midland Company for not ensuring
that their engines were supplied with properly graded coal,
and for permitting locomotives to work over so difficult a route
with trains of a weight approaching, or in excess of, their load
limit. Those in charge of the first train were gravely at fault.
Before the collision occurred the train had been standing for at
least seven minutes, yet no attempt was made to protect it in
the rear as required by the working rules. The accident was
primarily due to the failure of Driver Caudle and Fireman
Follows to observe the Mallerstang signals. The Colonel said
he appreciated the footplate difficulties which prevented their
seeing them, but having knowingly missed them, instead of
proceeding with great caution until they reached the next block
post, they took a chance that the road was clear and continued
at unreduced speed and without keeping a good look out. The
introduction of wick-type lubricators meant that it was no
longer necessary for a driver to leave his post and go round the
framing of his engine with an oiler while it was in motion. Yet
tradition died hard, and he understood that Midland drivers

made a habit of doing so at least once during the climb from Carlisle to Ais Gill. The Colonel thought it high time that this dangerous practice was discontinued. He also had a sharp word for Signalman Sutherland at Mallerstang. Although his action did not appear to have contributed to the disaster, he should not have lowered his home signal until he was quite positive that the train was obeying the distant signal. It was evident that Sutherland had not been quick enough with his hand signal and he recommended the Midland to follow the example of other companies by equipping their signalmen with detonator placers for use in such emergencies. By means of this device a signalman could put warning detonators on the rail by moving a special lever in his box. Colonel Pringle also suggested the revival of a very ancient idea – the issue to the guard of coloured warning flares for use in the event of a train coming to a stand in a section.

The circumstances of the Ais Gill accident reveal the many unrealized difficulties with which footplate men have to contend. The engine driver is no mere regulator pusher any more than his fireman is a mere coal heaver. For all its massive bulk, a steam locomotive is a machine as sensitive as a race-horse and, like Driver Caudle's obstinate injector, it needs humouring. And yet, despite the claims of the locomotive, the terrible responsibility of observing all signals must remain. Many new safety devices had, as we saw in the last chapter, been introduced by this time to ease the signalman's burden, but nothing at all had been done to mitigate the danger of a driver over-running signals. Everything still depended, as it had done in the first days of railways, on the vigilance of the men on the footplate. In his report on Ais Gill, Colonel Pringle made a number of suggestions for reducing this risk – automatic train stops as introduced on London's Underground and even the wireless control of trains. But he also referred to the system of automatic train control which had been developed by the Great Western Railway Company, and said he thought that this system deserved wider notice and trial.

The Great Western invention to which Colonel Pringle referred was first tried out experimentally on that Company's Henley branch in January 1906. It consisted of an insulated steel bar mounted on a baulk of timber and laid centrally between the running rails in the form of a ramp at each distant signal. This bar made contact with a spring-loaded shoe on the locomotive and so raised it. When the signal stood at 'clear' the bar became electrified, and the current, passing through the shoe, rang a bell in the engine cab. If, on the other hand, the signal was at danger, the ramp remained dead with the result that when the locomotive shoe was raised it broke an electric circuit on the engine and by so doing caused an alarm whistle to sound. It thus possesssed the essential virtue of all railway safety devices in that if the signal or the ground current failed the danger signal was automatically given.

So successful was this Henley experiment that a year later it was decided to give it a more extended trial on the twenty-two miles of the branch line from Oxford to Fairford. In this case the visible distant signals were removed and reliance was placed entirely on the audible warning system, only locomotives fitted with the device being allowed to work over the branch. Next, some of the main line locomotives having been suitably equipped, ramps were laid beside all distant signals between Reading and Slough in 1908 and between Slough and Paddington in 1910. The visible signals were not, of course, removed. Shortly afterwards the apparatus on the locomotive was modified so that it not only gave an audible danger signal but at the same time it opened an air valve and so applied the automatic vacuum brake to the train unless, or until, it was released by the driver. The invention therefore ceased to be merely an audible signalling device; it became as well a positive system of automatic train control (ATC). In this improved form it was introduced progressively on all the main lines of the Great Western Railway. Besides its obvious contribution to safe working, ATC made it unnecessary to post fogmen at distant signals provided all locomotives were suitably equipped. Train working in foggy weather was not only greatly assisted, but one of the signalman's worst problems was banished – the question as to whether or not he should call out fogmen.

It is entirely fitting that a Company with so proud a safety record should have been responsible for perfecting so simple and admirable a device. One might suppose that the other railway companies would speedily follow such an example, but no. In accident report after accident report we find the railway inspecting officers recommending the installation of ATC just as stubbornly as they had advocated continuous automatic brakes or block working fifty years before. Yet from the first experiment at Henley, forty-six years would pass by before their persuasions were crowned with success. Two world wars intervened, while owing to the effect of increasing road competition the railways had less money to spare for improvements which could show no direct return in traffic revenue. Yet this was not the whole story. The railways were growing old and suffering a certain hardening of the arteries. A sense of tradition is an admirable thing; but it can become too strong and lead to inertia, to a failure to keep mental pace with changing traffic conditions and demands. Because a home signal is a stop signal which must not be passed at danger under any circumstances, whereas the distant signal at danger merely gives an advance warning, there was a tendency to regard the former as the more important. In fact the reverse was the case, and as express trains increased in speed and weight the more vital did the distant signal become. But the Great Western Railway were for some time alone in recognizing this truth which was tragically emphasized by the disaster on the Great Eastern Railway at Ilford on New Year's Day, 1915.

The crew of the 7.6 am express from Clacton to London failed to see that the distant and home signals at Ilford East were at danger. Signalman Nichols endeavoured unsuccessfully to attract their attention by shouting and waving a red flag from the box. At the west end of the station the 8.20 am local train from Gidea Park to Liverpool Street was in the act of crossing from the up local to the up through line on which the express was running. The express came into violent side-long collision with the local train at the fouling point of the crossover. It struck and seriously damaged the seventh coach of the suburban train, completely destroyed the eighth and damaged four others. The four-coupled bogie engine of the Clacton train spun completely round and toppled into a lineside coal store, while the leading coach was also seriously damaged. Ten lives were lost and no less than 500 passengers complained of injury.

This collision [wrote Colonel Von Donop, in his report] which was attended with such sad results and which was mainly due to the fact of the driver not noticing that his distant signal was at danger, points to the desirability of the provision of some arrangement for giving a driver an unmistakable warning as to the position of his distant signal when he passes it. The Great Eastern Railway Company have placed a number of detonator machines at home signals in the London area, but it is at the distant signal that warning is specially needed.

How a driver may misread a complicated signals installation at a busy station with dire consequences was shown by the costly disaster at Darlington on June 27th, 1928. At 10.45 pm a passenger and parcels train from the north drew up at the south end of No 1 platform at Bank Top station. The train was hauled by a six-coupled bogie express locomotive, No 2369, in the charge of Driver Bell and Fireman McCormack. After discharging its passengers the train began to shunt, as was usual, before continuing, as a parcels train only, to North-allerton and York. In the course of these shunting operations No 2369 came to a stand on an up duplicate line at the head of a rake of ten carriage trucks, horse-boxes and vans which were to be transferred to No 1 platform and attached to the rear portion of the train which had been left standing there. This duplicate line eventually debouched on to the main through avoiding lines which enabled fast trains to by-pass Bank Top station. When a small-arm 'calling on' signal was lowered, Driver Bell moved forward in obedience. Now this signal did not authorize him to run forward through the crossovers on to the main line; before he could do this legitimately, signal No 18 'Up Home, Duplicate to Main' had to be pulled off. This signal stood at danger. Bell, however, was under the fatal impression that No 8, the little 'calling on' signal, entitled him to run out on to the main preparatory to setting back into No 1 platform. Michael Morland, a shunter who was riding in the third van, understood the limited purpose of the 'calling on' signal, and when he realized that the train was not stopping as it should he opened the Westinghouse brake valve in his van. Unfortunately, however, he then thought that his action had made Bell realize that he had made a mistake and that the train was coming to a stand. So he released the Westinghouse and took another look at the signals. He saw that they were definitely overrunning and still moving so he at once applied the brake again and brought the train to a stand. But by this time Driver Bell was well out on the main line, and almost immediately there was a violent collision. A return excursion train from Scarborough to Newcastle consisting of eleven eight-wheelers drawn by an 'Atlantic' type locomotive No 2164 had run head-on into Bell's engine at forty-five miles an hour. With one exception all the coaches of the excursion train were electrically lit and there was no fire, but very serious telescoping took place. The underframe of the third coach cut clean through five crowded compartments of the second, and in them twenty-five passengers died. Forty-five other passengers were seriously injured.

As a result of his inquiry, Colonel Pringle stated that he had come to the conclusion that Driver Bell's knowledge of signalling was insufficient to enable him to read correctly any complication of signals in a yard with which he was evidently unacquainted. He should have asked for advice or assistance from the staff. Something more, the Colonel thought, than a mere signature in a Road Book should be required as evidence that a driver was properly qualified to work over a particular route. Yet he acknowledged that the use of duplicate 'calling on' signals in such situations was confusing and suggested the substitution of a single three-aspect colour light signal. The yellow 'caution' indication would thus serve the purpose of the 'calling on' arm. It was most unfortunate that Shunter Morland, when he first saw that Bell had overrun the limit authorized by the 'calling on' signal, had not applied the Westinghouse fully and kept it on. Had he done so the collision would have been avoided. Referring to the effects of the collision, Colonel Pringle recommended the extended use of buck-eye couplings to prevent overriding and consequent telescoping.

1928 was one of those black years in railway history when, for no operational reason but by pure coincidence and ill-fortune, a number of serious accidents occurred. Such an unlucky sequence is invariably seized upon by popular newspapers as a heaven-sent opportunity to belabour the railways. 'What's wrong with our railways?' they ask in heavy type, while minor mishaps which ordinarily would not earn a paragraph are headlined as: ANOTHER RAILWAY ACCIDENT. They certainly found plenty of copy during the latter half of 1928. There were bad accidents at London Bridge and Ancoats, in the tunnel at Queen's Street, Glasgow, and at Dinwoodie. There was also another major disaster – at Charfield between Gloucester and Bristol on the West of England main line of the London, Midland & Scottish Railway.

On October 13th, in the early hours of the morning, the following four trains were proceeding on the down line from Gloucester towards Bristol in the order given:

(1) LMS 10.35 pm down through freight, Washwood Heath to Bristol.

(2) GWR 9.15 pm down fitted goods, Oxley Sidings to Bristol.

(3) LMS 12.45 am down parcels train, Leicester to Bristol.

(4) LMS 10 pm down passenger and mails, Leeds to Bristol.

The parcels train was overhauling the two goods trains and therefore the LMS goods was shunted clear when it reached Charfield and the Great Western goods when it arrived at Berkeley Road Junction. The parcels train then ran past them. When he had received the 'Out of Section' for the parcels train from Wickwar, Signalman Button at Charfield consulted his control at Fishponds, Bristol, and decided, first to send the LMS goods forward, and then to accept and pass the Great Western goods from Berkeley Road. He therefore signalled the LMS goods out of the lay-by, but the driver stopped in Charfield station for water. He was not booked to take on water there, nor had he advised Button that he wished to do so. There was a delay of five minutes which forced Button to change his plans. When the LMS train eventually drew away he realized that he could not now pass the Great Western train without seriously delaying the mail train (4) so he decided to shunt it. If only he had known that the driver of the first goods needed water he would have kept him in the siding and allowed the second to run through.

The block system on the line was controlled by three position instruments working on the rotary interlocking principle which enforces the proper rotation of signals: 'Line Blocked', 'Line Clear', 'Train on Line'. It was also so arranged that the signals could not be lowered to admit a train into a section until the train ahead had actuated a release treadle at the box in advance and the signalman at that box had given his consent. When the Great Western goods train ran into Charfield at 5.13 am it worked the release and Button cleared back to Berkeley Road. He then shouted down to the driver and guard to set back into the 'lay-by' siding and pulled off the shunting disc signal.

It now wanted little over an hour to dawn and into the clear and still autumnal air the early morning mist was rising in the fields and creeping over the tracks. But Signalman Button could still see his 'fog object'[1] and decided that there was no necessity for him to call out his fogmen. At 5.14 he accepted the mail train from Berkeley Road. He was perfectly correct in doing this, for the Great Western goods had passed the release treadle in advance of his clearing point signal and there was the necessary quarter mile interval between this signal and his down outer home signal which, like his distant and inner home, was standing at danger. The distant and outer home signals were invisible from the box so that their position was indicated by electrical repeaters. There was also a track circuit in rear of the outer home signal.

The Great Western goods had almost shunted clear of the main line and the 4.45 am empty freight, Westerleigh to Gloucester, which he had previously accepted from Wickwar, was approaching on the up line when Button happened to notice his down line track circuit indicator. It flickered from 'Clear' to 'Occupied' and then, to his alarm, back to 'Clear' again. This could only mean one thing – the mail was overrunning his signals. An instant later she roared into Charfield at a mile a minute. The Great Western locomotive and three wagons were still foul of the down line, while the empty goods train was running by on the up. Moreover at this point the line is in a cutting and spanned by a substantial brick overbridge. The express thus ran into a bottleneck in which there were two trains, both moving in the opposite direction. The mail included eight coaches varying in age from nineteen to forty-three years, all of them wooden-bodied and gas lit. The result was appalling. The locomotive, four-coupled Class 3, No 714, struck the Great Western train and then cannoned

---

[1] A fixed point, usually the back light of a signal, by which the signalman judges whether or not he should call up his fogmen.

off into the up goods train, cutting it in two behind the eighth wagon and falling on its side amid a welter of splintered wagon bodies. The coaches which followed were almost completely destroyed and their twisted frames reared themselves on end until the buffers of the leader overhung the parapet of the bridge high overhead. Part of the body and roof of this coach, indeed, shot right over the parapet and one of the victims of the disaster was found lying in the roadway. Almost immediately escaping gas caused fire to break out and the great pile of debris heaped against the bridge soon became an unapproachable furnace which, despite the efforts of the local fire brigades, blazed for twelve hours. Fifteen lives were lost in this, the latest, and it is to be hoped, the last, of the series of great train fires.

Twelve years had passed, wrote Colonel Pringle in his report on Charfield, since an accident with so many deplorable features had occurred.

> Elements of time and chance [he went on] have often been known to play a favourable part, either in averting or reducing the ill effects likely to arise from an accident. In this case all the conditions were hostile. Ten seconds later there would have been no obstruction. If the driver of the previous goods had told Button he needed water, the trains involved would have been cleared through. The existence of the bridge, the simultaneous movement of two trains in the opposite direction, the misty atmosphere and the early morning darkness combined to produce almost the worst conditions in which a collision at high speed could occur and rendered deplorable results inevitable.

At the inquiry the crucial question was: what was the position of the Charfield down distant signal? There could be no question of a mistake on Signalman Button's part. He could not have pulled off his down signals, for the section to Wickwar was not clear at the time and until it became clear the levers would remain locked. At the inquest the jury accepted the view that the disaster was due to the negligence of Henry Aldington, the driver of the express, in passing signals at danger. The unfortunate man was committed to Assizes on a charge of manslaughter but was very properly acquitted. For, as in the case of the later accident at Castlecary, considerable doubt remains in the mind as to the position of that signal. Neither Aldington nor his fireman, Frank Want, sought to excuse themselves, as they might so easily have done, on the grounds of sudden fog and absence of fogmen. On the contrary, both declared with convincing emphasis that, whereas they had admittedly failed to see the home signals, they saw the distant perfectly distinctly showing clear. Aldington said that owing to the misty conditions he had crossed the footplate and was standing behind his fireman, peering ahead. They had both seen the green light, about 50 yards away, at the same moment, for Want had immediately exclaimed, 'He's got it off, mate.' After the collision, in which he miraculously escaped serious injury, Driver Aldington helped in the work of rescue until the fire made it hopeless. He had then gone up to the signal box where he said to Button: 'What's the meaning of this? Your distant was off.' 'Impossible,' replied Button, yet when he looked at the distant repeater it was showing 'clear'. Investigation then showed that the arm of the distant signal was drooping 20 degrees owing to the wreckage of the collision lying upon the signal wire and that when this was removed it flew back to danger. Yet it seems strange that the repeater should show 'clear' if the arm was only inclined to an extent so small that the green spectacle would not be brought before the lamp. Yet the signal could not have failed at 'clear' unless some heavy object had fouled the wire – or unless the wire was deliberately pulled. The mystery – and the doubt – remains.

Once again the absolutely vital importance of the distant signal had been emphasized in most tragic fashion. Once again Colonel Pringle strongly recommended the adoption of Automatic Train Control as used by the Great Western Railway

'which,' he said, 'can alone prevent accidents of this kind.'
Referring to the fire, the Colonel said that the promised conversion from gas to electric lighting had not proceeded so
rapidly as they had hoped. Returns showed that half the rolling stock on the LMS was still gas lit, and he urged the
Company to speed up conversion and also the construction of
new steel rolling stock. Meanwhile he recommended the
marshalling of all steel vans at the front and rear of express
passenger trains.

There was one strange and poignant feature about the Charfield disaster. Among the victims were two young children.
Their charred bodies were unrecognizable and their identity
was never established. It seems unbelievable that two children should board a long distance express without someone,
parent, relative or guardian being aware of the fact, or missing
them if they were playing truant. Yet nobody came forward to
claim them, nor could they be connected with any of the other
victims of the accident. They were buried in an unnamed
grave in Charfield churchyard.

Within three months of Charfield, on the same line under
similar conditions and in almost precisely similar circumstances, a second collision occurred. In the early morning of
January 8th, 1929, the driver of an up express from Bristol to
Leeds overran signals in fog approaching Ashchurch Junction
and crashed at fifty miles an hour into a goods train which was
setting back over a trailing crossover from the up to the down
line. The material damage was almost equally catastrophic,
but fortunately there was no fire and there were only forty-five
passengers on the train so that the death roll was mercifully
light – two passengers, the driver and one Company's servant.
Once again the moral was stressed at the inquiry – the need for
'ATC'.

In spite of these repeated warnings the years slipped by and
still nothing was done by other companies to emulate the
example of the Great Western. On September 6th, 1934, two
passenger trains met in head-on collision at Port Eglinton

Junction near Glasgow for the same reason – the driver of one of them had missed the signals. In this case the driver of a local train from Paisley to Glasgow misread his signals owing to their changing perspective on the reverse curves by which he approached the junction and came into violent collision on the diamond crossing of the junction with another local train from Glasgow to Kilmarnock. Six passengers, both firemen and the driver of the Kilmarnock train lost their lives. In this case, however, as Colonel Mount pointed out, faulty operating was a contributory factor. The signalmen at Port Eglinton box had accepted the Paisley train up to the junction home signal only 147 yards away from the point where the crossing movement was about to take place – a space margin of safety perilously small. As long ago as 1892, two accidents, at Birmingham (Lawley Street) and Esholt Junction, had shown the importance of maintaining an ample clearance between converging lines.

From November 1890, when the broad gauge Cape Mail was wrecked at Norton Fitzwarren, until the outbreak of the second world war in 1939, the Great Western Railway did not suffer a single major disaster. Indeed the only accidents of any gravity were the collision at Slough in 1900 and the derailment at Llanelly in 1904. The fine safety record of the Great Western throughout its history is the more remarkable when we consider the unique conditions of working in the days prior to the abolition of the Broad Gauge. The increased complexity of mixed gauge track layouts would seem to multiply the risks of accident tenfold. Yet it was not so in practice.

The creation of that most individualistic and wayward of all Victorian engineers, Isambard Kingdom Brunel, the Great Western Railway remained from its prodigious birth until its tragic demise in 1948 the most individual of railways. The narrow gauge locomotives designed by George Jackson Churchward were as unique in their day as Gooch's broad gauge flyers and set a new standard of locomotive design which has since been widely flattered by less successful imitation. Their drivers drove from the opposite side of the foot-plate to those on the other lines, and in many other respects the western line was a cat that preferred to walk by itself. Working practices which were of everyday occurrence on other lines were never tolerated upon the Great Western. For example, the banking of passenger trains in the rear was discouraged, and if a passenger train required pilot assistance, then the pilot must be coupled to the train and the train engine attached in front of it. For it was rightly held that the driver in charge of the train should remain at the head of his train. Moreover, apart from pioneering ATC, the protection of through running lines from the risk of conflicting movement on the Great Western was more efficient and a model to other companies. But the most efficient safety devices and the most rigid rules cannot alone make a railway great. H. Raynar Wilson, in his analysis of railway accident statistics, came to the conclusion that the remarkable safety record of the Great Western was partly due to the efficiency and *esprit de corps* of the staff. Now that that individuality which paid such striking dividends is in process of being ironed out of existence to bring it in line with that uniformity which modern democracy demands, it is fitting that this belated tribute should be paid to it.

Yet even Homer nods, and it was against all the laws of probability that the happy immunity from serious accident which the Great Western had enjoyed for so long could continue indefinitely. It became even less likely when war broke out, when the black-out and the blitz created innumerable operational difficulties and subjected railwaymen everywhere to exceptional hazards and nervous strain. So it came about that the long record was broken one dark night in November, 1940. The train concerned was the 9.50 pm sleeping-car express from Paddington to Penzance and it was surely the strangest of coincidences that it should meet with disaster at Norton Fitzwarren, the very place where the Cape Mail had been wrecked almost exactly fifty years before. The accident was also remarkable for the fact that a second train had what was without doubt the most hairbreadth escape from certain destruction in all railway history.

The Penzance express consisted of thirteen vehicles including a twelve-wheeled sleeping car and it was drawn by locomotive No 6028, 'King George VI'.[1] This was the time of the blitz; it was also a very dark night, wet, with a strong west wind blowing and when No 6028 drew into Taunton she was one hour and eight minutes late. From Taunton westwards as far as Norton Fitzwarren, the West of England main line is quadrupled by relief lines, the junction of the down relief with the down main line west of Norton Fitzwarren station being protected by trap points. The Penzance express habitually used the down main line but on this occasion its late running brought about a change of plan.

Following the express was a newspaper train consisting of only five bogie vans drawn by another engine of the 'King' class. With this featherweight load her driver had made up for previous delays and was actually running ahead of time. Signalman Wadham at Taunton West box was aware of this situation, and as soon as the express arrived at Taunton he rang Athelney Junction to find out how the newspaper train was running. The latter was not booked to stop at Taunton, so on learning that it was still gaining time he very rightly decided to give it a clear run through on the main and to dispatch the express on the down relief. He accordingly pulled his down relief signals off for the express, and one minute later cleared his main line signals for the newspaper train. At 3.44 am the express pulled out and at 3.45 am the newspaper train ran through the station eight minutes ahead of schedule at about fifty-five miles an hour.

On leaving Taunton, the relief signals were placed to the left of that line, while the down main signals were to the right of it. The driver of the express now had a fatal aberration – he mistook the main line signals, which were cleared for

[1] Named 'King Henry II' when originally built.

the newspaper train, for his own. He was making speed rapidly, but the newspaper train continued to overhaul him and as they approached Norton Fitzwarren station the two 'Kings' drew level, one facing a clear road to the west, but the other open trap points only 350 yards ahead. It was only when the sister engine appeared beside him that the driver of the express realized his terrible mistake, shut off steam and applied his brakes, but by this time disaster had become a foregone conclusion. A second or so later 'King George VI' had ploughed her way into the soft ground off the end of the trap points, while the first six coaches of her train lay spread-eagled and telescoped across all four tracks. Of the 900 passengers on board the express, twenty-seven were killed and seventy-five injured. Meanwhile the tail-lights of the newspaper train were vanishing into the darkness, her crew unaware of the tragedy which had just taken place. Guard Baggett, who was travelling in the fourth vehicle of the train, did not even realize that they were passing the express, but he was alarmed when something flew through a window at the leading end of his van and struck him on the arm. Fearing that something was amiss with his train, Baggett applied the vacuum brake and brought it to a stand at Victory Crossing a mile beyond the scene of the disaster. After consultation with his driver they decided to proceed cautiously to Wellington station for examination where they heard the news of the accident but, finding nothing wrong, proceeded on their way.

The object which had hit Guard Baggett was subsequently found in his van – it was a rivet head from the bogie frame of 'King George VI'. Moreover, daylight revealed that the once familiar chocolate lower panels of the fifth and last van were scored and pitted by the ballast which had been flung up like grapeshot as the Penzance express left the rails. The newspaper train must have drawn clear a fraction of a second before the wrecked train reeled right across her path. Thus even in disaster the Great Western were fortunate, for had the newspaper train been but a few seconds later its massive locomotive, weighing 135 tons and running at nearly a mile a minute would have crashed into the crowded coaches of the express with consequences even more terrible than Quintins-hill.

The fireman of the express lost his life, but the driver had a miraculous escape, his engine turning over on its left side while he was on the right. He waded through flood water back on to the ballast and immediately hurried up the line for a mile to Silk Mill, the next block post to the east, his one immediate concern, as a good railwayman, being to protect the line. He said he feared he was responsible for the accident and was, according to the evidence of the Silk Mill signalman, 'agitated and dazed', as well he might be. We can only sym-pathize with, and pray that we may never share, the feelings of this most unfortunate man in the realization of the frightful consequences of his mistake. He was a driver in the 'top link' at Old Oak Common Shed with forty years' railway ex-perience and an intimate knowledge of the road, and in their report on the disaster Colonel Mount and Major Wilson treated him with understanding and sympathy. The cause of the disaster, they found, was psychological. They took into account the difficult operating conditions of the black-out and also the fact that the driver had recently suffered much hard-ship and distress owing to his house at Acton having been damaged by bombing. Two other factors had contributed to his tragic mistake. First, he had never before been diverted to the relief line at Taunton when working this train. Second, the arrangement of both sets of signals on the left side of the relief line was apt to be misleading. Had the down relief signals alone been on the left of that line and the main line signals on the right (*i.e.* to the left of the main line only) in accordance with more normal practice, such a mistake would become far less likely. In this case the track layout made such an arrange-ment of signals impossible, but the inspectors considered that this point should be borne in mind when any future track widenings were contemplated. There was no doubt whatever that the down relief signals approaching Norton Fitzwarren* were standing to danger. This meant that when he passed the distant signal the driver of the express should have heard the audible warning of the ATC siren and felt the automatic application of the vacuum brake. When 'King George VI' was extricated practically undamaged from the soft ground into which she had ploughed, the ATC apparatus was tested and found to be in perfect working order. The inspectors could only conclude that the driver, who had no recollection of doing so, had cancelled the warning subconsciously.

11

RECENT ACCIDENTS, 1944–57

DURING THE war years, in the difficult operating conditions of the black-out and under constant threat of enemy action, the railways of Britain did a magnificent job. To keep the traffic rolling under such circumstances called for vigilance, presence of mind and great courage and determination on the part of the railway staff. One incident alone may be taken as typical of this heroic contribution of the railways to the war effort.

On the night of June 1st, 1944, Driver Gimbert and Fireman Nightall were approaching Soham station on the Ely–Newmarket branch line with the 11.40 pm freight train, Whitemoor to Ipswich. Behind the tender of their 2–8–0 freight engine, WD7337, were fifty-one open wagons loaded with US aircraft bombs and components which had been transhipped at Immingham Dock the previous day.

The train had been examined before it left Whitemoor, while neither Signalman Francis, who watched the train pass through Ely Dock Junction, nor Signalman King at Barway Siding box noticed anything amiss. Barway Siding is only two and a quarter miles from Soham station and the train exchanged single line tokens there at 1.31 am. Yet a few minutes later as he was steaming past Soham up distant at fifteen to twenty miles per hour, Driver Gimbert noticed steam coming from his left-hand injector and leant out of the cab. As he did so, he saw that the leading wagon of his train was on fire. 'The flames,' he said, 'appeared to be getting all over the bottom of the wagon and seemed to be spreading very rapidly, which seemed to suggest that something very inflammable was alight.'

Driver Gimbert knew very well what his train contained. The blazing wagon was loaded with forty-four 500 lb bombs, equivalent to more than 5 tons of TNT. Behind it were thirty-four wagon-loads of 250 lb bombs. In these circumstances, Gimbert and Nightall had every excuse for losing their heads, jumping from the footplate and making for cover. Instead, their first thought was to separate the blazing wagon from the rest of the train, and to this end they acted with perfect coolness and presence of mind in face of extreme danger. Gimbert brought his train gently to a stand, and then instructed Nightall to uncouple the leading wagon. He advised him to take a coal hammer with him in case the link coupling was too hot to touch. Hardly a minute elapsed before Nightall was back on the footplate, his work done. Gimbert then restarted his engine and drew the wagon forward. As he entered Soham station he slowed to a crawl and shouted to Signalman Bridges at Soham station box, telling him what he proposed to do and that he must stop opposing traffic. He recollected Bridges coming down from the box on to the station platform with a fire bucket in his hand, but no more, for at this instant the wagon exploded.

The explosion blew a crater 66 feet in diameter and 16 feet deep which embraced both running lines and both platforms of Soham station. Only one buffer of the wagon was ever found; the rest of it was presumably driven into the ground. The engine tender was blown into a mass of twisted steel, but the engine, though derailed, sustained only superficial damage. The station buildings, the signal box and fifteen houses in the town of Soham were destroyed and thirty-six others rendered uninhabitable. Fireman Nightall was killed instantly and Signalman Bridges died the next day, but Driver Gimbert, though seriously injured, miraculously survived.

There is no doubt that the prompt and courageous action of the engine crew averted a major catastrophe, for the rest of their train contained 400 tons of bombs. As it was, only the leading wagons were damaged by flying splinters and there was no fire. Guard Clarke in his van looked out when the train slowed as they were approaching Soham distant signal and noticed, on the right-hand curve, that the leading wagon was on fire. He applied his van brake to assist the driver to stop. He was walking forward to give assistance when the blast of the explosion knocked him down and he lost consciousness. Although very dazed, when he came to his first thought was the safety of his train. He relit his van rear lamps which had been blown out and then walked back to Barway Siding box, putting down detonators as he went. In fact, these precautions were unnecessary, for the signalmen on either side of Soham had been alerted by the explosion and had stopped oncoming traffic.

The cause of the fire which led to the explosion was never positively established, but in course of the inquiry which followed, the previous movements of the ill-fated wagon were traced. These included a recent load of sulphur in bulk to Luton, and it was conjectured that a spark from the engine had ignited some fine residual sulphur powder on the wagon floor. This was the more probable because the wagon's sheet was not carried over the wagon sides as the regulations for loading explosives required, but only covered the load of bombs, thus making it easier for a spark to lodge. Furthermore, Sub-ganger Fuller of Soham, who saw the fire and was injured in the explosion, referred to the strong smell as 'something like the gasworks on fire', and said the flames had a pronounced blue colour, 'like the flame of a gas ring'.

The Inspecting Officer, Major (as he then was) G. R. S. Wilson, recommended that wagons should be specially examined and their floors cleaned before loading with explosives. 'There is no doubt,' he went on, 'that the two enginemen acted in accordance with the highest traditions of the Railway Service, and they were successful in preventing an incomparably greater disaster; I am very pleased to report that the George Cross has since been awarded to Driver B. Gimbert, and posthumously to Fireman J. W. Nightall.'

Britain's railways emerged from the war in bad shape. Equipment, particularly the permanent way, was suffering from deferred maintenance due to manpower and material shortages. Older staff were suffering from the strain of the war years, and they were joined by many inexperienced men returning from the forces. All this increased the risk of accidents. A speed limit of seventy miles per hour was imposed over the whole system, causing some dismay to the travelling public who did not appreciate the very high standard of permanent way maintenance required before speeds in excess of this figure can be authorized. This was underlined in 1946–7 by two derailments of express trains on plain main line track.

The first of these accidents occurred on December 27th, 1946, to the 2.20 pm up express, Bournemouth to Waterloo, drawn by engine No 851 'Sir Francis Drake' of the 'Lord Nelson' class. Travelling at sixty miles per hour on the up through line to Waterloo, the locomotive and its entire train of twelve coaches became derailed as it was passing through Byfleet station. The leading six coaches were fitted with buck-eye couplings and most fortunately the whole train remained upright and in line, with the result that only three passengers were injured, two of whom were taken to hospital.

Between 3.40 pm and 4.31 pm, when the accident occurred, four expresses hauled by 'King Arthur' or 'Lord Nelson' class locomotives, two of them travelling at sixty-five miles per hour, had passed over the same metals and none of their drivers had noticed any bad riding at Byfleet. But the line at this point was in a clay cutting with inadequate drainage, there had been melting snow and rain in recent weeks, the ballast was dirty and there were signs that a number of sleepers had been 'pumping'. Voids under the sleepers caused considerable variations in cross-level to develop very rapidly. These variations had synchronized with the hammer-blow of the locomotive, causing oscillation of increasing violence until the flanges of the driving wheels had mounted the rails. The Inspecting Officer had no recommendations to make because the Company was already applying the remedy – improved drainage and the 'blanketing' of the formation with a three-inch layer of fine stone chippings.

The second derailment occurred on July 22nd, 1947, and had more serious consequences. The train concerned was the 8.30 am down express, Euston to Liverpool, consisting of sixteen screw-coupled coaches drawn by Pacific locomotive No 6244 'King George VI'. The express was travelling at sixty-five to seventy miles per hour on the down fast line when the locomotive and fourteen of the coaches became derailed on the outside of a left-hand curve near Polesworth station. The engine and the two leading coaches overturned and the ends of the following six coaches were crushed together. The train was crowded with 800 passengers, four of whom were killed outright, while one died subsequently. Nineteen more were seriously injured. All four tracks were blocked, and only the down slow line was undamaged.

The length of track concerned was due for renewal in the 1948 relaying programme, but the Inspecting Officer found that those responsible had seriously underestimated its rate of deterioration. The fastenings were yielding in the eighteen-year-old sleepers and in an attempt to hold the rails to gauge the ganger responsible had refastened eleven sleepers three weeks before the derailment. In addition, the amount of side-cutting (wear) on the inside of the outside rail of the curve exceeded the permissible maximum, and there were considerable variations in cross-level. Failure of the fastenings was the prime cause of the derailment, but these were contributing factors which increased the stress on the fastenings. As a result of this accident, District Engineers were instructed to carry out a personal fortnightly inspection of the permanent way by engine riding, to impose speed restrictions wherever necessary and to initiate an immediate programme of turning side-cut rails on successive Sundays.

Two similar derailments occurred at Hatfield (July 15th, 1946), and Marshmoor (November 10th, 1946), on the LNER main line from King's Cross. In the latter case, the entire train of twelve coaches of the 4.45 pm express from Newcastle to King's Cross became derailed, but fortunately it remained upright and there were no serious casualties. Although similar permanent way defects were primarily responsible, in both cases locomotives of the 2–6–2 V2 class were involved, and did not escape criticism. The Inspecting Officer considered that the swing link control of the leading pony truck made the V2 unduly sensitive to minor permanent way defects in alignment and cross-level. He recommended a spring-controlled pony truck and his words took effect at Doncaster where, he reported, 'one engine has already been altered in this way, and twenty-five more will be dealt with as the necessary equipment becomes available'. Meanwhile the locomotives would be relegated from express duties as more 'Pacifics' entered service.

To restore the railways to their prewar state in which they were suitable for sustained high-speed running required an extensive programme of relaying and other civil engineering work. Inevitably, this work caused delays and the diversion of traffic to unaccustomed paths. This in itself increased the risk of accident, for although drivers are notified of all engineering works on their route by shed postings, and the works themselves are fully protected by signals, such departures from the normal carry the risk that long familiarity will breed forgetfulness. In this way, three serious accidents were indirectly caused by diversions.

In 1945, owing to engineering work in Watford tunnel, up expresses on the Crewe–Euston main line were being diverted by crossover from the up fast to the up slow line at Bourne End. This crossing movement was protected by a colour-light distant signal, one and a quarter miles in rear, which displayed a double yellow caution indication automatically when the points were set for the crossing movement. This was followed after a mile by an outer home semaphore at clear and then, after a further 440 yards by a 'splitting' pair of inner home semaphores which indicated the diversion.

In the early hours of September 30th Driver Swaby and

Fireman Jones took over locomotive No 6157 of the 'Royal Scot' class and the 8.20 pm Perth–Euston sleeping-car express for the final stage of its journey from Crewe to Euston. He was a very reliable man, of long experience of the road, who knew of the diversion. Yet for a reason that can never be known he ignored the warning lights of the distant signal and approached a crossover carrying a twenty miles per hour speed restriction at fifty miles per hour with catastrophic results. The 'Royal Scot' overturned in a field some 9 feet below the line and the six leading coaches piled up against it and were completely destroyed. Of the fifteen vehicles, only the last three remained on the rails and all four lines were blocked. Thirty-eight persons, including the driver and fireman, were killed on the spot and five more died later. In addition, sixty-four were seriously injured.

Why did Driver Swaby ignore the warning of the colour-light distant? It was a fine, clear morning with some haze, and the low sun was shining directly in his eyes. Several drivers who had driven up to Euston that morning testified that they had found the colour-light distants difficult to see and said that they preferred semaphores under such conditions. But this does not explain Swaby's lapse; he knew of the diversion, and a man of his experience could hardly have mistaken his whereabouts in daylight.

The working rule then applying to colour-light distants read:

> In some cases colour-light signals will exhibit two yellow lights. This indication means – pass next signal at restricted speed, and if applicable to a junction *may* denote that the points are set for a diverging route over which the speed restriction shown in the appendix applies.

Although it probably had no bearing on the accident, the Inspecting Officer, Lieut-Colonel Sir Alan Mount, criticized the ambiguity of the word 'may' in this rule and it was accordingly deleted. He also recalled that the diversion of trains from fast to slow lines had led to two previous accidents on this route (at Leighton Buzzard and Great Bridgeford) and that this emphasized the need for some form of ATC at the distant signal.

On the afternoon of Sunday, October 27th, 1947, a similar accident occurred at Goswick on the East Coast main line between Berwick and Newcastle where, owing to engineering work on the up main line, trains were being diverted from the up main to the up independent line. Notice of the diversion had been posted at Edinburgh Haymarket shed, and Signalman White at Goswick, with the assistance of Lengthman McIntyre, was controlling the crossing movement by means of his upper quadrant semaphore signals. His procedure was to leave his distant signal at caution, and lower his home signal when he saw that the train had slowed, so as to draw it slowly forward to his starters at danger. He would then clear the starter applicable to the crossing movement and display a green flag from the box.

At 12.45 pm on the day in question, White received the 'Train entering Section' from Scremerston for the 11.15 am Edinburgh–King's Cross express and remarked to McIntyre that the up Scotsman was approaching. When White first sighted the locomotive, Class A3 Pacific No 66 'Merry Hampton', steam was pluming from the safety valves. It appeared to him that steam had been shut off and that the train was slowing. Most unfortunately, therefore, he cleared his home signal. A moment later he shouted to McIntyre, 'Good God, he will not pull up!' threw the home signal back to danger and pulled over his detonator placer lever. The detonators exploded under the wheels of the locomotive, but their warning came too late. The engine and eight of the leading nine coaches reeled over the crossing and plunged into a ditch beside the track. The fourth coach, the leading member of a triple articulated set, broke away from the rest and, taking with it its leading bogie, slid for 70 yards along the line before coming to rest on its side, blocking all lines. Twenty-seven passengers were killed and fifty-nine, including the driver and fireman, were seriously injured.

Once again the driver was an experienced man, but he admitted he had not read the diversion notice when he booked on duty at Haymarket shed. He also admitted that he had not seen the distant signal because, he alleged, it was obscured by steam from his engine, but, seeing the home signal come off, he assumed he had a clear run through on the main. It emerged at the inquiry that he had taken an unauthorized person with him on the footplate and he was criticized for this as it probably distracted his attention. But once again the Inspecting Officer pointed out that had there been an ATC warning device at the Goswick distant signal the disaster would not have occurred.

The most inexplicable of this series of accidents occurred on Sunday, January 23rd, 1955, at Sutton Coldfield. Because of permanent way relaying on the normal route to Birmingham via Tamworth, the 12.15 pm express from York to Bristol was diverted at Wichnor Junction to the secondary route to Birmingham via Lichfield and Sutton Coldfield. The train consisted of a 4–6–0 Class 5 mixed traffic locomotive and ten coaches. The regular driver did not know this alternative route, so Driver Allen came on to the footplate at Burton to act as conductor driver to Birmingham. Because he complained that the rough riding of the engine was tiring him, the regular driver left the footplate at Lichfield and took his seat in the train, leaving Driver Allen in charge.

Allen was used to Class 5 locomotives and he was well acquainted with the road. Sutton Coldfield station is approached from the north by a short tunnel on a rising gradient of 1 in 101; this is followed immediately by a curve of 15 chains radius between the station platforms over which there is a *permanent* speed restriction of thirty miles per hour. Allen must have known this, and if by some inexplicable aberration he had forgotten his whereabouts the tunnel should have reminded him. Yet according to witnesses on the train he passed through the tunnel at fifty to sixty miles per hour. No one at Sutton Coldfield saw the train, but Station-Inspector Overton who had lived in the station house for twenty years, judged that the vibration and noise was unusual, so much so that he remarked to his daughter: 'If he keeps up that speed he will be in trouble.' A moment later he heard the shattering noise of the crash and ran out to see the locomotive and tender on their side on the down platform and the leading six coaches piled in hideous confusion on or between the platforms, with part of the station awning on top of them. Seventeen lives were lost, including the footplate men, and twenty-three more were seriously injured.

Lieut-Colonel Wilson could find no explanation for Driver Allen's extraordinary lapse, but he strongly criticized the regular driver for leaving the footplate at Lichfield. He was still nominally in charge of his train, and even though he did not know the road, his presence on the footplate with Allen might have averted the disaster.

Between 1949 and 1951 a remarkable series of fires occurred on express passenger trains. The first fire gutted two coaches of an Edinburgh to King's Cross express at Penmanshiel tunnel on the evening of June 23rd, 1949. It was a fine, warm summer evening and the train was about two and a half miles beyond Cockburnspath on the East Coast main line when fire broke out in the corridor of the tenth, brake-composite coach and spread with such extreme rapidity and fierceness that within seconds the whole coach was enveloped. The train was stopped within one and a quarter minutes of the outbreak, but by this time the fire had already spread to the trailing end of the coach next ahead. Most of the passengers escaped by running to the guard's compartment or forward along the corridor, but some were forced to break the glass in their compartment windows and jump down to the track. In doing so, one lady passenger was seriously injured.

The train staff acted with admirable promptitude and coolness in this emergency. They managed to uncouple the two blazing vehicles from the rest of the train. They were first uncoupled from the rear portion, so that the driver, by setting back, could isolate the last four coaches. He then drew forward before uncoupling again and proceeding with the leading eight vehicles to Grantshouse station.

The second fire occurred near Beattock summit, on the main line between Carlisle and Glasgow, on the afternoon of June 8th, 1950. The train involved in this case was the 11 am express from Birmingham to Glasgow. At 4.53 pm when the train passed Greskine box between Beattock station and the summit, the signalman there noticed nothing unusual, yet three minutes later the communication cord was pulled in coach 4851 and smoke was seen to be pouring from the windows and sliding ventilators at the middle and rear end. The train was stopped in twenty seconds, but within half a minute the rear end of 4851 and the gangway of the coach next to it were burning fiercely. Once again the train crew took prompt action to isolate the two burning vehicles. A ganger named Moffat twice entered the burning coach. On the first occasion he rescued a woman passenger, but on the second occasion fumes and intense heat forced him to his knees and compelled this very gallant man to beat a retreat. In this remote moorland situation, help was not readily forthcoming, but the Moffat Fire Brigade reached the scene in thirty-four minutes and, with the aid of brigades from Abington and Lanark who arrived later, the blaze was extinguished by six o'clock. Only then was it possible to discover whether any passengers remained in the burning coaches. The bodies of one man, two women and two children were then found in one compartment. From the repose of their attitudes it was believed that all had been killed instantly by a sudden blast of intense heat.

The third in this series of fires occurred at Huntingdon on July 14th, 1951, the train concerned being the 3.45 pm express from King's Cross to Leeds, the 'West Riding'. The four leading vehicles of this train consisted of two articulated centre vestibule twin-sets. Three-quarters of an hour after leav-

ing London, a woman passenger in the rearmost left-hand seat
of the leading twin-set noticed a wisp of smoke rising between
the arm-rest of the seat and the side of the coach. She told a
passing pantry-boy who reported to the restaurant-car conductor. The conductor went forward and leant out of the
nearby vestibule window to see if he could detect signs of
smoke. He could not, but he reported the matter to the guard
who, in turn, came forward. He noticed smoke seeping between the edge of the carpet and the coach side, and he too
readily diagnosed a hot axle box. He then passed back down
the train with the intention of throwing out a message at
Huntingdon station requesting that the train be stopped for
examination. Meanwhile there was growing alarm in the
affected coach as it filled with smoke. The carpet under the
seat was hot to the touch and part of the rubber underlay had
melted. When a small flame appeared there a male passenger
decided it was high time the communication cord was pulled
and after some delay he found the cord in the coach vestibule.
The driver then made a full brake application and brought the
train to a stand in 700 yards. As it drew to a halt the flames
suddenly spread wih frightening rapidity up the coach sides
and along the roof. The central corridor became blocked by
passengers trying to escape and some broke windows and
jumped through them. In this way twenty-two passengers were
injured by burns and cuts, but mercifully everyone came out of
this perilous situation alive.

The train staff endeavoured to isolate the leading twin-set,
but owing to the intense heat they could not uncouple it and
were forced to divide the train behind the second twin-set,
with the result that all four coaches were destroyed.

What was the cause of these three fires and why did they
spread with such frightening rapidity? This was the question
that the Railways Inspectorate had to answer. In the case of
the Beattock fire the Inspecting Officer was satisfied it had
originated in an empty smoking compartment which had been
vacated at Carlisle. A cigarette end or a lighted match, falling

down behind the seat, had set fire to the accumulated dust and rubbish in the inaccessible space beneath the seat and behind the steam-heating radiator. All the way from Carlisle the fire had been gaining ground, eating away the unprotected deal boarding of the partition and climbing up the space between it and the back of the seat. But there had been insufficient oxygen supply in the closed compartment for it to burst into open flame until the heat broke one of the corridor side windows. At once a great volume of highly inflammable gas poured into the corridor to meet a strong current of air from the open ventilators. The corridor acted like a blow-lamp and at once became a roaring inferno of flame. The Inspecting Officer recommended redesign of the coaches so that there were no inaccessible pockets under the seats where rubbish could accumulate.

At Penmanshiel it was believed that the fire originated in a cigarette end or lighted match flung down against the partition wall of a cross corridor. At Huntingdon it was discovered that A3 Pacific No 60058 that was hauling the 'West Riding' had a missing firebar and it was thought that a hot ember, lodging in a hole in the coach floor carrying a lavatory vent pipe, was the origin of the fire. But the cause of the rapid spread of the fire was, in both cases, the same. The corridor walls of coaches 1498 and 1148 at Penmanshiel had been sprayed with nitro-cellulose lacquer. On the twin-sets of the 'West Riding', interior walls and roof were lined with fabric impregnated with nitro-cellulose. What happened when the Inspecting Officer, Colonel Walker, carried out an experiment in a coach corridor treated with this lacquer is best told in his own words:

A lighted match was thrown into a corner. After a pause of ten seconds the surface of the wall suddenly burst into strong flames about 2 feet in length; the root of the flames climbed up the first 2 feet of wall in fifteen seconds, by which time the flames extended to the roof, and reached the top of the wall in the next ten seconds. The entire corridor

was now in flames and the fire had to be extinguished
immediately.

After further tests by the Joint Fire Research Organization,
that body reported that, for inflammability of surface, the
material used in coach 1148 at Penmanshiel was, by a very
large margin, the worst they had ever recorded.

The use of nitro-cellulose lacquer was forbidden; existing
coaches so treated had to be withdrawn for rectification at the
first opportunity. A danger more deadly than the old gas lighting, because it was more insidious, had been recognized and
eliminated.

Automatic safety devices erect a formidable fence against
human error on the part of drivers and signalmen, particularly
in situations where traffic is dense and the headway between
trains is therefore small. They are, however, inflexible in their
operation and it is an essential feature of their design that, in
the event of mechanical or electrical failure, they can only
display a danger indication or its equivalent. Consequently,
some means have to be provided whereby, in the event of
failure or other exceptional circumstances, the human element
can overrule the mechanical in order to keep traffic moving.
Although these emergency means are subject to the strictest
safeguards, they permit the human element to take control and
the lesson of four recent accidents is that such emergency
means provide a loop-hole through which human error can
creep in.

London's Underground system is protected by two aspect
colour-light signals, operated automatically by continuous
track circuiting. These function in association with an automatic line-side train-stop which, if a train should overrun a
signal at danger, switches off the motor current and applies the
Westinghouse brake. On April 8th, 1953, the hook of a loose
side chain used for emergency coupling struck and damaged
the train stop at signal A491 in the Central Line tunnel between Stratford and Leyton stations. This trifling mishap re-

sulted in the only serious accident in the history of London's tube railways. It caused signal A491 and the stop signal next in rear at Stratford station, No 489, to exhibit a permanent red. This failure brought into operation the 'Stop and Proceed' rule. After being notified of the failure at Stratford, this authorized a driver, after waiting for one minute and giving one long warning whistle to: 'Proceed cautiously as far as the line is clear or to the next stop signal in advance at such a speed as to enable him to stop short of any obstruction there may be, having regard to the prevailing conditions . . .' The station staff at Stratford did not know that signal A491 was also displaying a permanent red; had they known, their warning to drivers might have been more explicit.

Eleven trains were worked safely through the section under this rule. The eleventh train, No 39, had stopped at signal A491 before drawing forward as required by the rule, and the twelfth, No 71, had stopped behind it. No 39 had moved off and No 71 was about to draw forward to the signal when it was struck heavily in the rear by the thirteenth train, No 59. The driver of train No 59 insisted that his speed was only five to eight miles per hour and that his vision had been obscured by a sudden cloud of dust, but the extent of the damage showed that he had either ignored the wording of the 'Stop and Proceed' rule or woefully misjudged his speed in the tunnel.

The damage [wrote Colonel McMullen] greatly exceeded that ever experienced in any previous accident to tube stock. The leading driving cab of the first car of train 59 was wrecked and the headstock was forced down with such violence that the whole end of the car was lifted and became jammed between the track and the roof of the tube, buckling itself in the process. This had two results – firstly, the whole of the energy of the train was dissipated at that point instead of some, at least, being expended in pushing train 71 further forwards; and secondly, the lifting of the front end caused the rear end to be lowered, enabling the buffer of the second car to ride over that of the first car and to telescope into it for a distance of 6 feet.

Both trains were crowded with rush-hour traffic, and in the darkness and confusion nine passengers lost their lives and three more received fatal injuries.

A similar accident had occurred eight years earlier at Northwood on the Metropolitan and Great Central Joint Railway where, on December 31st, 1945, a London Transport electric locomotive-hauled train from Baker Street to Aylesbury crashed into the rear of an electric multiple unit train from Aldgate to Watford, causing a fire in which three lives were lost. In this case, thick fog and a signal failure at Watford South Junction had disorganized traffic and the driver of the Aylesbury train had been authorized to pass a signal correctly showing a red indication at Northwood Hills under the 'Stop and Proceed' rule. He had clearly disobeyed this rule by proceeding at much too high a speed having regard to the foggy conditions.

At this time traffic over the busy London suburban lines of the Southern Railway had been controlled for many years with great reliability by the Sykes lock-and-block system. In this system the signal levers are interconnected with the block instruments in such a way as to ensure that only one train at a time can occupy a block section. When signalman A offers a train forward to signalman B, if the latter is in a position to accept it he presses a plunger on his home signal instrument. This frees the starting signal at A and when signalman A pulls off the lever controlling it, it becomes back-locked. The plunger in box B also becomes locked and at the same time the lower of two tablets in the instruments moves from blank to 'Train On'. When signalman B pulls off his home signal, the upper tablet changes from 'Free' to 'Locked'. When a train passes the starting signal at A, it actuates a treadle which releases the back-lock on that signal and changes its tablet indication from 'Locked' to 'Free'. The lever can then be returned to danger and cannot be pulled again until a second release is authorized by B. When the train has passed the home signal at B, the return of the home signal lever restores the lower tablet from 'Train On' to blank, but the plunger remains locked until B's starting signal is freed in the manner described above. As additional precautions, a semaphore indicator shows when the section is occupied and a switch hook is placed over the plunger which prevents its attempted use and also serves as a visible reminder that a train is occupying the section concerned.

It will thus be seen that Sykes 'lock-and-block' is a formidable defence against error, but its Achilles heel is the release key by which a signalman can release the plunger lock and so overrule these mechanical and electrical safety devices. It is necessary to provide this key in case a fault should develop in the train-actuated treadle release, or in the event of a train being offered forward and then cancelled, but needless to say use of the key is governed by the most stringent regulation which states:

> Signalmen are specially cautioned not to use the Release Key or other means of release unless they have clearly ascertained that no train is in the section and that such release is absolutely necessary and can with safety be given.

Yet in 1947 and 1955 two major disasters were caused through misuse of the release key by inexperienced signalmen.

The first occurred between Purley Oaks and South Croydon Junction at the height of the morning rush hour on October 24th, 1947. Owing to fog, visibility at the time was reduced to 50 yards. Signalman Jones (as I will call him) in Purley Oaks box accepted the 7.33 am electric passenger train, Haywards Heath to London Bridge, from Purley North Box but neglected to offer it forward to South Croydon. In default of South Croydon's acceptance Jones's starting signal therefore remained locked at danger. He brought the train nearly to a stand at his home signal before allowing it to draw forward into the station platform and up to the starter. He neglected to place the switch hook over the plunger controlling the Purley North starting signal, so he was without this additional reminder that he was not free to accept another train. The Haywards Heath train was held at the platform for six or seven minutes. It was invisible to Jones, and during this period he forgot it. He was then offered the 8.4 am train from Tattenham Corner to London Bridge by Purley North. Glancing at his tablet instrument he saw that the lower tablet showed 'blank' (it had been restored to this position by the return of his home signal), but that the upper tablet showed 'Locked'. He wrongly assumed from this that the instrument had failed, used his release key to free the plunger which released the Purley North starting signal, and accepted the 8.4 am train. At the same time he offered it forward to South Croydon who accepted it and actuated the plunger which released Jones's starting signal. Seeing the starting signal come off, the forgotten 7.33 am train at the platform moved forward and as it did so it actuated the treadle which changed the tablet indication from 'Locked' to 'Free'. Jones noticed this, but thinking it was due to a fault in the mechanism, he restored the instrument to the 'Locked' position. A few moments later, running under clear signals, the Tattenham Corner train passed through Purley Oaks station and at 8.36 am Signalman Walder at South Croydon received the 'entering section' signal from Jones who advised him by telephone that the train was approaching. One minute later Walder heard through the fog the noise of a violent collision and took immediate steps to block all lines. He telephoned Jones to ask whether the Tattenham Corner train had been overrunning signals at danger. 'No,' he replied, 'it was all my fault.' Both trains were crowded, and in the collision thirty-one passengers and the motorman of the following train lost their lives and many were seriously injured.

A similar accident occurred at Barnes Junction on the night of December 2nd, 1955, when the 11.12 pm four coach elec-

tric train from Waterloo to Windsor and Chertsey collided
with the rear of a forty-two-wagon steam freight train, Batter-
sea to Brent, which had been stopped at the Barnes Junction
down local home signal and was slowly moving forward. Electrical arcing set fire to the wooden bodywork of the leading
coach and eleven passengers, the motorman and the guard of
the freight train lost their lives. The freight train was normally
routed on the down through line, but because of late running
due to a power failure earlier that evening, the signalman at
Clapham Junction had diverted it to the down local line. In
this case, the signalman at Barnes had forgotten the freight
train and accepted the Windsor train from Point Pleasant by
using his release key. The Point Pleasant signalman had contributed to his confusion by offering the Windsor train forward
without having first received the 'Train out of Section' signal
from Barnes for the freight.

On January 7th, 1957, near Welwyn Garden City station on
the East Coast main line, an up express from Aberdeen to
King's Cross overran signals at danger and collided with the
rear of a six coach commuter train from Baldock to King's
Cross which, according to instructions, had been given prior
right of way over the express. Only one passenger was killed
and five injured in the last coach of the local train. But death
and destruction, as has been shown in earlier chapters, depends
on chance circumstances – the location of the collision or the
imminence of opposing traffic – which can all too easily trans-
form a minor accident into a major disaster. So it was that
similar errors on the part of drivers of express trains in 1952
and 1957 brought about two of the worst disasters in the whole
history of Britain's railways.

On the morning of October 8th, 1952, the 7.31 am local
passenger train from Tring to Euston crossed from the up slow
to the up fast line at Harrow and Wealdstone station and came
to a stand at the up fast platform. This was in accord with
normal working procedure which was to give urban commuter
services priority over late running expresses from the north.

The train of nine non-corridor coaches drawn by a 2–6–4 tank engine was packed with 800 passengers and there were many more waiting for it on the platform. It had been standing for one and a half minutes when there burst upon the scene the Perth–Euston sleeping-car express drawn by Class 8P Pacific No 46242 which had passed a colour-light distant and two semaphores at danger in patchy fog and was travelling at fifty-five to sixty miles per hour. The express ran through the trailing points of the crossover and dashed into the rear of the local train with such violence that the last three coaches were compressed into the space of one. The locomotive of the express came to rest fouling the down fast line 78 yards beyond the point of impact, with two leading vans and the first three coaches of its train piled up behind it.

The Harrow signalman was severely shocked by the sight, but he retained sufficient presence of mind to throw all his signals to danger and send out the 'obstruction danger' signal. But he was too late; before the accident occurred he had accepted the 8 am down Euston to Liverpool and Manchester express. He had also thrown his detonator lever as soon as he saw the Perth express coming at him through the mist. The driver responded to the warning crack of the detonators by making an emergency brake application, but by then it was too late. Having done all he could, the Harrow signalman was forced to stand helplessly at his levers as disaster followed disaster.

The Liverpool express consisted of fifteen bogie coaches and four vans in rear. It was drawn by Class 8P Pacific No 46202 piloted by Class 6P 4–6–0 No 45637 which was working back to shed. With such ample motive power, the train made a rapid start from Euston and it approached Harrow station at sixty miles per hour, a matter of seconds after the first collision had taken place. The two locomotives struck the derailed engine of the Perth express, mounted and crossed the down fast platform and overturned fouling the up electric line from Watford which islanded the platform. By so doing they

cut off the traction current and so stopped an approaching
electric train. The three rear coaches of the local train, the
three leading vehicles of the Perth express and no less than
seven coaches of the Liverpool express were now compressed
into a compact mass of wreckage 45 yards long, 18 yards wide
and 30 feet high between the station platforms. And underneath it all was the engine of the Perth train. 'Damage to the
three express engines and destruction of rolling stock was
altogether exceptional,' said Lieut-Colonel G. R. S. Wilson,
the Chief Inspecting Officer. The wooden-bodied coaches of
the local train had suffered most, but he praised the way the
rear coaches of the Liverpool express, which were of all steel
construction with buck-eye couplers, had stood up to the
shock. In such a catastrophe the death-roll was proportionately
heavy; a total of 112 lives were lost and ten died later from
their injuries. Casualties included the engine crew of the Perth
express and the driver of the pilot engine, a toll that was
second only to Quintinshill.

There were thick, drifting fog banks over the southeastern
suburbs of London on the evening of December 4th, 1957,
which delayed the crowded rush-hour trains on the Southern
Region Kentish lines as they groped their way out of London.
These are the most densely occupied lines in the world and it
was estimated at that time that a total of 990 trains passed St
Johns signal box at Lewisham every twenty-four hours. This
box also controls traffic on the Nunhead–Lewisham loop which
crosses over the Kent coast main line on a steel lattice girder
bridge at this point. This traffic increases the total to 1,115
trains a day. There is no manual block working, traffic being
governed by four aspect automatic or semi-automatic colour-
light signals controlled by continuous track circuiting. The
semi-automatic signals are operated from the signal boxes, but
when this control was exercised by the signalmen in acceptance of a train, they would only clear to the aspect dictated by
the state of the track circuits – double yellow, yellow or green
as the case might be. Double yellow (YY) means that the

driver may expect to find the next signal at single yellow, an indication which, of course, means that the next signal may be at red. Thus adequate braking distance between trains is always maintained. There were nineteen of these four aspect signals in the five miles of line from Cannon Street to Parks Bridge Junction where the Mid Kent line diverges from the old South-Eastern main line to Dover and Ramsgate. There were only two signal boxes in this five miles, St Johns and North Kent East Junction.

The 4.56 express to Ramsgate via Folkestone left Cannon Street three-quarters of an hour late. The locomotive, 'Battle of Britain' class Pacific No 34066 had had to run light from Stewart's Lane Depot to Rotherhithe Road Carriage sidings to pick up the empty stock and then propel it into Cannon Street with a pilot engine at the head. The fog had seriously delayed these operations and as a result, by the time the train was due to leave, the tender tank of the Pacific was half empty. Because of this the driver said he would have to make an unscheduled stop at Sevenoaks to take on water. For this reason he was anxious to make up time to offset this further delay.

The relevant signals are situated to the right of the line, while the Pacific was driven from the left of the footplate and had a special narrow cab suited to the restricted clearances on the Kent Coast line. Consequently, despite their penetrating beam it was difficult, if not impossible, for the driver to see the signals in fog from his side of the footplate with his close view of them cut off by the streamlined bulk of the boiler casing.

The fireman read the signals until the train was approaching St Johns outer and intermediate home signals. Because these two signals are on the outside of a left-hand curve they were normally within view of the driver, and for this reason, as was his custom, the fireman ceased to look out, but began firing in readiness for the long climb to the summit of the North Downs at Knockholt. But the driver did not see these two signals, nor did he cross the footplate in order to do so. Asked why, having missed them, he failed to slow down, he could only reply that he had never experienced a signal check at this point. The signals were showing a double yellow and a yellow indication respectively. The fireman paused from his firing in time to glimpse the St Johns home signal and shouted to the driver, 'You've got a Red,' whereupon the driver instantly made an emergency application of the vacuum brake. Too late; 138 yards beyond the signal the Pacific crashed into the rear of the 5.18 pm ten coach electric train, Charing Cross to Hayes, which was standing at the Parks Bridge Junction home signal.

Two unfortunate factors magnified the destruction caused by the collision. In the first place, owing to a rising gradient at this point, the electric train was standing with its brakes on. This caused severe telescoping. The underframe and body of the ninth coach was driven right through the eighth, completely destroying it. In the second place, the collision occurred directly beneath the girder bridge carrying the Nunhead–Lewisham loop. The locomotive itself was not derailed, but its tender and the leading coach were thrown to the left where they struck and brought down a $14\frac{1}{2}$-ton steel column that supported the bridge. The bridge girders and deck weighing 350 tons thereupon collapsed on to the wrecked train, completing the destruction of the leading coach and crushing the forward half of the next.

Two minutes after the disaster occurred, the 5.22 pm eight coach electric train from Holborn Viaduct to Dartford approached the fallen bridge. Fortunately it was moving slowly up to a signal at red and the motorman, seeing the track had subsided in front of him, stopped very promptly, with his leading coach on the tilt. But for this prompt action another chapter of death and destruction might have been added to the Lewisham disaster in which ninety lives were lost and 109 persons seriously injured.

In his report on Lewisham, Brigadier Langley[1] felt that

[1] Lieut-Colonel G. R. S. Wilson died while the report on Lewisham was being prepared and Brigadier Langley succeeded him as Chief Inspecting Officer.

its lesson should be borne in mind when new or replacement over-line bridges were designed, but above all he stressed that this disaster, like the previous one at Harrow and Weald-stone, would have been prevented by some form of ATC, or AWS (Automatic Warning System) as it is now called, at the distant signal. With this device the accidents at Bourne End, Goswick and Welwyn Garden City would almost certainly not have occurred. It would also have prevented the accidents at Ilford on January 16th, 1944, and Gidea Park on January 2nd, 1947, when a total of fourteen lives were lost, both of which were due to trains overrunning signals in fog. Altogether, in the forty-six years from 1912 to 1957, 31 per cent of the fatalities in railway accidents would have been saved by Warning Control.

The absence of any mention of the Great Western Railway in this chapter is not without significance. In his report on the Harrow disaster, the late Lieut-Colonel Wilson wrote in his summing up:

Credit must be given to the former Great Western Railway Company for developing their contact system (of ATC) so early, and installing it so extensively without pressure from Government recommendations, and there is no doubt that it contributed in no small measure to their notable safety record which has been continued on the Western Region.

When the railways were nationalized the GWR system of AWS was rejected in favour of a development of the Hudd electro-magnetic apparatus which was then in use on the Tilbury–Southend line, and extensive development work was done on the East Coast main line. The result is a device which not only gives the driver an audible but a visual warning that he has passed a distant signal at Caution. Moreover, even if the driver cancels the warning subconsciously, as was the case at Norton Fitzwarren, this visual warning remains displayed as a reminder until it is cancelled by the next track magnet apparatus.

Installation of this apparatus is an immense and costly task which is now well advanced. Together with the fog-penetrating beam of modern colour-light signals, AWS greatly reduces the risk of a driver overrunning signals.

Yet if this chapter has a moral, it is that no matter how many ingenious safety devices are introduced, in the last analysis our safety on the rail depends largely, as it has always done, upon the skill and vigilance of the railwayman. That vigilance has made railways the safest form of transport ever devised by man. The railwayman's rare lapses, the patient thoroughness with which such lapses are investigated, and the steps taken to prevent a recurrence should be contrasted with the free-for-all on our congested roads and the annual slaughter to which it leads.

APPENDIX 1

To the: Right Honble H. Labouchere,
   President of the Board of Trade

Sir,

Since my examination before the select committee on Railways I see the difficulties you have to contend with from the opposing members to your Bill in bringing forward a measure for the management and better regulation of Railways. I am quite sure that some interference on the part of Government is much wanted. Perhaps I ought to be the last man to admit this (the whole system of Railways, and Locomotive Engines having been brought out by my exertions) but when I see so many young engineers, and such a variety of notions, I am convinced that some system should be laid down, to prevent wild, and visionary schemes, being tried, at the great danger of injury or loss of life to the public. I consider it right that every talented man should be at liberty to make improvements, but that the supposed improvements should be duly considered by proper judges. Then the question follows, from the opponents to the Bill, who are those judges to be? I beg to lay before you my views on this point.

Suppose any Engineer has any improved plan for the better working of Railways to propose, he should submit his plan to the Engineer belonging to the Board of Trade, but before that Engineer should give his decision as to the utility of the scheme, he should have full power to call together the chief Engineers of the principal Railways of the Kingdom, and after the subject has been duly discussed, votes should be taken for and against the measure: the discussion should be laid before the Board of Trade, accompanied with the observations of the government Engineer, and if approved of should be then placed into his hands to carry out.

I should propose for the consideration of the different Engineers that the speed of Locomotives should not exceed forty miles per hour on the most favourable Lines, excepting on special occasions: curved Lines to diminish in velocity according to the radius. I am quite aware that this cannot be carried out to any great nicety, but still it would be a check upon the Drivers. Collateral Lines require government consideration is a very strong point of view.

Uniformity of signals is another desirable point.

As several persons are now turning their attention to self-acting breaks, it will soon appear that great benefit and safety to travelling will be found by their adoption. In the meantime no train should be allowed to travel which has not two breaks-men, and four coaches in each train should be provided with breaks to allow for contingencies. It is my opinion that no contrivance can be found out by which the breaks can be dispensed with.

Six-wheeled Engines and carriages are much safer and more comfortable to the travellers than four; any person riding one hundred yards upon an engine or coach constructed upon this plan would discover the difference. The rim of all Railway wheels ought to be made the same width, and the axle trees for all coaches of a strength approved of by the Engineers, both wheels, springs, and axles should bear the government stamp, to being made of the best materials, as every practicable means ought to be made use of in order to have these made of the best iron.

All disputes between Railway Companies should be decided by the Board of Trade.

It appears to me that the above suggestions might be carried out with success, without interfering injuriously with Railway property. I hope that you will not consider that I am intruding by sending you these observations.

I am, Sir,
Your Most Obt Servant,
(Sgd) Geo Stephenson

Tapton House
Nr Chesterfield,
March 31st, 1841

APPENDIX 2

THE FIRST REQUIREMENTS OF THE INSPECTING OFFICERS OF RAILWAYS

Railway Department,
Board of Trade,
Whitehall, S.W.
29th April, 1858

Sir,

Several cases have recently occurred in which the opening of New Lines of Railway has been postponed because certain of the requirements of the Inspecting Officer had not been completed.

In order to prevent as far as possible the disappointment which such postponement must occasion to the Companies, the Lords of the Committee of the Privy Council for Trade have considered it desirable to forward the accompanying statement which sets forth some of these requirements, a deficiency in which has generally caused the opening of new lines of Railway to be postponed.

I am, Sir, Your Obedient Servant,
(Sgd) Douglas Calton

The Secretaries to 79 Railway Companies

At the Stations

Platforms to be not less than 6 feet wide, and when raised, the descent at the ends should be by means of ramps, and not by steps.

Clocks to be provided in a position where they are visible from the line.

Signals and distant signals in each direction to be erected.

The lever handles of switches and signals to be placed in the most convenient position, and to be brought as close together as possible, so as to be under the hand of the person working them. The switches to be provided with double connecting rods.

No Facing Points, except on single lines or at double junctions. In the case of Facing Points at junctions, it is most desirable that the signals should be connected with the points so as to be worked in conjunction with them, and to indicate whether they are open or shut.

Sidings, if falling towards the line, or on a level, to be provided with locked chock blocks, or locked points, leading into a blind siding.

Turntables for engines to be erected at terminal stations.

As Regards the Line Generally

No standing work above the level of the carriage steps to be nearer to the rail than 3 feet 6 inches, where the carriages are not above 7 feet 4 inches in width, outside measurement.

The interval between adjacent lines of rails, and between lines of rails and sidings, must not be less than 6 feet.

When stations occur on, or immediately contiguous to, a viaduct, a parapet wall on each side, 3 feet high, should be built, with a hand railing or a fence on the top sufficient to prevent passengers from falling over the viaduct in the dark.

At all level crossings of turnpike roads or of important public roads, the gates must be so constructed as to be capable of closing across the Railway as well as across the road.

A fixed signal, either attached to the gate or otherwise, to be placed at every level crossing, and when the level crossing is so situated that an approaching train cannot be seen for a sufficient distance, distant signals will be required.

Main signals and distant signals for each line are required, at all junctions.

Where the lines are single, an undertaking will be required, to be signed by the Chairman and Secretary of the Company, that the line shall be worked in such a manner that only one engine in steam, or two or more when coupled together and forming part of a train, shall ever be upon the single line, or upon defined portions thereof at one and the same time.

BIBLIOGRAPHY

Accident Reports of the Railways Inspecting Officers, Board of Trade and Ministry of Transport, 1840–1940. (State Papers and HMSO.)

Acworth, W. M.: *The Railways of England* (John Murray, 1890).

Blythe, Richard: *Danger Ahead* (Newman Neame, 1951).

Great Western Railway, Rule Book (GWR, 1933, with later amendments).

Holt, G.: 'Railway Accidents' (Institution of Railway Signal Engineers, Proceedings, 1923).

Langley, C. A.: *History and Methods of Government Regulation of Railway Safety in Great Britain* (Bulletin of the International Railway Congress Association, 1953).

Lascelles, T. S.: 'The Signal Engineer and Safety Legislation' (Presidential Address, Institution of Railway Signal Engineers, Proceedings, 1952).

MacDermot, E. T.: *The History of the Great Western Railway*, 2 vols (GWR, 1927, 1931).

Ministry of Transport: *Requirements for Passenger Lines and Recommendations for Goods Lines of the Minister of Transport in Regard to Railway Construction and Operation* (HMSO, Rep, 1952).

Pendleton, J.: *Our Railways*, 2 vols (Cassell, 1894).

Thomas, J.: *Obstruction-Danger* (Blackwood, 1937).

Wilson, G. R. S.: 'Safety on the Railways' (Address to the Royal Society of Arts, 1933).

Wilson, H. Raynar: *Railway Accidents* (Author, 1925).

CHRONOLOGICAL INDEX OF ACCIDENTS MENTIONED IN THE TEXT

(Accidents described in full detail shown in heavy type)